HIDDEN GOSPELS

HIDDEN GOSPELS

*How the Search for Jesus
Lost Its Way*

PHILIP JENKINS

OXFORD
UNIVERSITY PRESS

229.8
JEW

OXFORD
UNIVERSITY PRESS

Oxford   New York
Auckland   Bangkok   Buenos Aires
Cape Town   Chennai   Dar es Salaam   Delhi   Hong Kong   Istanbul
Karachi   Kolkata   Kuala Lumpur   Madrid   Melbourne   Mexico City   Mumbai
Nairobi   São Paulo   Shanghai   Taipei   Tokyo   Toronto

First published by Oxford University Press, Inc., 2001
First issued as an Oxford University Press paperback, 2003
198 Madison Avenue, New York, New York 10016
www.oup.com

Oxford is a registered trademark of Oxford University Press

Library of Congress Cataloging-in-Publication Data
Jenkins, Philip, 1952-
Hidden Gospels: how the search for Jesus lost its way/Philip Jenkins
p. cm.
Includes bibliographical references and index.
ISBN 0-19-513509-1 (cloth); ISBN 0-19-515631-5 (pbk.)
1. Apocryphal Gospels.
2. Christianity—Origin.
I. Title.
BS2851 J46 2001
229.8—dc21
00-040641

1 3 5 7 9 10 8 6 4 2
Printed in the United States of America

Contents

Acknowledgments

I am grateful to Kathryn Hume and William Petersen for their always valuable advice; needless to say, they take no responsibility for the arguments made here, nor for any errors of fact or faith. Thanks also to other colleagues who have made helpful comments, including Paul Harvey and Gary Knoppers, and I'd also like to acknowledge the excellent research assistance provided by Peter Lawler.

HIDDEN GOSPELS

1

Hiding and Seeking

I know a certain gospel which is called *The Gospel according to Thomas*, and a *Gospel according to Matthias*, and many others have we read—lest we should in any way be considered ignorant. . . . Nevertheless, among all these, we have approved solely what the church has recognized, which is that only the four gospels should be accepted.

ORIGEN

SCHOLARS OF THE NEW TESTAMENT often argue as to which of the words attributed to Jesus might plausibly have come from his mouth. One criterion used in this debate is that of difficulty, namely that a passage which would have seemed baffling or off-putting to early Christians is more likely to be authentic, since no early writer would have dared to invent it. Early editors recorded the story because a strong tradition linked it to Jesus himself, so that it was not to be denied or tampered with lightly. By this standard, some scholars feel that one saying that is likely to be genuine concerns the woman who carries a jar full of meal. Unknown to her, the jar cracked while she was walking home, and by the time she arrived home, the jar was empty. The story ends provocatively, irritatingly, at that point, allowing hearers to deduce from it any meanings which might seem appropriate. In his book on current views of Jesus, Russell Shorto describes this as "one of the strangest and most alluring of the parables," a prime example of the startling, counterintuitive, and even frustrating teachings of the Master. According to the Jesus Seminar, that body of critical scholars whose attempts to determine the actual words of Jesus have been so widely publicized, this parable is classified as probably authentic, which is a rating higher than that given to the vast majority of the best-known sayings in the New Testament (not a word of the Gospel of John receives so positive a judgment).[1]

Though this story echoes many well-known parables attributed to Jesus, it is not familiar to most readers, even to those with a thorough knowledge of the New Testament, simply because it is not found in our Bibles: the account of the woman with the jar of meal comes instead from a text called the *Gospel of Thomas*. In other words, at least some contemporary scholars present as probably genuine a saying of Jesus which is not recorded in the writings of Matthew, Mark, Luke, or John, but which is exclusively found in a document of which most people had never heard before the 1950s. Nor is this example unique. *Thomas* is widely quoted as authoritative in modern studies which seek to rediscover the historical Jesus, and these same works cite a battery of other gospels with unfamiliar titles, gospels attributed to Mary Magdalen, Peter, and others. Gospel texts bear the names of the Egyptians and the Hebrews, and dozens or hundreds of others are known, at least by name, and some survive in fragmentary form.

For nonspecialist readers, the very existence of texts with such names can be tantalizing, if not shocking. Not much Bible literacy is needed to know that there are, or should be, only four gospels, so just what are *Thomas* and the others? Did Mary Magdalen really have a gospel devoted to her? Or did Thomas, Philip, Peter, or some other disciple write such a thing? Not only do these other gospels exist—though they are certainly not by the actual apostles—but distinguished scholars treat these works as serious historical sources. For the lay public, respectful references to *Thomas* and the rest are puzzling, since the concept of "gospel" is so embedded in our culture and language. Still, after decades of secularization, gospels symbolize an absolute standard of truth: people swear on the gospel, and the very phrase "gospel truth" indicates unwavering certainty. The existence of newly discovered gospels suggests that the Bible itself might not be as clearly defined as most people believe. And if the other gospels existed, why have such treasures been lost or hidden in the first place: was it because they contained unpopular or subversive truths? Other questions come to mind: are these other so-called gospels true in anything like the same sense as the texts we know, as valuable perhaps as the documents in the New Testament? Do they tell us anything new or startling about Jesus himself? And does the existence of such alternative gospels require a radical revision of what we think of as Christianity?

In many ways, the answers to these questions are disappointing. Though the rediscovered texts are very informative about the byways of early church belief, in very few cases do they reveal anything of significance about the times of Jesus and the apostles, or indeed about the first century of the Christian era. Even the few exceptions to this statement, namely, *Thomas* and the hypothetical text known as the Q gospel, tell us much less about the earliest ages than their advocates like to believe. The vastly exaggerated claims made on behalf of these gospels are more revealing about what contemporary scholars and writers would like to find about the first Christian ages, and how these ideas are communicated, accurately or otherwise, to a mass public. The alternative gospels are thus very important sources, if not for the beginnings of Christianity, then for what they tell us about the interest groups who seek to use them today; about the mass media, and how religion is packaged as popular culture; about how canons shift their content to reflect the values of the reading audience; and more generally, about the changing directions of contemporary American religion.

Other Christianities

Discussions of the "other gospels" generally focus on the spectacular haul of over fifty texts which were discovered at Nag Hammadi in Egypt in 1945. These documents had been concealed in the late fourth century, presumably by someone who felt (reasonably enough) that if they were not concealed, the texts would be destroyed by heresy-hunting vigilantes. The best-known text from the Nag Hammadi treasure trove was the *Gospel of Thomas*, which in the last two decades has widely, if controversially, been attributed a degree of authority little less than that of the four gospels—and perhaps a great deal more. Other items in this collection supplied countless alternative views of Christianity: though only four explicitly bore the title of "gospels," dozens claimed to record the words or deeds of Jesus. New Testament scholar Marvin Meyer has described the Nag Hammadi collection as "just as precious, and perhaps even more precious" than the texts in the New Testament.[2]

Unlike the Dead Sea Scrolls, which were discovered in Palestine two years later, the Nag Hammadi collection quickly became available to the general public. *Thomas* was translated into English in 1959, and over the coming years the work excited a flurry of media attention. A new wave of interest followed in the late 1970s, when all the Nag Hammadi texts were made available in translation as *The Nag Hammadi Library in English* (1977), and

Elaine Pagels published her influential account of *The Gnostic Gospels* (1979).[3] Pagels's book, a masterpiece of popularization, immediately became a favorite item in church reading groups no less than college classrooms.

Since the 1970s, scholars working on Jesus and Christian origins have made much use of the Nag Hammadi collection, as well as other related texts such as the *Gospel of Mary*, which had been known previously, but which only now became generally available. Based on these long-lost texts, countless popular books and media reports suggest a picture of Christian origins quite at variance with standard accounts, and present the hidden gospels as the precious remains of a whole lost world of ancient Christianity. The suppressed gospels indicate the existence of alternative currents within the startlingly diverse Jesus movement, or The Way, as it was probably known before anyone coined the term Christianity.[4]

The impact of the new sources is not hard to comprehend. Traditionally, the story of primitive Christianity told how the church developed organically from the time of the apostles: though this community had to fight off some serious rivals over the years, the voice of true Christianity was always associated with one clearly identifiable mainstream church. There was never any doubt about which was the one true path, namely, orthodoxy, and which were the byways, the heresies. Rival groups with unfamiliar names such as the Gnostics and Montanists, Ebionites and Marcionites, were deviant breakaway sects, historical dead-ends doomed to extinction. In the case of some heretical factions, scholars even doubted whether they were Christian in anything more than name. Today, though, we commonly read that there existed in the first Christian centuries an enormous range of doctrines and practices, all equally legitimate, all with equal right to boast a link to Jesus and his first apostles. No particular path should ipso facto be labeled orthodoxy or heresy. What later became orthodoxy, the Catholic Church, originally held no privileged position, but was just one strand of opinion among many: it was not a case of the mainstream versus the heresies, but rather a struggle of competing mainstreams. Following the subtitle of a recent book, this is a story of "How Jesus Inspired Not One True Christianity, but Many."[5]

In the modern vision, too, the classic four gospels have lost their privileged position. Traditionally, a clear and straightforward division separated the classic four gospels, which were early and reliable sources for the life of Jesus, and the apocryphal texts, which were late and spurious. The word *apocrypha* comes from the same root as crypt or cryptic, and literally signifies that the works in question are "hidden." In modern English usage, an apocryphal story is one of dubious origin, far removed from reliable fact. To speak of a story as apocryphal is to label it a rumor, perhaps an urban legend, so how could an apocryphal text possibly claim to possess gospel certainty? Already in the second and third centuries, some orthodox Fathers of the early church used "apocryphal" as synonymous with "forged" or "false." Today, though, it is argued that the other currents of early Christianity also had their own gospel traditions, quite distinct from those we have known over the centuries. These works might even be "apocryphal" in the positive sense of that word found among other ancient religions, namely, material that was hidden from anyone unqualified to receive these weighty mysteries.[6]

The existence of these early gospels raises troubling questions about the limits of the New Testament and its approved list of contents. Since the fourth and fifth centuries, twenty-seven books constitute the New Testament canon, which is the Greek word for "rule": literally, the canonical texts are the "regular" books. But why is Luke canonical, and *Thomas* not? With so many hidden gospels now brought to light, it is now often claimed that the four gospels were simply four among many of roughly equal worth, and the alternative texts gave just as valid a picture of Jesus as the texts we have today. When we read the gospel texts found at Nag Hammadi and elsewhere, we are rediscovering quite authentic records of the earliest Christianity—or should we rather speak of Christianities?

According to the modern account of the emerging church, the spectrum of acceptable Christian opinions narrowed dramatically over time. As orthodoxy won, it proceeded to destroy its rivals and their texts, in which the vindictive mainstream church found so many subversive ideas. The winners then declared their favored texts canonical, and the losers became apocryphal. The four gospels survived a kind of Darwinian struggle because they were favored by the churches and religious traditions which eventually arrogated to themselves the names of catholic and orthodox, by the Great Church that achieved political power when the Roman Empire was converted in the early fourth century. To quote a book produced by the Jesus Seminar, "With the Council of Nicaea in 325, the orthodox party solidified its hold on

the Christian tradition, and other wings of the Christian movement were choked off."[7] If political accident had resulted in the
triumph of other groups, then presumably the distinctive texts of
these "other wings of the movement" would have become the
Christian norm. In that eventuality, perhaps, works such as Luke
and Mark would then have vanished from view, with the last surviving copies buried in a jar in some Egyptian desert or Judaean
cave. At the same time, our histories would relegate the uphold-
ers of what we call orthodoxy to the position of minor heretical
thinkers, on the margins of Christian development. The winners
chose the canon, and on grounds of political expediency rather
than historical judgment.

While the implacable orthodox church felt that destroying its
rivals was necessary to preserve the purity of true Christianity
from Satanic pollution, many modern scholars have a far greater
sympathy for the texts and ideas which, often literally, went
underground. Elaine Pagels writes that today, "We now begin to
see that what we call Christianity—and what we identify as Christian tradition—actually represents only a small selection of specific sources, chosen from among dozens of others. Who made
that selection, and for what reasons?"[8] The loss of the almost limitless diversity of early Christian thought is commonly seen as a
lamentable suppression of much that was most valuable in the
Jesus tradition. Conversely, modern accounts portray the mainstream church as suspect and devious, and the canonical gospels
as weapons wielded by the powerful.

While the newly found documents have enriched our understanding of the early Christian movement, many scholars also
believe that they have revolutionized the study of the world of
Jesus himself. The pioneering Quest of the Historical Jesus followed the emergence of critical historical methods in the nineteenth century, which was described in a classic book by Albert
Schweitzer. The second quest followed in the 1960s and 1970s,
and was swiftly followed by a distinct "third quest" in the 1980s
and 1990s.[9] (We can debate whether each of these supposed
events was a discrete phenomenon, or whether it was in fact a
phase in a continuing endeavor.) In large measure, this latest
quest is distinguished from its predecessors by the discovery of
new sources of information, above all, the hidden gospels.
According to some scholars, we finally have access to documents
and other resources which had been unavailable since not long

after the time of the apostles: only at the end of the twentieth century did it become possible to gain an understanding of Jesus and his age infinitely superior to that of the past sixty or seventy benighted generations. To quote Stevan L. Davies, "For nineteen hundred years or so the canonical texts of the New Testament were the sole source of historically reliable knowledge concerning Jesus of Nazareth. In 1945, this circumstance changed" (the reference is to the finding of the complete text of *Thomas*).[10]

Much of the attention received by the hidden gospels reflects the advocacy of the Jesus Seminar. Fundamental to the Seminar's approach is what the group's founder Robert Funk has called "the end of canonical imperialism," the determination not to be constrained by only those sources approved by imperial and ecclesiastical authorities over the centuries.[11] In 1993, the Seminar group published their new edition of *The Five Gospels*, in which they state that "foremost among the reasons for a new translation is the discovery of the *Gospel of Thomas*."[12] Throughout the writings of Seminar Fellows, *Thomas* is used as a yardstick to assess the accuracy of words attributed to Jesus. Seminar members have also been diligently engaged in publishing other suppressed texts, and have presented a major collection which boasts the title *The Complete Gospels*. This volume "presents for the first time anywhere all twenty of the known gospels from the early Christian era. . . . Each of these gospel records offers fresh glimpses into the world of Jesus and his followers."[13] This effort is advertised as an attempt to restore the suppressed scriptures to the lay public, much as Luther and the early Protestant reformers gave the people the Bible in their own vernacular tongue.

If we can believe some claims about the hidden gospels, then this historical Jesus was utterly different from what most of us would have imagined until very recently. According to readings of *Thomas* and its like, the earliest Jesus Way was nothing like the religious system which it ultimately became, the world of Churchianity. Instead of focusing on concepts such as sin and judgment, redemption and otherworldly salvation, early Jesus followers were seekers after mystical illumination, of heavenly Wisdom. Neither hierarchical nor liturgical, the movement was individualistic, egalitarian, and intoxicatingly diverse. Based on *Thomas*, it is claimed that Jesus' "message is strongly counter-cultural: he shuns materialism and directs the reader towards the simple life, a spiritual existence. . . . Jesus here is not a messiah but a social radical, telling listeners to reject society's phony piety and the hollow

values of the business world."[14] This Jesus teaches that the kingdom of God is present and attainable here and now, within each
follower: he mocks concepts of eschatology, any hopes or fears
about the end of the world. The rejection of the apocalyptic Jesus
is probably the greatest single insight derived from the hidden
gospels, and presented as unshakable fact, the idea pervades contemporary critical New Testament scholarship. For the radical
scholars at least, the change of attitude toward the nature of
Jesus' core message represents a full-scale paradigm shift. Early
Jesus followers were not even "Christians," as that term implies a
belief in the concept of the messiah (*christos,* or anointed one),
with all its theological baggage. Jesus was neither Christ, nor a
Christian.

Though the controversial "Quest for Jesus" has been widely
publicized, no less significant for contemporary Christians is the
equally subversive Quest for the Earliest Church, a search which
depends entirely on insights from the hidden gospels. In rediscovering the real Jesus, scholars ask how the subversive inner kingdom which he preached gave way to the all too worldly power of
the institutional churches. In this process, it is claimed, Jesus'
principles of love and individual self-discovery were transformed
by ideas of law and patriarchy; a popular spiritual movement
became an authoritarian empire; democracy gave place to hierarchy, spontaneity to ritualism, gender equality to misogyny.
According to this view, triumphant catholicism concealed the revolutionary origins of the Jesus Way, and labeled as heretics those
groups and individuals who had the courage to maintain the pristine vision. The true Jesus tradition was not primarily found
within the Great Church, but was rather preserved within the dismissively named heresies. In only a few isolated areas could a
pure Jesus-oriented spirituality survive the constricting pressures
of the bureaucratic church. In a currently popular view, one such
area of resistance was the Celtic church, which flourished in Ireland and Western Britain during the early middle ages, and which
has proved immensely attractive to many moderns, both Christians and New Age adherents.[15]

For Elaine Pagels, perhaps the most important of these submerged early traditions was Gnosticism, the followers of *gnosis* or
spiritual knowledge, who were most active in the second and
third centuries, and whose ideas permeate the Nag Hammadi
writings. Viewed through her wistful account, Gnosticism was a
glorious historical might-have-been, which is both relevant and

attractive to a modern audience. This was a forgotten movement of mystics unfettered by dogma, who followed Jesus in their rejection of institutions and hierarchies. Gnostic believers practiced "equal access, equal participation and equal claims to knowledge," to the extent of allocating clerical functions by lot at their ceremonies. Like other so-called heresies, Gnosticism gave women a far higher status than did orthodoxy. Gnostic spirituality is easily reconciled with the insights of modern psychotherapy, as the heretics believed that the conflicts and dramas described in the Christian world-view occurred within the mind of the individual. Gnostic writers were intuitive and subjective, and "considered original creative invention to be the mark of anyone who becomes spiritually alive."[16] It is implied that the historical Jesus would have been far more at home in these circles than in the stodgy and authoritarian church which claimed to speak in his name. The very early date of the lost scriptures gives the Gnostics and their like a plausible claim to rank as a genuine form of early Christianity and, who knows, perhaps even the one true voice.

Supported by such laudatory reviews, dense mystical texts written 1800 years ago by obscure Syrian and Egyptian heretics have demonstrated real appeal for a modern mass audience. The alternate gospels play a central role in the "Jesus books" published by the major commercial publishing houses, which give the impression that *Thomas*, *Peter*, and the rest do in fact represent gospel truth, that they even predate the famous four evangelists. The picture of early Christianities described here has been popularized not just through academic books and articles but through many popular presentations, in television documentaries such as the PBS series *From Jesus to Christ*, broadcast in 1998.[17] Through such means, texts like *Thomas* have become a familiar presence in religious debate and consciousness. As one orthodoxy is established, so older ideas are relabeled as deviant or marginal: in terms of understanding early Christianity, the heretical has virtually become orthodox, and vice versa.

Evaluating the New Gospels

But are the new views true? In fact, the iconoclastic views of early Christianity so often proposed in recent years can be challenged in many ways, so many in fact that it is amazing that these ideas have achieved the wide credence they have. One basic problem is the claim that the hidden gospels contain a wealth of information which is new and incendiary. To the contrary, much of what was uncovered is not relevant to Christian origins, while what is relevant is not new, still less inflammatory. Conservative scholars such as Luke Timothy Johnson and John P. Meier have fired powerful counterblasts against the whole historical methodology of the New Quest, particularly as practiced by the Jesus Seminar. As one aspect of this counteroffensive, and by no means the central one, conservatives largely reject the evidence of the various hidden gospels on which so much of the radical scholarship relies. Both Johnson and Meier attack the claims advanced on behalf of an early date for the gospels of *Thomas* and *Peter*, which also attract convincing rebuttal in the collection of essays entitled *Jesus under Fire*.[18] Conservatives cite an impressive array of specialist scholars who are thoroughly unconvinced by arguments for the revolutionary significance of the lost gospels, even outstanding texts like *Thomas*.

Despite the claims of their advocates, the problems with taking the hidden gospels as historical sources are, or should be, self-evident. The idea that these documents have opened a window on the earliest days of Christianity stands or falls on whether they were written at a primitive stage in that story, and much depends on determining the dates at which these texts were written. The scholarly literature offers a very broad range of datings for these texts, but the consensus is that most of the works found at Nag Hammadi belong to the late second and third centuries. This is much later than the canonical gospels, on which the Gnostic works can often be clearly shown to depend. While the Gnostic texts are ancient, their value as independent sources of information is questionable, so that the canonical gospels really are both more ancient and authoritative than virtually all their rivals.

Far from being the alternative voices of Jesus' first followers, most of the lost gospels should rather be seen as the writings of much later dissidents who broke away from an already established orthodox church. This is not a particularly controversial statement, despite the impression that we may get from much recent writing on the historical Jesus. The late character of the alternative texts is crucial to matters of historicity and reliability. Historical research is as good as the sources on which it relies, and to the extent that the latest quest for the historical Jesus is founded on the hidden gospels, that endeavor is fatally flawed. To take a specific example, it is wildly unlikely that the parable of the woman with the jar derives from the historical Jesus, stemming as it does from *Thomas* alone, unsupported by any other source. The most remarkable point here is why any scholar should have assumed differently.

For the same reasons of history and chronology, it is difficult to see the hidden gospels as crucial new sources about the development of the church, or the relationship between orthodoxy and heresy. These texts depict a world of individualistic mystics and magi whose unfettered speculations are unconstrained by ecclesiastical structures, and it is common to suggest that this freewheeling situation represented a primitive reality which was ultimately destroyed by the emerging hierarchical church. But the institutional church was by no means an oppressive latecomer, and was rather a very early manifestation of the Jesus movement. We have a good number of genuinely early documents of Christian antiquity from before 125, long before the hidden gospels were composed, and these give us a pretty consistent picture of a church which is already hierarchical and liturgical, which possesses an organized clergy, and which is very sensitive to matters of doctrinal orthodoxy. Just as the canonical gospels were in existence before their heterodox counterparts, so the orthodox church did precede the heretics, and by a comfortable margin. And for all its flaws, that church has by far the best claim to a direct inheritance from the apostolic age. Despite all the recent discoveries, the traditional model of Christian history has a great deal more to recommend it than the revisionist accounts.

Nor are the "new" findings touted in recent years all that new: contrary to some recent writings, the scholarly world did not flounder in darkness until illumination came from Nag Hammadi. Basic to the dramatic account of the rediscovered gospels is the idea that they restored to the world knowledge which had been lost for many centuries. At last, we are told, after 1600 years, we finally hear the heretics speak for themselves. The problem with this approach is that many of the insights about early Christianity found in the lost texts had been known for many years before the Nag Hammadi discoveries, and had in fact already penetrated a mass audience.

With few exceptions, modern scholars show little awareness of the very active debate about alternative Christianities which flourished in bygone decades, so that we have a misleading impression that all the worthwhile scholarship has been produced within the last thirty years or so. To the contrary, much of the evidence needed to construct a radical revision of Christian origins had been available for many years prior to the 1970s, if not the 1870s. Through the nineteenth century, the idea that Gnostics might have kept alive the early truths of Jesus was familiar to critical religious thinkers, some on the far fringes of academe, others more respectable. Even the theory that Jesus was an Essene mystic, a member of the group that probably wrote the Dead Sea Scrolls, was familiar over a century before those documents were uncovered and ignited so much popular speculation. Speculations about the Essenes overlapped with ideas about the Gnostics, and both were seen as close to the earliest Christianity: even a century ago, people dreamed of finding actual documents to verify these theories.

Particularly between about 1880 and 1920, a cascade of new discoveries transformed attitudes to early Christianity, both the mainstream and the heretical fringes. The most exciting find involved portions of the *Gospel of Thomas* located in Egypt, and then known simply as the Sayings of Jesus. Though the work did not have quite the revolutionary impact that it has on modern scholars, quotations from *Thomas* were appearing in works of popular piety long before the Nag Hammadi finds. And just as modern writers claim *Thomas* as a fifth gospel, so many experts a hundred years ago awarded a similar laurel to the recently found *Gospel of Peter*. Many of the insights and observations which have been based on the recently found Gnostic texts were also well known before 1900. Even the special role of women disciples, which has attracted so much comment in recent years, was already being discussed in that epoch. The image of Jesus choosing Mary Magdalen as his especially beloved disciple runs through a large Gnostic work called the *Pistis Sophia*, which was available in a popular English translation as far back as 1896. The notion was quoted in feminist and New Age writings of the early twentieth century— and though this tends to be forgotten in modern writings, both feminists and New Age adherents wrote extensively on early Christianity in this period.[19] Radical perspectives on religion were not an innovation of the 1960s. Far from being decently concealed in abstruse academic journals, the new speculations reached a mass audience through magazines, newspapers, and novels: they were thoroughly familiar to any reasonably well-informed layperson.

Over the last two or three centuries, scholars and activists have periodically rediscovered the notion that the historical Jesus was a subversive individual mystic whose suppressed doctrine survived in the teachings of lost heresies and hidden gospels. This lengthy prehistory must affect our view of the latest quest, making it difficult to see current interests as simply a natural response to the outpouring of data from the rediscovered texts: there really is nothing new about the Jesus reconstructed from texts such as *Thomas*. To the contrary, the search for alternative Christianities has been a perennial phenomenon within Western culture since the Enlightenment: it has never vanished entirely, though in different eras, it has attracted larger or smaller degrees of public attention.

The American Gospel

But if the ideas were so familiar, why should there have been such an upsurge of interest and enthusiasm in the Gnostic gospels over the last twenty years? One reason for their importance is that the sheer volume of available texts grew impressively after the Nag Hammadi finds, encouraging vastly more writing on the topic, while the expansion of the universities and the religious studies profession since the 1960s has swelled the ranks of academics and graduate students in search of topics. This has been a genuinely exciting academic field which has established many careers.

Even so, the most important change seems not to have been the new volume of information, but a fundamental change of attitude among scholars, and in the institutions in which they worked. The academic profession engaged in studying the Bible was transformed, above all by the influx of large numbers of women scholars, but also by the impact of postmodern and feminist theories. These changes had a revolutionary impact on attitudes to issues of canon and the nature of history, and to movements once regarded as peripheral and heretical. Scholarship on Gnosticism and alternative Christianities now revived, after a period of some decades in which these ideas had fallen into disfavor, probably because the subject had been so overworked in earlier years. From the 1960s, the fringe movements suddenly returned to view as essential for understanding Christian origins. Once that transformation had occurred, new and existing materials were reinterpreted accordingly, and scholars reexamined texts and ideas with which they had long had a nodding acquaintance. The discovery of the noncanonical scriptures marks a change of perception and ideology, rather than a balanced or objective response to a new corpus of evidence. As the cynical saying declares, "If I hadn't believed it, I wouldn't have seen it with my own eyes." If we can borrow the language of detective stories, the new gospel finds provided the *means* for new directions in research, while the expansion of the academic world supplied the *opportunity*: even so, a *motive* was still required, and this came from the new intellectual currents and theories which focused attention on topics once relegated to the academic fringe.

Radical ideas can be proposed and discussed without causing much disturbance outside the closed ranks of academe, but what has been remarkable about the recent study of Gnosticism and its gospels is how broadly and rapidly these matters have affected a general audience. At the end of the twentieth century, as at its beginning, a broad general public demonstrated an avid interest in the new gospels and the lessons which can supposedly be drawn from them. The reasons for this development are not hard to seek, since the scholars and writers presenting the "real Jesus" and his followers were making them sound so precisely compatible with strictly contemporary concerns, so relevant to modern-day debates. The marketing of alternative Christianity represents a model case study in effective rhetoric, in which a potential audience is first identified, and a message is then tailored to its particular needs and interests.

Despite its dubious sources and controversial methods, the new Jesus scholarship of the 1980s and 1990s gained such a following because it told a lay audience what it wanted to hear. For some ideological perspectives, the new view of early Christianity has been almost too good to be true, in validating postmodern approaches. The hidden gospels have been used to provide scriptural warrant for sweeping new interpretations of Jesus, for interpreting theological statements in a purely symbolic and psychological sense, and for challenging dogmatic or legal rules on the basis of the believer's subjective moral sense. Generally, the hidden gospels offer wonderful news for liberals, feminists, and radicals within the churches, who challenge what they view as outdated institutions and prejudices. And this is by no means true of the churches alone: since Christianity is so fundamental a component of Western culture, any radical reinterpretation of the movement's core message is bound to reverberate through contemporary issues and debates. Though proponents of the radical view usually write as scholars, there is rarely much pretense of objectivity, in the sense that orthodoxy and the institutional church are regularly blamed as authoritarian, patriarchal, and narrow, while the heresies suppressed were egalitarian, creative, and libertarian.

The rediscovered texts help shift the whole ground of debate within the churches, permitting liberals to argue from their own distinctive version of the primitive gospel. Feminist scholars in particular note the central role which women play in texts like the *Gospel of Mary*, which is believed to show that women were apostles, leaders, and teachers in the earliest Jesus movement: if this is the case, how can modern churches refuse to grant priestly authority to women today? Apart from the obvious appeal for women, the new portrait of Gnosticism is profoundly attractive for modern seekers, that large constituency interested in spirituality without the trappings of organized religion or dogma. For such an audience, texts like *Thomas* are so enticing because of their individualistic quality, their portrait of a Jesus who is a wisdom teacher rather than a Redeemer or heavenly Savior. Modern readers are drawn by the work's presentation of the mystical quest as a return to primal innocence, an idea that recalls the psychological quest for the inner child. Regardless of the work's historical value, reading *Thomas* undoubtedly can provide the basis for meditation and spiritual insight, as well as justifying diverse forms of contemporary spirituality. As N. T. Wright remarks, the emphasis on the "real" Jesus of the alternative gospels "appears to legitimate precisely the sort of religion that a large swathe of America yearns for: a free-for-all, do-it-yourself spirituality with a strong agenda of social protest against the powers that be and an I'm-OK-you're-OK attitude on all matters religious and ethical. You can have any sort of spirituality you like (Zen, walking labyrinths on church floors, Tai Chi) as long as it isn't orthodox Christianity." Some have given this eclectic creed the suspect title of "flexodoxy," flexible orthodoxy.[20]

Equally appealing for modern believers, the Jesus of the hidden gospels has many points of contact with the great spiritual traditions of Asia. This concept makes it vastly easier to promote dialogue with other great world religions, and diminishes any uniquely Christian claims to divine revelation. Pagels has written that "one need only listen to the words of the *Gospel of Thomas* to hear how it resonates with the Buddhist tradition. . . . these ancient gospels tend to point beyond faith toward a path of solitary searching to find understanding, or *gnosis*." [21] She asks, "Does not such teaching—the identity of the divine and human, the concern with illusion and enlightenment, the founder who is presented not as Lord but as spiritual guide—sound more Eastern than Western?" She suggests that we might see an explicitly Indian influence in *Thomas*, perhaps via the Christian communities in southern India, the so-called Thomas Christians.[22] The statements of this Jesus even have something of the quality of Zen koan: stories like the woman with the jar of meal are obvious examples. Coincidentally or not, the Jesus movement was initially known as the Way, which is the same self-descriptive term used by other great religions and philosophical systems, including Buddhism and Taoism. Jesus thus becomes far more congenial to modern sensibilities about both gender and multiculturalism.

This Jesus meshes very well indeed with contemporary concerns, but the whole "hidden gospels" theme also echoes older traditions in American society, particularly its thoroughly Protestant assumptions. Even people reluctant to identify with historic orthodoxies still need the comfort of knowing that they are acting in the traditions of "real" Christianity, and that there are genuine early Gospels, written texts, to validate these beliefs: Protestants have long been stirred by the dream of restoring the true church of the apostolic age.[23] Also quintessentially American is the distrust of external authorities such as the clergy, and the sense that through their affected learning, the priests have hidden the truth from the people. This was a key element in the anti-Catholic fears which blazed for so long in the nation's history. In the late twentieth century, such ideas spread quite widely among Catholics themselves, whose dissents over matters of authority and sexuality have so often put them in opposition to ecclesiastical hierarchies.

Over the last century, the literature on hidden gospels, genuine and fraudulent, has been pervaded by conspiratorial speculations which suggest that some powerful body (usually the Roman Catholic Church) is cynically plotting either to conceal the true gospel, or to plant bogus documents to deceive the faithful. Such ideas run through the many novels and fictional presentations on this theme: in the Hollywood film *Stigmata*, the Vatican is shown desperately trying to suppress a "Jesus Gospel" which is unmistakably modeled on the *Gospel of Thomas*.

In an episode of the TV show *The X-Files*, a forger produces a bogus "Gospel of Mary Magdalen," which records a sexual relationship between Jesus and Mary. Convinced of the document's authenticity, a cardinal who is considered a likely candidate for the papacy purchases the supposed gospel in order to suppress it. Ultimately, the cardinal murders the forger. However bizarre this may sound, the story is based on events that occurred in Utah in the 1980s, when a real-life forger produced documents purporting to expose embarrassing secrets about the nineteenth-century origins of Mormonism. He then tried to blackmail senior officials in the Mormon church, who wished desperately to keep these supposed discoveries from public gaze. Presumably the writers of the *X-Files* episode ("Hollywood A.D.") felt that giving this tale an anti-Catholic slant would appeal much more directly to popular prejudices about religious trickery.

Much contemporary discussion of the earliest church is laden with age-old anti-Catholic rhetoric, with its imagery of power-hungry popes and book-burning prelates, set against heroic dissidents clinging to their scriptures of liberty. These ideas have an added significance for liberal and feminist scholars whose most cherished issues so often involve conflict with contemporary religious conservatism. In matters such as abortion, contraception, homosexuality, or women's ordination, the main enemy is the Roman Catholic Church, which is stereotyped in terms of reaction and misogyny. A related form of anticlericalism focuses on evangelical Protestant groups like the Moral Majority of the 1980s or the Christian Coalition of the last decade.[24] When contemporary accounts attack the oppressive ecclesiastical establishment in early Christianity, the writers seem motivated at least in part by these contemporary political concerns and stereotypes, which are read back into the first centuries. Conversely, many of these scholars openly identify with the Gnostics and other sectarians who resisted the Great Church; in our own age at least, the title of heretic is an honorable one.

Ironically, the liberal emphasis on restoring the presumed "early Christianity" by means of its authoritative texts bears a strong resemblance to traditional fundamentalist approaches, which are instead based on the canonical scriptures. The whole issue of canons is critical here. Postmodern thought holds that no text should be privileged or authoritative, as each reflects the ideological stance of a particular hegemonic group. Scholars claim a duty to challenge the received canon of approved and valued texts, whether in literature or in religion. Radical critics seek to dethrone the canonical authority of the New Testament, yet in a way which substitutes an alternative range of scriptural authorities. Though these new texts are more acceptable to current tastes, they are still treated with the same kind of veneration once reserved for the Bible. Particularly with some of the feminist approaches to texts such as *Mary*, we find what can only be described as a kind of inverted fundamentalism, a loving consecration of the noncanonical.

The Gospel Myth

The whole idea of hidden gospels and lost Christianity has a still deeper resonance, in that it appeals at the level of myth, using that word in its anthropological sense, rather than in its popular connotation of something which is a lie or a fiction. Myths emerge, or are reconstructed, to meet the changing needs of a society, particularly at a time when values are in flux or when ideological conflicts become acute. Myths summarize profound truths in the form of stories, which become popular and memorable through their use of familiar themes and plot elements. These stories usually offer a simplistic morality with sharply defined good and evil, with few intermediate shades of gray: they tell of heroes and villains, presented with familiar folktale themes. Sometimes, myths are built upon the framework of actual historical events, and such constructed histories guide the actions of contemporary politics and modern-day activists. This is a familiar enough idea in the context of strife-torn regions like Ireland and the Balkans, but in North America, too, history has repeatedly served its political function. Academics can play a critical role in generating and spreading such historical mythologies, which are frequently bookish and literary in their origins.[25]

It may seem curious to use the word mythology in the context of the hidden gospels which have had so much impact in our own day, which are not mythical in the sense of being fictitious. The texts certainly exist, and do represent the ideas of early Christian groups: for all the attacks on the historical reliability of the contents, no one has ever suggested that the Nag Hammadi hoard contains forgeries. Yet the associated story tells how the real Jesus was hidden behind the deceptive facade of Christianity, until hidden documents were found which exposed the truth and overthrew a conspiracy that had lasted for centuries. Phrased in this way, modern perceptions of Christian history sound less like scholarly reconstruction than the sort of mythology common to many societies, with their tales of original innocence, catastrophic fall, and fortunate redemption. This mythical framework adds immeasurably to the authority which is claimed for the lost gospels, and contributes to their power in galvanizing contemporary movements.

The process by which history becomes serviceable as a modern mythology is exemplified by Nachman Ben-Yehuda's model sociological account of how the first-century siege of Masada became the crucial national myth of the state of Israel, a myth that developed from the 1940s onward: as we see below, the mythologizing of Masada has many analogies with contemporary ideas about the hidden gospels.[26] Ben-Yehuda shows how the events of an actual siege and massacre were thoroughly distorted in subsequent retellings to fit the interests and ideological concern of modern-day factions. The story was systematically repackaged over time, which meant simplifying a complicated tale, ironing over moral ambiguities; ideologically useful themes were highlighted while inconvenient messages were omitted or distorted. Certain historians and scholars played a critical role in advocating the particular version of the story which gained credence, and they became what in sociological terms are known as moral entrepreneurs, the inventors and purveyors of the myth. Of course, they could not have succeeded as fully as they did if the story did not appear relevant to multiple modern constituencies, and the new account was precisely tailored to the concerns and prejudices of the contemporary audience. As the process of ideological reconstruction continued, so both historical scholarship and archaeology adjusted the facts to fit the desired purpose, to promote a version suitable for popular consumption. Ben-Yehuda then shows how this invented history developed a life of its own as a full-blown contemporary mythology. It served to "develop a new sense of identity both individual and national," as modern Israelis modeled their actions on those attributed to the warriors of old. The story offered a crucial sense of antiquity and continuity: since the event permitted Jews to assert their long continuity in the land, it provided an additional justification for the reoccupation of Palestine under the Zionist movement. Whatever the objective basis of the events concerned, they have become an immovable and indeed cherished component of collective memory.

Similarly, scholars have used the hidden gospels to construct an effective and useful myth of Christian origins, however great the effort required to make the Gnostics and their writings fit the desired framework. Just as Israeli historians had to make Masada's defenders nobler and more patriotic than they actually were, less bloodthirsty and terroristic, so the Gnostics are viewed with rose-colored spectacles as paradigms of tolerance and skepticism born 2000 years before their time: the reality was much less appealing, since the actual sect was highly elitist and anti-Jewish, and its thought-world was thoroughly misogynistic. As in the case of Masada, academics led the way as moral entrepreneurs in the effort to reconstruct early Christianity: the critical scholars of the Jesus Seminar have to a striking extent become the architects of historical memory in this field. The story they told, a well-rounded liberal mythology, has gained such influence because it permits modern-day activists to identify with their early predecessors, and demonstrates the ancient roots of current concerns. Just as the Gnostics and their like supposedly fought tenaciously to defend authentic Christianity, nondogmatic and woman-friendly, so modern students of the hidden gospels continue the good fight at the beginning of the twenty-first century. It remains to be seen whether the mythology attached to the hidden gospels will achieve the kind of hegemony over popular perceptions of religion that the idea of Masada acquired in Israeli life and culture.

Much of the appeal of the hidden gospels is in the very fact of their hiddenness, with all the intrinsically dramatic implications of secrecy, persecution, escape, refuge, rescue, buried treasure, even burial and resurrection. The visceral, mythical power of these notions can be appreciated by a hypothetical exercise. Let us imagine the commercial fate of a scholarly project which announced the goal of publishing a collection of Biblical and doctrinal texts by a separatist Jewish sect from the intertestamental period, probably from the first two centuries before the Christian era. The idea sounds utterly lacking in popular appeal, and unlikely to interest a nonspecialist public. Of course, the collection in question does exist under the celebrated title of the Dead Sea Scrolls, and the story of its concealment and discovery is known in broad outline to most literate people. The very name of the Scrolls has become uniquely evocative: "the term is redolent of enigma, of intrigue, perhaps even of sacred mysteries; hovering in the background are images of caves, scrolls, barren deserts and intense scholars hunched over tiny scraps of leather."[27] Largely because of the seductive narrative attached to this tale, this arcane collection has repeatedly been published in best-selling popular editions, and has frequently been discussed in related books and magazine articles. Anything concerning the Scrolls is guaranteed an instant market across the reading spectrum, from technical scholarly books to supermarket tabloids. Much of their mass appeal derives from the fact of their burial, which raises the suspicion that they must contain something worthwhile. They are validated by the fact of their concealment: if they didn't contain vital secrets, why were they buried in the first place?

The concealment theme has particularly rich connotations in a religious context. The idea of a religion being restored or revitalized by an amazing discovery of lost texts has many parallels over the centuries, and might well be an inevitable component of any religion which sets such a high premium on literacy and the importance of scriptures. Lost or hidden texts are the most obvious and potent means of justifying a revolutionary change or revival, in which the purity of ancient religious truth is restored. Such a device is all the more necessary in early societies, which are deeply suspicious of deliberate innovation, or departure from tradition: in the words of the *Tao Te Ching*, "Woe to him who willfully innovates." In ancient Egypt and Mesopotamia, change was so often justified by claims of a miraculous textual discovery that the motif of book-finding becomes a cliché in inscriptions and historical records.[28] In a society which venerates a closed corpus of inspired scriptures, such a "rediscovery" can be an ideal means of effecting doctrinal change. At a stroke, it adds more congenial texts to the existing canon, while simultaneously challenging the uniqueness and authority of the traditionally accepted writings.

Judaism itself was fundamentally reshaped by the finding of a hidden book, which reputedly occurred in the seventh century B.C. The story tells how a priest of the Jerusalem Temple stumbled across an ancient text which described "the Law of the Lord given through Moses," which is probably the book which we today find in the Pentateuch as Deuteronomy.[29] When this book was read to the king, Josiah, he was appalled to find how far his people had strayed from the divine commandments, and was inspired to launch a moral and religious reformation, destroying the popular shrines and cult sites which violated the worship of the one true God, who dwelled in Jerusalem. According to most historians, this book of the law was a recent composition by the priests of the Temple, who had a revolutionary vision of an uncompromising monotheism which had no real precedents in the land. Such a radical departure from traditional ways could only be justified by an invented text, which was palmed off on the ancient national hero, Moses. This successful forgery inspired a tectonic shift in Israelite religion, and also contributed to a general rewriting of Hebrew history. The story has had a vast impact on generations of both Jews and Christians.

Similar patterns and narrative themes occur in other religions and spiritual movements. Much of modern occultism claims descent from the Rosicrucian movement, an invented phenomenon of the early seventeenth century, when a scholar reported the discovery of texts which revealed the secrets of magic and mysticism. These documents had been buried in the tomb of an ancient sage, who had gained his learning in Egypt and elsewhere.[30] The restoration of a pristine truth can even be seen as an apocalyptic sign, a portent of the end times, as God offers his people a final chance to repent. Some evangelical writers have noted the coincidence that the Dead Sea Scrolls were discovered only the year before the establishment of the state of Israel, an event believed to fulfil so many messianic prophecies.

The most famous American example of a rediscovered gospel is Joseph Smith's discovery of the buried gold plates from which he reputedly translated the *Book of Mormon*.[31] According to the story, the plates had been deposited after a climactic battle in which one population group of early America had been all but exterminated, leaving only these records. The religion founded upon this particular hidden gospel, the Latter Day Saints, spread rapidly in response to the messianic and millenarian hopes prevalent in the America of the 1830s and 1840s, and the movement now claims perhaps 10 million members worldwide. The church continues to thrive by the promise of revealing lost wisdom, a new gospel for the end times. Its most successful advertising materials ask outsiders whether they would like to know even more words and deeds of Jesus, before offering them access to "another Testament of Jesus Christ," namely, the *Book of Mormon*. As an interesting counterpart to the Nag Hammadi finds, Smith's plates were written in the "Reformed Egyptian" tongue. Euro-American culture has long idealized Egypt as the appropriate home for lost secrets and ancient wisdom: witness the eye-in-the-pyramid design on the Great Seal of the United States.

Seeing the new version of Christian origins as a mythical tale helps explain the often misleading emphases of contemporary accounts of the lost gospels, as the facts of the particular case are modified to fit the expected formulas and narrative themes. Above all, the discovery must be revolutionary, something that radically changes our concept of the world, and so the newness of the material discovered must be emphasized and, often, grossly exaggerated. It will not do, for example, to say that these finds are somewhat valuable for specialists, but that they really tell us little more than we already knew; they have to be earth-shattering. The unparalleled importance of the material must also be stressed. In the context of a historical find, it must be given a date which is extremely early, and should ideally be directly associated with some famous individual or event. The Nag Hammadi texts are presumed to reveal truths about the core events of the Christian faith, rather than merely shedding light on church conflicts two or three centuries after Jesus' time. We repeatedly find attempts to push the dates of the alternative gospels ever earlier, to give them an authority superior to the canonical books.

Ideally, the story of both the concealment and the discovery should be as dramatic as possible, involving secrecy, subterfuge, and perhaps violence. Nag Hammadi offers rich pickings for anyone in quest of such themes, as the documents may well have been hidden to save them from the fanatical monks who used violence to enforce the strictest orthodoxy. The discovery of the collection in the 1940s is quite as dramatic, involving as it does a tale of murder, blood feud, and revenge killing among the Egyptian peasants who stumbled across the documents.[32] The process of exposing the new finds should also involve conflict, perhaps against some entrenched institution which seeks to prevent the truth emerging, so that an element of conspiracy theory will commonly enter in. The power of this idea is obvious from the story of the Dead Sea Scrolls, discovered in 1947, but not fully released until the early 1990s. The long delay inevitably generated conspiracy stories, claiming that the committee which controlled these documents was seeking to hide some embarrassing or explosive fact, usually involving Jesus or the origins of Christianity. Largely because of its dramatic qualities, the story of the Scrolls' eventual "liberation" generated huge media interest, incomparably greater than might have been expected for any other archaeological or documentary find in living memory. Though no such drama surrounded the Nag Hammadi texts, iconoclastic New Testament scholars often claim that they are struggling against established powers in the churches and the academy in order to present unpopular truths suppressed for almost two millennia, and the media generally report such claims quite uncritically. Heretics today fight to vindicate the heretics of an earlier generation.

Against this background, it is not difficult to understand the power of the whole notion of hidden gospels. The story offers people something they dearly want, namely, additional information about the "real Jesus" and the primitive church in a manner that precisely fits American assumptions about authority in religion. The information comes complete with a powerful dramatic narrative with heroes and villains, secret societies, buried scriptures, a struggle against oppressive priests, and other elements that seem borrowed direct from folktale. It is an extraordinarily attractive package; the only problem with it is that, at more or less every step, it is misleading, or simply wrong.

Fragments of a Faith Forgotten

Now in Benares, Jesus tarried many days and taught.

THE AQUARIAN GOSPEL OF JESUS THE CHRIST, 29: 29

WHAT DID THEY KNOW and when did they know it? Though the documentary finds of mid-century have encouraged scholars to map the alternative vistas of early Christianity, it is striking how little truly new information emerged from those texts, or how few are the discoveries which would have surprised earlier genera- tions. This may sound strange, given the tendency of modern New Quest scholars to assume that their predecessors simply lacked the critical sources they needed to understand the com- plexity of early Christianity; sometimes, too, we find the added charge that earlier scholars were too hidebound by religious pre- conceptions to speculate about such matters. In the Jesus Semi- nar's edition of *The Complete Gospels,* the editors claim that until very recently, anyone interested in finding out about Jesus was confined to the New Testament texts: "Many interested in Jesus were not even aware of the existence of other gospels, or if they knew of them, did not know where to find them."[1]

Accounts of the finds at Nag Hammadi are said to have caused astonishment not just among the unenlightened masses, but also among scholars themselves. Elaine Pagels writes that "until the discoveries at Nag Hammadi, nearly all our information concern- ing alternative forms of early Christianity came from the massive orthodox attacks upon them. . . . Now, for the first time, we have the opportunity to find out about the earliest Christian heresy; for the first time, the heretics can speak for themselves. . . . we may have to recognize that early Christianity is far more diverse than nearly anyone expected before the Nag Hammadi discoveries."[2] Jesus Seminar founder Robert Funk agrees that "for the first time,

we have ample actual documents produced by the so-called
heretics, rather than reports about them written by their accus-
ers."[3] In the 1998 PBS program *From Jesus to Christ*, the narrator
declares that "what the [Nag Hammadi] books showed was that
early Christianity was even more diverse than scholars had
expected, with many different ways of interpreting Jesus."

Yet most of the radical new interpretations of Jesus arising from
the recent discoveries are no such thing. In broad outline, these
ideas were known to scholars and polemicists at the end of the
nineteenth century, and ever since that point there has been
lively popular interest and speculation about Christian origins. A
vigorous literature has long presented a supposed "real Jesus"
who had been concealed by the sinister tricks of orthodoxy, and
who was revealed by various hidden gospels, genuine or imagi-
nary. A number of these other gospels were available for general
consumption, and were widely read. Then as now, the real
Jesuses who emerged from contemporary speculations varied
kaleidoscopically in character depending on the tastes and ideological predilections of the observer. Virtually all the seemingly
modern insights about the early Jesus movement were arrived at
by skeptical and liberal critics quite independently of the historical
sources which have recently become available to us. Long before
Thomas and the other gospels came to light, the materials lay to
hand for a thorough reconstruction of early Christianity and a
corresponding vindication of the heretics.

Remembering the Heretics

Despite suggestions that the Nag Hammadi documents permitted
us to hear the voices of the heretics "for the first time," the
ancient polemics contained a surprising amount of authentic literature from the heretics themselves, and these materials have been
widely known for centuries. From the earliest days of Christianity,
successive sects, heresies, and movements arose, and many
claimed access to the truths of the religion superior to those
offered by the official or majority churches. For much of Christian
history, scholars devoted themselves to studying the church
Fathers, who so regularly denounced the rival traditions which
they labeled as heresies, and those authors provided a vast
amount of historical evidence in the process (unwittingly, as their
goal was to eradicate their enemies from human memory). Much
could be learned about these sects from patristic scholars such as
Tertullian and Clement of Alexandria, and the various early writ-

ers preserved in the fourth century *Church History* of Eusebius. One of the most comprehensive polemics was the *Adversus Haereses* ("Against the Heresies") of Irenaeus, who was Bishop of Lyon around the year 180.[4] While these writings made no pretense at objectivity, they were richly informative about the core ideas of the various movements, and as more heretical texts have been found, we can see that the Fathers were quoting their enemies' opinions quite fully and accurately. Partly, the Fathers were demonstrating a sense of fairness by quoting their enemies objectively, but in addition, orthodox writers plausibly felt that the views they were quoting were so contorted and ludicrous that the heretics were best condemned out of their own mouths.

From the middle of the second century, the orthodox saw themselves as under assault on several separate fronts. Many believers were agitated by the relationship between the new Christian revelation and its Jewish roots. Around 140, Marcion drew a line of radical separation between Jews and Christians, rejecting the Old Testament and its evil god while extolling the good deity of the new covenant, and his messenger, Jesus: Love confronted Law. Marcionites favored jettisoning the Hebrew Bible in favor of a new entirely Christian collection. Marcion was apparently the first individual to attempt to define a canon of Christian texts, and his tendentious effort directly provoked the orthodox to create their own canon, which eventually became the New Testament. At the other extreme from Marcion, the Jewish-Christian Ebionites tried to retain the food laws and other aspects of Jewish ritual piety; they also viewed Jesus as the son of Joseph and Mary, rather than the outcome of a miraculous conception. Other hotly contested issues at this time included the continuing nature of revelation, and the Montanist sect of the 160s and 170s earned the label of heresy by following the prophecies of their inspired charismatic leaders.

The most persistent enemy identified by the early Fathers was Gnosticism, a movement which drew on Christian, Jewish, Egyptian, and Hellenistic roots.[5] While the first recorded leaders and teachers can be dated to the first century, the great Gnostic thinkers such as Valentinus, Basilides, Carpocrates, and Cerdo flourished between about 135 and 165, an age of furious controversy over the definitions and boundaries of Christian doctrine.[6] Their ideas would have a particular influence in two of the richest and most populous regions of the Roman Empire, namely, Syria and Egypt, but the cosmopolitan nature of that empire meant that both activists and texts traveled freely, and crossed paths in the city of Rome itself. Followers of the Egyptian Valentinus posed a serious ideological challenge to the orthodox church through the early third century. Gnostic thought flourished until the end of antiquity, and survived up to modern times in the teachings of secretive Middle Eastern sects such as the Druze, Mandaeans, and Alawites; a kind of Gnostic tradition may also survive in the Jewish tradition of the Qabalah. Both Marcionite and Gnostic thought contributed to the powerful dualistic movement known as Manichaeanism, which emerged in the third century and flourished across Europe and Asia for over a millennium. Like its predecessors, this system saw Jesus as the representative of a good God of Light and spirit who warred with the evil forces of matter, darkness, and the Old Testament.

Like Marcion's followers, Gnostics thoroughly rejected the Jewish tradition.[7] They saw the material world as the product of evil forces, though scattered fragments of the higher spiritual realm had tragically become enmeshed in this dark world. Trapped in matter and subordinate to the powers of destiny, human beings were slaves to powerful cosmic forces, or archons—"rulers"—a subjugation which could be overcome by liberating the inner spark of the divine within the individual believer. This was achieved by learning the mystical practices, spells, and words of power which would allow the initiate to ascend to the highest spiritual realms of light and truth. Gnosticism offered an elaborate mythological system with a hierarchy of many spiritual forces who together comprised the "fullness," or *pleroma*, and Christ was one being among this great array. At the lowest level of this hierarchy was a deranged god called the Demiurge, the God of the Old Testament, who created our deeply flawed material world. Gnostics consequently exalted the figures from Hebrew lore who had rebelled against the evil creator: one sect, the Ophites, or Naassenes, took its name from the serpent in the Garden of Eden. According to the Gnostic myth, the personified power known as Sophia, Wisdom, had fallen into the world of matter and error, from which she could be freed only by the gracious Redeemer, Jesus. Unlike orthodox Christianity, Gnostics saw the coming of Jesus as a spiritual manifestation rather than an incarnation: his death was equally illusory. Like the Montanists, the Gnostics refused to believe that the age of revelations had ended with the apostles: they held that the Resurrection of Jesus was not just a historical event but a continuing phenomenon which occurred within believers.

Many of the rival movements possessed their own gospels or sacred scriptures, which the mainstream church tried to extirpate, but the surviving fragments would intrigue generations of later religious thinkers. Reading the Fathers indicated the existence of alternative gospels which presented pictures of Jesus quite alien to that found in the familiar scriptures, and these apocryphal texts were commonly associated with one of the heretical traditions. Sometimes, the rival gospels are quoted with enough respect to suggest that the quotation in question might have some validity, even though the gospel as a whole was suspect. Clement of Alexandria, a venerated leader of the orthodox church in Egypt around 200, knew and cited a variety of texts that would later be condemned. In the fourth century, Saint Jerome several times cited variant readings that occur in the "Jewish Gospel," the scripture of a Jewish-Christian sect. Origen introduces one saying with the caveat, "And if any accept the *Gospel of the Hebrews*—here the Savior says, 'Even so did my mother, the Holy Spirit, take me by one of my hairs and brought me to Tabor, the holy mountain.'" These infuriatingly incomplete quotations sometimes showed Jesus engaged in long mystical discourses with the disciples, especially with women followers such as Salome and Mary Magdalen. In the *Gospel of the Egyptians*, Salome asks Jesus, "How long will death have power?" only to be told, "So long as you women bear children."[8] By the nineteenth century, these piecemeal quotations—the Salome fragments and the Mount Tabor saying—were so widely quoted in academic and popular writing on Christian origins that they had become clichéd.

Scholars also knew of scattered sayings, or agrapha, some of which sounded as interesting and puzzling as anything in the New Testament: one text recalled Jesus as saying "Those who are with me have not understood me," while Clement of Alexandria reported that Jesus had said, "Ask for the great things, and God will add to you what is small." Muslim sources remembered other sayings of Jesus, such as, "The world is a bridge: Go over it, but do not install yourselves upon it."[9] Some sounded very close to orthodox teaching, while others were alien or shocking to contemporary sensibilities. A few of these phrases would later prove to be part of the *Gospel of Thomas*, and became familiar components of Christian literary culture long before the complete version of that text was found at Nag Hammadi. Examples included the sayings, "He who is near me is near the fire; he who is far from me is far from the kingdom" and "When the two shall be one, and the outside as the inside, and the male with the female, neither male or female—these things, if ye do, my Father shall come."[10] The wide range of Jesus sayings, the *logoi* or logia which had not found their way into the Gospels, became familiar in English through several popular books and novels.[11] The existence of the logia, which often stemmed from highly regarded church fathers, confirmed that authentic materials about Jesus could still be found outside the pages of the New Testament, and inspired nineteenth-century readers to ask what else of value might have been preserved in the lost apocryphal texts.

Out of the Sands

In addition to known ancient texts, newly discovered documents fueled speculations about early Christianity. The mid-nineteenth century was a revolutionary age for the science of archaeology, in which whole lost civilizations were rediscovered, together with forgotten languages and literatures. The decipherment of Egyptian hieroglyphics was followed by the translation of cuneiform texts, and mining the libraries of Assyrians, Hittites, and Babylonians produced exciting finds which shed new light on the origins of the Bible, proving, for instance, the ancient origins of the tale of the Flood.[12] If legendary civilizations such as Troy and Mycenae could be uncovered, who knew what archaeologists might find about the Nazareth or Jerusalem of Jesus' time? Might a fifth gospel yet be discovered?

Scholars did indeed produce some critical finds relating to the New Testament. One celebrated event occurred in 1859, when Constantine von Tischendorf found an astonishing treasure at the monastic house of Mount Sinai: this was the *Codex Sinaiticus*, a fourth-century New Testament manuscript, which also included two long-lost second-century Christian texts, namely, the *Epistle of Barnabas* and part of the *Shepherd of Hermas*. In 1873, a manuscript found in Constantinople included the liturgical text known as the *Didache*, or the Teaching of the Twelve Apostles.[13] All were soon available in English translation. In the early church, *Barnabas*, *Hermas*, and the *Didache* had been serious candidates for inclusion in the New Testament, and all were priceless witnesses to early Christian thought.

The most evocative of the new finds were the unfamiliar logia, the "Sayings of Jesus" which emerged from the deserts of Egypt during the 1890s. These Oxyrhynchus Papyri showed once again the enormous range of writings about Jesus which had been excluded from the church's canon. The very title given to a 1904 publication of the new findings stirred excitement by its promise of major discoveries: *New Sayings of Jesus and Fragment of a Lost Gospel from Oxyrhynchus*: new sayings *and* a lost gospel, together in one volume! The fact that these manuscripts were dated to around 200 immediately made them a century closer to the time of Jesus than any other writing then available.[14] Scholars were divided as to whether the new Sayings came from one of the gospels described by patristic authors, but few realized that what they actually possessed was a substantial portion of the *Gospel of Thomas*. Already at the start of the century, therefore, readers had access to about a fifth of the *Thomas* sayings, twenty-one verses out of 114, which gave them a solid sample of that gospel's radical teaching that the true kingdom was within the believer, rather than a supernatural or apocalyptic state which was yet to come. The new sayings also cast light on the other lost gospel source, Q, which is believed to lurk behind the text of our existing gospels of Matthew and Luke. Some scholars immediately proposed that the new sayings *were* a version of Q. A significant overlap between the Oxyrhynchus Sayings and Q indicated a very early dating for the sayings, perhaps making them actually older than the canonical gospels. As we see below, arguments about the possible relationship between Q and Thomas have been seminal for New Testament scholarship since the 1970s, but the core ideas were present soon after 1900, and had already been discussed exhaustively by the great Bible researcher Kirsopp Lake. The Oxyrhynchus finds would have an influence on public opinion at the start of the twentieth century comparable to that of the Nag Hammadi documents at its end.[15]

In addition to "the vastly important logia," several other gospel fragments were discovered at this time.[16] Oxyrhynchus produced fragments of narratives which were close to the canonical gospels in tone, yet disconcertingly unfamiliar in their contents. One fragment known as Papyrus Egerton 2 was published in 1935: this had a powerful resemblance to portions of the gospel of John, but included an otherwise unknown miracle in which Jesus responds to a question by sowing water on the ground, which amazingly produces fruit (details of the story's reconstruction are controversial). Such texts were regarded as possible building blocks of the canonical gospels, conceivably as remnants of first-century Christianity. By the early 1930s, scholars had access to the large collection of early New Testament papyri in the Chester Beatty collection, which dated from around 200.[17]

Also widely publicized was the ancient *Gospel According to Peter*, a fragment of which was found in Egypt in 1886. A few scholars still believe that *Peter* dates from the beginnings of Christian literary activity, and that portions of the work might predate the canonical gospels, though this is a minority view today. A hundred years ago, though, *Peter* received much wider scholarly respect, and it aroused popular hopes reminiscent of those stirred by *Thomas* in recent years. As the great scholar J. Rendel Harris remarked in 1899, "if some are quite certain that the gospel in question is merely a pendant from and adaptation of the four canonical gospels, others have been equally positive that a fresh line of tradition has been disclosed, and that we are face to face with a canonical fifth gospel (or one that was something very like canonical in the second century)."[18]

Other discoveries of this age transformed the study of the Hebrew Bible, and the Jewish tradition, and in so doing raised unnerving questions about Christian origins. Most significant was the finding of the tens of thousands of manuscripts in the Cairo Genizah, a kind of synagogue archive, the importance of which was recognized in 1896. Among other treasures, this collection produced the first document from the group or sect which had written the Dead Sea Scrolls: this latter collection would be unearthed in 1947, near what is presumed to be the Essene settlement of Qumran. Like the later Scrolls, the early manuscript finds portrayed a venerated leader known as the Teacher of Righteousness. Even before the First World War, some scholars were arguing that this Teacher was either Jesus or John the Baptist, and that among the nameless enemies and traitors described in the texts was Paul, who betrayed Jesus' message. These are exactly the ideas which have been proposed in various controversial books of the last decade, although neither now nor then do they command any kind of consensus.[19]

Cumulatively, the various discoveries were impressive. In 1930, Edgar Goodspeed listed the texts which had come to light just since the 1870s: "the *Teaching of the Twelve Apostles*, the *Gospel of Peter*, the *Revelation of Peter*, the *Apology of Aristides*, the *Acts of Paul*, the *Sayings of Jesus*, the *Odes of Solomon*, and the *Epistle of the Apostles*—all from the second century."[20] Between about 1890 and 1910, lengthy and well-informed articles about the new finds appeared in many English-language magazines and periodicals, including the *Contemporary Review, Outlook, McClure's*, the *Nation, Nineteenth Century, Harper's Weekly*, and the *Independent*, as well as popular papers such as the *New York Journal* and the *Sun*.[21] Books on new gospels and freshly discovered Jesus sayings also proliferated in these years, reaching a peak in the opening years of the new century. This activity is worth stressing in view of the statements by some modern scholars that their predecessors were afraid to divulge too much about the new frontiers of New Testament research for fear of outraging the faithful and jeopardizing their careers. Robert Funk, for example, writes that before the 1980s, "scholars . . . limited their pronouncements to the classroom or buried their considered judgments in scientific journals and technical jargon. They have hesitated to broadcast the assured results of historical critical scholarship out of fear of public controversy and political reprisal."[22] The events of the 1890s show the absurdity of such comments: both the information and the interpretation were there for any literate person who wanted them. Likewise, anyone interested in the New Testament who "did not know where to find" alternative gospels must have been living as a hermit.

Media reports aroused popular expectations about the potential for revolutionary new finds which could shed light on earliest Christianity, and contributed to making the archaeology of religion a genre in twentieth-century popular culture. To quote a *Nation* article from 1897, "The uppermost feeling of the Christian world seems to be an ardent hope that investigation may be pushed, and other of the lost logia brought to light."[23] People were speculating hopefully on what might be learned from other lost texts, even from such apparently ludicrous examples as the Gospels of *Eve* and *Judas Iscariot*, which did once exist, and are known from ancient sources.[24] With so many materials of this sort known or actually available, by the end of the nineteenth century an influential school of thought already disparaged the canonical sources while placing extravagant hopes in their rivals, in the hidden gospels. As E. J. Dillon wrote, sweepingly, in 1893, "nowadays, no impartial critic, or even enlightened theologian, holds to the once general belief that the four gospels of the Christian canon either headed the list of written narratives of the living and working of Jesus, or absorbed the vast mass of tradition which speedily gathered around his name." The canonical four "were neither the first nor the last links of the series of written sketches in which the features of the Son of Man were limned."[25]

Nor was Dillon unrepresentative. J. Rendel Harris remarked on the existence of a substantial school of thought which held that "our existing gospels are a selection and a survival out of a great mass of similar attempts at gospel writing, and it is inferred that they owe their success not simply and purely to their superior excellence and accuracy but in part at least to the accidents which make some books popular and permanent, and relegate others to obscurity." Revisionist writers could be just as dogmatic as the strictly orthodox, and in a note which sounds very modern, Harris commented that "the two extreme views are seen to be strongly divided from one another; the one school minimizing or reducing actually to zero the Gospels which lie outside the canon, the other maximizing them."[26] He was scornful of what he regarded as the powerful tendency of his contemporaries to leap on every new extracanonical fragment as if it overturned all the accepted truths of Christianity, and urged restraint in accepting new finds. A century later, Harris's comments evoke a powerful sense of déja vu.

The Gnostics Again
Some newly found texts shed light on Gnosticism and other ancient heresies, and caused scholars to redraw the frontiers of the early Christian movement. In 1842, the long-lost *Refutation of All Heresies* was found in a monastic house on Mount Athos. This text was written by the early third-century Bishop Hippolytus, a pupil of that great foe of heresy, Irenaeus. Published in English in 1868, the *Refutation* vastly expanded available knowledge about the Gnostics because of the author's long quotations from the works of several heretical schools, and his elaborate retelling of Gnostic celestial mythologies. Among other things, Hippolytus was familiar with many texts which sound very much like the documents found at Nag Hammadi. Other finds revealed the heretics in their own words: in 1896, a codex purchased in Egypt supplied texts of the *Apocryphon of John,* the *Gospel of Mary, The Wisdom of Jesus Christ,* and other ancient Gnostic texts, and other codices offered fragments of similar works.[27] On closer examination, long-familiar apocryphal sources such as the Syriac *Acts of Thomas* were shown to be deeply imbued with Gnostic sentiment, and this particular work offered a number of Gnostic or Gnosticized passages, including the "Hymn of the Soul," and whole liturgies, prayers, and sacramental formulae.[28]

The most intriguing of the new discoveries was the *Pistis Sophia* ("Faith Wisdom" or "Faith of Wisdom"), an allegorical account of the Gnostic world system, which some wrongly attributed to Valentinus himself.[29] Purchased in the 1760s, this Coptic text remained barely noticed in the British Museum until in 1851 it was made available in Latin and Greek. By 1896, English readers had access to a translation by G. R. S. Mead, a prolific author who became the great contemporary popularizer of the lost heresies, rather like Elaine Pagels a century later. Mead's publications included the eleven-volume *Echoes from the Gnosis* (1906-8), a comprehensive edition of every Gnostic writing then known, while *The Gnostic John the Baptizer* (1924) translated the psalms of the Mandaean sect.[30] Mead was consciously publicizing these texts as hidden gospels: he described *Pistis Sophia* as a Gnostic gospel, and the text was commonly recognized as "a sort of Gospel coming from some early Gnostic sect."[31]

Pistis Sophia initiated the modern rediscovery of the Gnostic gospels. Because it is so elaborately detailed (it runs to some 300 pages in translation), the work offers a thorough introduction to Gnosticism, including many of the aspects which have attracted the most attention in the Nag Hammadi gospels. *Pistis Sophia* claims to report the interactions of Jesus and the disciples after the Resurrection, but it differs radically from the canonical texts in its account of the spiritual powers ruling the universe, its belief in reincarnation, and its extensive use of magical formulae and invocations. The Jesus depicted here is a mystic teacher, whose main interactions are with powerful female disciples such as Mary Magdalen. Much of the book concerns the stages by which Jesus liberates the supernatural (and female) figure of Sophia, heavenly Wisdom, from her bondage in error and the material world, and she is progressively restored to her previous divine status in the heavens. Characteristic of these gospels, the events described occur symbolically and psychologically, in sharp contrast to the orthodox Christian concern with historical realities. Much like the Nag Hammadi texts a century later, *Pistis Sophia* aroused widespread excitement among feminists and esoteric believers, and aspiring radical reformers of Christianity.

Spreading the Word

Because the heretical texts provided such an odd slant on the endlessly fascinating question of Christian origins, they were often translated and published. Even at the start of the twentieth century, it was feasible to possess a whole library of Gnostic texts. From 1904 onward, German readers were uniquely fortunate in the range of sources available to them; for example, Richard Reitzenstein published his series of massive surveys of

Gnostic thought, drawn from Hermetic and alchemical works as well as from writers such as Hippolytus.[32] Even so, a substantial literature was available to any English-speaking reader with the means to purchase them. Publishers knew that a solid market for religious literature existed among clergy and theological students, and the number of popular editions indicates the wide general market for such works. One reliable source for the new discoveries was the British Society for the Promotion of Christian Knowledge, which in the 1920s published cheap translations of Hippolytus, *Pistis Sophia*, the *Didache*, and others. Translations of *Pistis Sophia* also appeared from mainstream houses such as Macmillan.[33]

Editions and translations of the apocryphal texts could be found in every seminary and countless private libraries. Several alternative gospels, mainly late and legendary, were well known through their inclusion in the popular *Ante-Nicene Christian Library*, which first appeared in the 1870s, and was expanded as new texts were discovered.[34] By the end of the century, this collection included the Gospels attributed to Nicodemus, Peter, Pseudo-Matthew, and the so-called *Protevangelium*, or "First Gospel" of James. Also translated was a *Gospel of Thomas*, though this is distinct from the famous Gospel of the same name discovered at Nag Hammadi. The Ante-Nicene collection included numerous apocryphal *Acts* of the apostles, including those of Thomas, John, Paul, Peter, Philip, and Andrew.[35] Selections from the same range of Acts and gospels appeared in M. R. James's *The Apocryphal New Testament* (1924), which became the standard English-language resource on early heresies. We also find here several apocalypses distinct from the famous Book of Revelation which we know from the New Testament. James quotes or discusses the apocryphal gospels of the *Hebrews*, the *Ebionites*, and the *Egyptians*, and the works named for Philip, Peter, Matthias, and Nicodemus. He describes the existence of Gnostic tracts such as the *Gospel of Mary*, though he did not find this worthy of discussion at length. Unknowingly, James also published major selections from the primitive *Gospel of Thomas*, though he gave them the neutral title of the "Oxyrhynchus Sayings of Jesus." James's collection helped give added public visibility to the intriguing logia, which acquired an appeal far beyond the scholarly world: sayings from *Thomas* were already by the 1930s appearing in devotional collections aimed at a lay public.[36]

Many works summarized the new texts for a general public. In

1864, Charles W. King published what became a standard book, *The Gnostics and Their Remains*, which, apart from summarizing the standard patristic texts, also described the large corpus of available Gnostic gems and amulets. [37] King's work was superseded in 1900 by G. R. S. Mead's mammoth and much-reprinted *Fragments of a Faith Forgotten . . . A contribution to the study of Christian origins based on the most recently recovered materials*. The subtitle indicates the already common idea that the heretical texts might shed much light on the earliest days of the faith. The *Fragments* included extensive translations from the Gnostic writings themselves, including the *Pistis Sophia*, the *Books of the Savior*, and the *Gospel of Mary*. Another popularization was Francis Legge's *Forerunners and Rivals of Christianity* (1915). Legge already regards the apocryphal Gospels as a very familiar source, referring, for instance, to the dialogue between Jesus and Salome from the *Gospel of the Egyptians* as "the well-known saying of Jesus," and allotting a substantial chapter to the *Pistis Sophia*.[38] From the 1890s onward, access to such sources inspired academic debate about Gnosticism and other heresies, as scholars argued whether Gnosticism was an offshoot of Christianity or of Judaism, or an entirely independent religion.[39]

The Uses of Heresy

The early heresies attracted interest because so many texts now became available and promised to shed light on matters of huge general concern. Then as now, studying deviant forms of Christianity became a gripping topic because it seemed to speak so precisely to current controversies. However far nineteenth-century culture believed itself to be drifting from traditional religious certainties, the society was still so deeply rooted in Christian assumptions that even the most radical innovators felt a need to justify themselves in terms of revised interpretations of that religion. Whether they advocated socialism or feminism, eugenics or vegetarianism, it was desirable to argue that this particular theme had been at the core of the early Christian message, before it was betrayed by a corrupt church and clergy. Within the churches, too, rediscovered gospels proved a vital weapon in the liberal arsenal.

Several distinct motives aroused interest in early Christian diversity. Early heresies and schisms were a critical issue for the catholicizing movements which developed in Protestant churches from the 1830s onward, the intellectual trend represented by the

English Oxford Movement. Scholars such as J. H. Newman (the later Cardinal) were fascinated by the ancient heretics' claims to authenticity precisely because this raised such troubling questions about the position of other Christian bodies separated from the Roman communion. An interest in finding the true church goes far toward explaining the outpouring of scholarly studies in the English-speaking world in the mid-nineteenth century. In 1875, Henry Longueville Mansel's *The Gnostic Heresies of the First and Second Centuries* provided a scholarly overview of the movements of Basilides, Valentinus, Marcion, and others.[40] About the same time, the well-known Bible commentaries of Bishop Lightfoot proposed that references to Gnostic thought could be found in various parts of the New Testament, especially the Epistle to the Colossians.[41] Many Biblical scholars in the late nineteenth century were aware of the extreme diversity of early Christianity and showed familiarity with the complex and long-running dialogue between what became orthodoxy and heresy. And many of the most active scholars were themselves clergy, including highly placed members of the English church establishment such as Mansel and Lightfoot.

The revolutionary critical scholarship emerging from Germany in the nineteenth century provided another incentive to rediscovering the losing side in the historical battles. Under the influence of Hegelian thought, German Bible scholars declared that the origins of Christianity should be sought in a clash between competing models or systems, which were ultimately resolved in a new synthesis. It was held that the Jewish Christianity of Jerusalem struggled with the gentile thought of Paul, until the synthesis was found in the new Catholic Church of the second and third centuries. According to this view, some parts of the New Testament were more Jewish than others, more primitive, and thus closer to the authentic Jesus than, say, the mysticism of the Gospel of John. As today, the quest for the "real" Jesus meant giving preference to gospels and other documents which seemed less supernatural and thus less offensive to contemporary sensibilities.[42] German scholars also prefigured modern attitudes in their belief that so-called heretical movements might contain ancient truths. Supposedly, the ancient Jewish Christianity of the apostles did not vanish without trace, as it survived in the Ebionite sect, which was so regularly condemned by the Church Fathers. This approach raised questions about other condemned movements, and their relationship to the official church of the catholic tradition: were these condemned groups really heresies, or should they better be regarded as alternative Christian realities? And if the Ebionites contained a core of Jesus' authentic teachings, why not the Gnostics?

For scientific critics, too, the attack on ecclesiastical positions further helped to justify their rejection of the religious orthodoxies of their own day. In Europe especially, many were strongly anticlerical and anti-Catholic, and saw Roman Catholicism as a pagan perversion of authentic Christianity. Historically, they believed, Catholicism had won not because it was morally or historically correct, but because it cynically won political power, eliminated its rivals, and all but destroyed any trace that they had existed. When scholars attacked the compromises which gave rise to "early Catholicism," they were also attacking the Catholic Church of their own time. As in the matter of alternative gospels, scholarship on the early Church often contributed to contemporary polemic.

Skeptical ideas acquired a mass audience at the end of the nineteenth century, as the growing modernist movement within the Protestant churches inspired a new interest in the diverse currents of ancient Christianity. In North America as in Europe, Biblical criticism had raised doubts about the uniqueness or historical value of the New Testament canon, while comparative religious studies expanded awareness of alternative spiritual traditions, and modernist ideas came to dominate the great divinity schools and seminaries. Modernists disparaged the more mystical elements of the scriptures, such as the Book of Revelation, which they saw as unworthy accretions to the core gospel of Jesus, and were duly sympathetic to suppressed groups which kept alive the early spirit, such as the Ebionites. The legitimacy of historical method and the higher criticism was symbolized by the establishment of the American Society of Biblical Literature, in 1880, and in the early 1890s, critical ideas were popularized through the writings of Washington Gladden and Charles A. Briggs. Harold Frederic's popular novel *The Damnation of Theron Ware* (1896) demonstrates the subversive impact of the new ideas on ordinary believers—in this case, chiefly daring new insights about the Pentateuch. Not surprisingly, modernism inspired a fierce counterattack: in 1892, Briggs was subjected to a nationally publicized heresy trial within his denomination, and in the same year, Presbyterians drew up a first draft of what later became the *Fundamentals*, basic articles of faith to be accepted by both clergy and teachers. Other Presbyterian Biblical scholars were silenced as the decade progressed. These events provide an essential context for understanding the excitement over the Oxyrhynchus finds in 1897, since this discovery was widely taken as a vindication of the whole method of higher criticism: scholars had hypothesized the existence of the early gospel source Q, and the papyri seemed to contain fragments of just such a document. Such a successful prediction appeared to give Biblical criticism the status of true science. Also in the 1890s, the florid claims made for the authority of *Peter* suggested the limitations of the approved gospel canon, and the extent to which the canonical gospels had achieved their status through political factors rather than divine inspiration.[43]

Skeptical approaches culminated in the assertion that neither catholic orthodoxy nor its distinctive texts had originally held any privileged position. Though this idea seems like an insight of recent years, it has a long pedigree. In 1934, Walter Bauer's influential *Orthodoxy and Heresy in Earliest Christianity* argued that numerous interpretations of Christianity coexisted across the Greco-Roman world, and in many areas, so-called orthodoxy was weak or nonexistent: Marcionites and Bardesanites were dominant in Syria, Gnostics in Egypt, Jewish Christians in parts of Asia Minor, and these heterodox movements claimed ancient and even apostolic roots comparable to those of the emerging Catholic Church. Bauer claimed that in parts of Syria and Mesopotamia, the term "Christians" long referred to what we would call a heretical school of thought, probably Marcionite. Around the great Syrian city of Edessa, orthodox believers were in such a minority that they could be dismissed as a fringe sect under the name of the "Palutians." In different areas, too, each group made use of its distinctive gospels, so that Jewish Christians used the Gospels of the Hebrews or the Nazarenes, others the Gospel of the Egyptians, and so on, while Gnostics were well supplied with texts such as the *Apocryphon of John* and the *Gospel of Truth*.[44] There was no intrinsic reason to see any of these works as any less authentic than the canonical texts, which were thereby deprivileged, to use a contemporary term.

According to Bauer, Catholic traditions and hierarchies scarcely existed in many areas until around 200, and orthodoxy did not triumph until it received the imperial seal of approval under Constantine in the fourth century. The heresies were not fatally weakened until the Muslim conquest of the Middle East several centuries later. It was in Constantine's age too that Eusebius compiled the *Church History* that for the next 1500 years would provide the standard interpretation of Christian origins, though Bauer's evidence suggested that this venerated account involved a substantial amount of retrospective myth-making. Many aspects of Bauer's interpretation have been criticized over the years, but he did raise important questions about older traditions and commonplaces. After Bauer, it was no longer possible to accept without question the automatic primacy of the catholic tradition and the canonical gospels.[45]

The Jesus of the Cults

Outside the academic world, heresy gained a popular audience in large measure through its appeal to occult and esoteric movements, who saw the early Gnostics as their spiritual ancestors. Ironically, the Gnostics became such heroes precisely because their deadliest enemies, the Church Fathers, had been so scrupulous in recording their beliefs and doctrines: Origen had quoted an entire liturgy of the Gnostic Ophite sect, complete with its secret names of power. He would have been horrified to know that such excerpts would be taken up enthusiastically by later occultists such as Aleister Crowley, who led a whole neo-Gnostic revival at the end of the nineteenth century. Crowley's Gnostic Catholic Church practiced a mass or liturgy in which the canon of commemorated saints included Basilides, Valentinus, Bardesanes, and the others "that transmitted the light of the Gnosis to us, their successors and their heirs." Crowley recommended the *Pistis Sophia* to his disciples as "an admirable introduction."[46]

Another influential vehicle for Gnostic revivalism was the Theosophical movement, which was cofounded by Madame Blavatsky in the 1870s, and which would influence most of the occult sects of the twentieth century. While Theosophy grew from older esoteric roots, much of its appeal derived from its seeming congruence with the science of the day, particularly notions of evolution. Theosophists told of the rise and fall of successive races through millions of years, and also depicted the progress of the human soul through successive lives: at the summit of spiritual evolution were divine redeemers, avatars, or Christs. The Theosophical Christ had a great deal in common with the Jesus of the Gnostics, the heaven-sent Redeemer dispatched to liberate the forces of light from their prison of matter. In presenting her picture, Blavatsky drew on the scholarship on Gnostic and early Christian heresy available in her own day, and her magnum opus,

Isis Unveiled (1877), borrows extensively from King's *The Gnostics and Their Remains*. Her assumption throughout is that the Gnostics represent the earliest and most authentic doctrines of Christianity, which were later perverted by the so-called orthodox.[47] Following the Gnostics of old with remarkably fidelity, Blavatsky and her contemporaries interpreted Christ's death and resurrection as a symbolic and psychological reality, which reflected transformations within the soul of the believer: in this view, "Christ" was not a historical personage, but a title given to any true initiate. As Theosophist Anna Kingsford declared in the 1880s, "religion is not historical and in nowise depends upon past events. . . . The Scriptures are addressed to the soul, and make no appeal to the outer senses."[48]

For Victorian occultists such as Kingsford and Annie Besant, Theosophy represented a whole tradition of esoteric Christianity, which had been taught to ancient initiates. These inner teachings were passed on orally, and appeared in the teachings of movements condemned by the orthodox church. The esoteric Christianity supposedly preached by this New Age Jesus has had a long life, since it was invented in the 1870s and is by no means extinct today.[49] Some occult thinkers published serious scholarly editions of early texts, and Theosophical publishers presented Gnostic and occult works to a mass market. G. R. S. Mead himself was secretary of the Theosophical Society, and his editions of the *Pistis Sophia* and the *Echoes from the Gnosis* were first published by the Theosophical Publishing House.

The Gnostic Jesus particularly appealed to those who heard in his voice echoes of the Asian religions that were in such vogue at the end of the nineteenth century. Blavatsky integrated her Gnostic insights into a wider framework drawn from Asian religions: she declared Jesus to be an avatar of the divine, a messenger from above comparable to Buddha or Krishna. Like many esoteric writers, she argued that the titles of Christ and Krishna were essentially identical. Her Jesus taught the law of karma, and revealed to humanity the principles of spiritual progress and perfectibility, achieved over many lifetimes. The theory that early Christianity had drawn on Asian and specifically Buddhist thought was a commonplace for nineteenth-century German thinkers, and these ideas were affecting the English-speaking world by the 1880s. It was argued that the unification of the known world under Alexander the Great had created an ideal environment for Buddhist missionaries to spread their ideas to the West. Possible east-west connections proved highly attractive for the esoteric com- munity: in Theosophical literature, Jesus was believed to have traveled widely in India, Tibet, Persia, Egypt, and elsewhere, where he acquired the mystery teachings of the respective tradi- tions. The idea of cross-cultural pollination gained popularity as imperial contacts gave Victorian scholars an increasingly global- ized perspective and permitted them to draw on the lessons of comparative religion. Asian movements such as Hinduism and Buddhism increasingly attracted mass Western audiences follow- ing the World's Parliament of Religions, which was held in Chicago in 1893.[50]

Theories of a possible Asian influence on the Jesus movement usually focused on the Essenes. Even orthodox scholars such as Dean Mansel argued that Buddhist monks and missionaries had provided the inspiration for the monks and ascetics whom we find recorded in the Middle East before the coming of Jesus, like the Essenes and the related Egyptian sect of the *Therapeutae*.[51] Some writers explored the idea that Jesus himself might have drawn on these esoteric traditions, as suggested by the title of Arthur Lillie's 1887 book, *Buddhism in Christendom; or, Jesus, the Essene*. In 1880, Ernst von Bunsen argued that Christian messianic concepts derived from a common fund of tradition that was shared by Bud- dhists and Essenes.[52] The Essenes, it was thought, provided a cru- cial link between Eastern mysticism and Western heresy, with Jesus as the pivot between the two trends. If Jesus had access to Buddhist ideas, and the Gnostic sects themselves preached rein- carnation and other Asian themes, then once again this was evi- dence that Jesus' earliest teachings were best preserved among the so-called heresies.

The idea of a connection between Jesus and the Essenes sounds remarkably modern, in that a possible link between Jesus and this sect has often been proposed since the discovery of the Dead Sea scrolls. (The idea that the Gnostics might have drawn ideas from the Essenes has been much discussed since the finding of the Scrolls, though it remains controversial.) However, the Essenes have fascinated scholars and amateurs since the Enlightenment. Frederick the Great asserted that "Jesus was really an Essene; he was imbued with Essene ethics." Ernest Renan, author of the most famous nineteenth-century life of Jesus, proclaimed that Christianity was simply a version of Essenism that happened to have survived. Blavatsky agreed that "the Gnostics, or early Chris- tians, were but the followers of the old Essenes under a new name." Legge in 1915 discusses the Essenes as "pre-Christian Gnostics," and quotes the (by then) familiar arguments "that St. John the Baptist was an Essene and that Jesus Himself belonged to the sect."[53] Already in the early twentieth century, G. K. Chesterton could mock the old-fashioned idea that Jesus was "an ethical teacher in the manner of the Essenes, who had apparently nothing very much to say that Hillel or a hundred other Jews might not have said; as that it is a kindly thing to be kind and an assistance to purification to be pure."[54] The Essenes were old hat long before the finds at Qumran.

For well over a century, Christians and non-Christians alike have been fascinated by the dream that somewhere, buried in a cave or lost in an ancient library, there might exist a document which would prove once and for all the truth about Jesus, his teachings, and his mission. Just what this truth would be depends on the attitudes of the individual responsible for the speculation: Jesus might be proved the son of God or an impostor, a political rebel or a victim of misguided hopes, but somewhere, this final truth must be found. And so great are these hopes that very frequently over the last century, people have tried either to concoct new gospels to supply this information or to imagine (plausibly or not) that these secrets are contained in genuine documents.

As if the surviving ancient texts had not raised enough sedi-tious questions, many writers from the early nineteenth century onward claimed to have discovered altogether new sources, new "hidden gospels," in order to justify their own beliefs; the *Book of Mormon* is a case in point. Exactly how this work was composed remains a matter of debate, but most non-Mormons would dis-miss it as outright forgery. The process of invention continued apace through the late nineteenth century, inspired by news of the genuine finds from Egypt and elsewhere: Tischendorf's dis-coveries at St. Catharine's inspired a whole generation of counter-feiters. In the 1890s, *The Archko Volume* purported to offer the offi-cial records of the trial and death of Jesus, with letters attributed to Pilate, Caiaphas, and others. This imagined treasure trove was subtitled "The archeological writings of the Sanhedrin and Tal-muds of the Jews . . . from manuscripts in Constantinople and the records of the senatorial docket taken from the Vatican at Rome." Typical of such works, this volume offered a plausible-sounding scholarly pedigree: a later *Gospel of Peace of Jesus Christ by the Disciple John* claimed to be based on secret manuscripts in the Vatican and the imperial library of the Habsburgs. Pseudo-Essene documents were published regularly, usually validated by claims that they had been discovered in some ancient library. The Vatican was a common candidate, on the assumption that the Roman Catholic Church was most likely both to know and to have concealed the ultimate truth.[55]

Occult and esoteric writers were particularly fertile in the process of invention, and many felt compelled to fill in the missing years in Jesus' life, that period of adolescence and early adulthood which preceded the start of his public ministry. Some of these attempts would be immensely influential. At the turn of the century, Nicholas Notovich published *The Unknown Life of Jesus Christ, from Buddhistic Records*, which reported the author's alleged visit to the Tibetan city of Lhasa. Notovich claimed to have found there abundant documents concerning the life of Jesus, who had preached his first sermons in India during his teens. The book includes a complete gospel, here published as "The Life of Saint Issa [Jesus], best of the sons of men." News of Notovich's alleged find resurfaced sporadically over the following decades, causing a minor furor in the American press as late as the 1920s.[56]

In an age fascinated by spiritualism and mediumship, it seemed natural that such revelations would be obtained through what would today be called channeling. New details of Jesus' life and thought were made familiar through books such as Levi Dowling's long-popular *Aquarian Gospel of Jesus the Christ*, Rudolf Steiner's *The Fifth Gospel*, and Edgar Cayce's channeled tales of Jesus, all of which drew to some extent on Notovich. All were very popular: between 1908 and 1995, the *Aquarian Gospel* alone went through fifty-two printings in hardbound editions, and thirteen in paperback. The full influence of these books is hard to trace too specifically because they were so widely plagiarized and imitated: with minor modifications, the *Aquarian Gospel* became the holy scripture of the Moorish Science Temple, America's first domestic Muslim movement. In recent years, the best-known examples of this esoteric tradition have been the works of Elizabeth Clare Prophet, who draws on Notovich to describe Jesus' occult career in Tibet and elsewhere.[57]

The proliferation of pseudo-gospels raised difficulties for the nonspecialist public, who had no reliable way of telling whether the new offerings represented genuine archaeological discoveries scrupulously edited by conscientious scholars, or spurious fictions. Once published, moreover, these books went through

many subsequent editions, so that apocryphal gospels were probably more numerous and widely read in 1920 than they had
been since the time of the Emperor Constantine. By 1931, Edgar
Goodspeed wrote *Strange New Gospels*, his exasperated survey of
the thriving genre, in which he highlighted *The Archko Volume*,
Notovich's *Unknown Life*, the *Aquarian Gospel*, as well as a "Confession of Pontius Pilate," the "Letter of Benan," and a 29th chapter of Acts, which described St. Paul's visit to Britain.[58] Goodspeed tried to provide potential readers with practical criteria by
which they could distinguish between genuine new finds and flagrant inventions.

Though these various pseudo-gospels have no claim to historical validity, they popularized many of the ideas which have
become commonplace in the last quarter-century, namely, that
Jesus preached mystical teachings related to those of various clandestine orders and traditions, and that early Christian doctrine
involved Buddhist teachings such as reincarnation and meditation. Moreover, these works present Jesus in traditional Gnostic
mode as the revealer of mysteries whose deeds have a symbolic
rather than historical importance. To a nonspecialist, there are
close resemblances between the mystical teachings of authentic
early texts such as the *Gospel of Truth* found at Nag Hammadi and
Dowling's spurious *Aquarian Gospel*. The seeming degree of plausibility of such forgeries need cause no surprise, since the forgers
were usually drawing on the authentic early Gnostic texts which
had become such a commonplace part of popular culture. While
they had little impact on the mainstream churches, these radical
interpretations reached a wide audience through the diverse esoteric movements that attracted so many millions of Americans
and Europeans in the first half of the century.[59] Long before the
discoveries at Nag Hammadi, a remarkably large public was condi-
tioned to accept the dramatically different portraits of Jesus contained in the new gospels: indeed, lay people with New Age interests may have been more disposed than scholars to accept the radical image of Jesus presented therein.

Gospel Fictions

Radical ideas about the origins of Christianity were also popularized through avowedly fictional literary works, which proliferated
in the early twentieth century.[60] Though such works have
received scant attention from either Bible scholars or literary critics, they were a principal vehicle for spreading the scholarship of

the intellectual elites to ordinary readers. These fictions did much to raise awareness of the possibility of newly found gospels, and the alternative visions of Jesus these might contain.

The direct ancestors of most of these fictions were two works published in the late eighteenth century by the German writers Karl Friedrich Bahrdt and Karl Heinrich Venturini. Both Bahrdt and Venturini describe Jesus' career in the context of plots by the Essenes, who are imagined as a vast international secret society pledged to revolution: the Essenes are portrayed in terms of the Illuminati who played such a role in the conspiracy theories at the time of the French Revolution. Writing at the start of the twentieth century, Albert Schweitzer remarked that since the publication of Venturini's work, few years had passed without some new book which either plagiarized or adapted his ideas. We can still today agree with Schweitzer that "when one knows two or three of them [the imaginative *Lives* of Jesus] one knows them all. They have scarcely altered since Venturini's time."[61]

Some of the fictional texts found their way into other languages, where they were occasionally taken as authentic. A German work that appeared in 1849 was subsequently translated into French, and was published in America in 1880: this was *The Crucifixion and the Resurrection of Jesus, by an Eyewitness*. It bore the subtitle, "a discovered MS. of the old Alexandria library giving, almost complete, a remarkable and lengthy letter, full, detailed, graphic and apparently truthful account by an eyewitness and friend of Jesus, an elder of the Essene order, to which Jesus belonged, showing Jesus did not die upon the cross but six months later; with much additional and explanatory matter concerning the Essenes and the crucifixion story."[62] During the twentieth century, this tract became a regular item in the inventory of esoteric publishers and bookstores.

The fictional genre inspired by Christian origins developed two quite distinct tracks, conservative and liberal, and each in its way became a significant presence in popular culture. On the conservative side, the central theme was the potential effects of a newly found hidden gospel, which might yet emerge from the Middle East. By 1900, any reasonably well-informed reader knew about the vast array of alternative Christianities that had once existed, and also had reason to suspect that fresh evidence might appear any day. Orthodox believers had coped well with the recent discoveries, and could argue that both the Old and New Testaments were receiving external confirmation from the records of other civilizations. Even so, there was nervousness about what else might be awaiting discovery: what if some new text raised doubts about Jesus' reality as a historical figure, or challenged the Resurrection?

One attempt to exploit the rediscovered gospel phenomenon was Guy Thorne's now-forgotten novel *When It Was Dark* (1903), which became a transatlantic best-seller by cashing in on the excitement aroused by the finds at Oxyrhynchus. This thriller describes the devastating effects on society when archaeologists discover a text purporting to record Joseph of Arimathea's confession that he faked the resurrection of Jesus, and indicating the real site of the tomb. The new gospel provokes a secular apocalypse, with a general outbreak of crime, rape, rioting, suicide, and moral collapse across the Christian world. However, the affair proves to be a hoax devised by a wealthy Jewish conspirator, an Antichrist figure. In passing, the book reflects the popular excitement of the day about textual discoveries, and the hope that they might confirm scriptural truths: people avidly follow news of "The Higher Criticism, the fact that it is not only in science that 'discoveries' can be made, the excavations in the east and the newly discovered manuscripts with their variations of reading, the possibility that the lost Aramaic original of St. Matthew's Gospel may yet be discovered."[63]

Thorne's theme of the cataclysmic impact of a forged gospel has been reused repeatedly. In 1940, an evangelical novel called *The Mystery of Mar Saba* drew heavily on *When It Was Dark* in order to update the notion of a diabolical plot against Christianity.[64] In this case, the villains seeking to discredit the Resurrection are the Nazis, who hope to use a forged gospel text called the Shred of Nicodemus to disprove the Resurrection, and thereby to undermine Allied morale in the face of German invasion. As in the Thorne novel, righteousness and the Resurrection both triumph, and the conspirators are defeated. Similar ideas would reappear in the 1960s with the furor over the discoveries of the Dead Sea Scrolls and the Nag Hammadi texts, and a genre of Bible-forgery fiction continues to this day.

These novels were conservative in their assumption that anything challenging the fundamentals of Christian belief must be a put-up job, perhaps even a means of testing the faithful. However, a quite distinct fictional tradition helped disseminate radical ideas about Christian origins. During the nineteenth century, pioneering German scholars had drawn a sharp distinction between the

Jesus of history and the Christ of faith, with the implication that the church's Christ was a mythological creation utterly different from the real Jesus, representing views alien to that historical individual. In such accounts, St. Paul normally occupies the role of principal villain and distorter-in-chief.[65] Novelists in Germany and elsewhere explored these ideas by imagining what might have occurred if the real Jesus had survived the crucifixion, and lived long enough to see his ideas transformed and contaminated by the emerging church.

In the first half of the century, several English writers perpetuated this tradition, including George Moore, Robert Graves, D. H. Lawrence, and Frank Harris. All had at least some acquaintance with contemporary Biblical scholarship, especially in the German tradition, and all were self-consciously exploring the implications of that research. And although their texts take the form of fictions or fantasies, it is remarkable to see how they anticipate many key beliefs of the modern Jesus Quest, including what today seem some of the most daring and far-reaching ideas drawn from the hidden gospels. Readers of this subgenre became familiar with the idea that Jesus was in dialogue with other world religious traditions, including those of India; that Christianity had much in common with the Essenes; that Jesus' life was by no means as devoid of sexuality as the New Testament portrayed; that the heresies preserved substantial traces of original truth; and that Pauline Christianity marked a pernicious deviation from Jesus' intentions. Throughout, we find images of Jesus very different from the conventional Christian image of the Messiah and Son of God: he is instead historicized as sage and royal pretender, Essene and mystic.

The first fictional effort to domesticate the ideas of the continental Jesus quest for an English-speaking audience was Moore's hugely popular *The Brook Kerith*, which was published in 1916 and went through many subsequent editions. The book tells the story of Jesus of Nazareth, both before and after the crucifixion, which Jesus survives. Indeed, his most important character growth occurs after his supposed death, as he realizes with horror the hatred and drive for power which had motivated much of his mission. He comes to realize that the ultimate truth is the nonreligious philosophical view that "there is but one thing . . . to learn to live for ourselves, and to suffer our fellows to do likewise."[66] Moore portrays Jesus and his followers as deeply interested in the intellectual movements of the ancient world, including the ideas of Heraclitus and the Greek philosophers, and the rich melange of ideas to be found in Alexandria. Much of the novel involves the Essenes and their "cenoby" (monastery) of Kerith, in which Jesus both begins his mission and spends his latter days.

Like other authors, Moore argues that Christianity was founded on fundamental mistakes, both about the resurrection of Jesus and his original goals. In his retirement at the cenoby, Jesus is visited by a sinister and power-hungry Paul, who informs him about the directions in which his new religion is leading, and presents the incomprehensible new doctrine of "the death and resurrection from the dead of the Lord Jesus Christ, raised from the dead by his Father." An Aramaic-speaking Jesus has to ask the meaning of the unfamiliar term "Christ," only to be informed that it is a newly coined Greek word. Discovering the imposture that has occurred in his name, Jesus must be dissuaded from going to Jerusalem to state and prove that he was not raised from the dead by any supernatural means: "the lie has spread . . . and will run all over the world even as a single mustard seed."[67] Ultimately, he joins the itinerant Indian monks who have been evangelizing the Judaean countryside, and travels with them back to their homeland.

The same idea about the perversion of Jesus' goals is presented in Frank Harris's story "The Miracle of the Stigmata," in which, again, Jesus survives the crucifixion, and lives on quietly as Joshua, a carpenter and smith.[68] Gradually, his town falls prey to the fanatical and ludicrous cult spread by the evil Paul, which is portrayed in terms of the most florid evangelical enthusiasm. Jesus is amazed by the myths spread about him, raises rational objections to every point of the emerging mythology, and modestly points out that Paul knew very little of what went on in Jerusalem. As the only one immune to the excesses, Jesus is ostracized by the community and abandoned by his wife, who despises him for his hostility to religion. After his death, however, Jesus/Joshua's neighbors find the vestigial marks of the crucifixion on his body, and conclude that he had been miraculously visited by the stigmata, proving that God's miracles can touch even so unworthy a skeptic. Many new converts find faith through this marvelous deed performed on "the last unbeliever in Caesarea."

Lawrence's story "The Man Who Died" also presents a picture of a resurrected Jesus who has abandoned his religious mission and is determined to live as a normal man, despite the self-deluding follies of his disciples. In this tale, Jesus emerges from his tomb through no supernatural means, but just because "They took me down too soon, so I came back to life." No longer a teacher or savior, he can resume the everyday life for which he was intended, which in this case means beginning a sexual relationship. He meets a pagan priestess of Isis, who believes him to be an incarnation not of the Jewish God, but of Osiris, that other dying and rising deity. The two have a sexual relationship, in order to generate a child who will be Osiris reborn: Jesus announces his erection with the line, "I am risen!" [69]

If the whole system of Christianity was indeed founded on delusion and ignorance, then we might argue with George Bernard Shaw that the last Christian died on the cross. Some writers, though, claimed that the authentic truth preached by Jesus might have been maintained by movements later categorized as heretics. This was the theme of Graves's *King Jesus*, which appeared in 1946, after the discoveries at Nag Hammadi, but written with no knowledge of those documents. *King Jesus* is Graves's pseudogospel, the sort of biography of Jesus which should have appeared if the evangelists had been rational Greco-Romans rather than superstitious Jews and Christians. After Jesus survived his apparent death on the Cross, his loyal Jewish followers survived as the Ebionite sect, who maintained their ancient scriptures and awaited the day when the twelve tribes of Israel would be restored and reunited in Jerusalem. The story is told through the words of the last surviving Ebionite bishop, who has seen these cherished truths polluted by Gentile intruders. In contrast to the Ebionites, current Gentile Christians were "unaware on what insecure historical ground their doctrine rests," and their views are outlined in a chapter entitled "Simpletons."[70] The received Christian scriptures are presented as partial and slanted, and Graves uses the fragments of lost ancient gospels such as the Gnostic *Descent of Mary* and the *Gospel of the Egyptians* to support his arguments. The epigraph to the book is the Salome fragment from the *Gospel of the Egyptians*. As in *The Brook Kerith*, an Essene monastery plays a crucial part throughout the action as Jesus' seminary and refuge.

Though Graves's fiction rarely ventures far into historical plausibility, he does show how, even before the documentary finds of the 1940s, it was possible to place Jesus into the broad context of Mediterranean societies, and to propose that the heretical movements possessed at least as much of the secret of true Christianity as did the orthodox churches. Far from being a new insight of the late twentieth century, the extraordinary complexity of early Christianity was familiar a century before, both to scholars and to the general reading public.

3

The First Gospels? Q and *Thomas*

These are the secret sayings which the living Jesus spoke and which
Didymos Judas Thomas wrote down. . . . Jesus said, Let him who seeks
continue seeking until he finds. When he finds, he will become troubled.
When he becomes troubled, he will be astonished, and he will rule over
the All.

GOSPEL OF THOMAS, PROLOGUE AND SAYING 2

ALTHOUGH THE EXISTENCE of other gospels was no surprise,
the Nag Hammadi collection vastly increased the range of documents available for study. This find supplied the full texts of fifty-
two documents, including a wide variety of sources from various
Gnostic and heterodox schools. Some of the new texts were only
tenuously linked with any Christian tradition, while a few had no
Christian credentials whatsoever, but a core of the documents was
written by people who incontestably saw themselves as followers
of Jesus. (It is an open question who actually formed or owned
the collection of texts: we will never know whether we are dealing with the cherished library of a particular Gnostic sect, or
whether orthodox scholars collected these works in order to
refute them.) The finds were important for what they suggested
or, rather, confirmed, about the diversity of belief and practice in
early Christianity.

By common consent, the most exciting find from Nag Hammadi was a complete Coptic text of the *Gospel of Thomas*. Of all the
ancient Christian texts that have been discovered over the last
century, it is *Thomas* which, according to its many advocates,
promises to cause the most sweeping revision of our views of
Christian origins.[1] *Thomas* has many resemblances to another
ancient source commonly called Q, and for some scholars, these
two documents, Q and *Thomas*, are the definitive standard by

which to judge the historicity of alleged words of Jesus, as well as the foundation for any attempt to reconstruct the surrounding events. Together, the two texts seem to show that the earliest Jesus Way was quite different from anything like what became the later Christian Church, and that the earliest Jesus followers knew little of what would later be called Christianity.

If not exactly as shattering as the fictional discoveries of *When It Was Dark* or *The Mystery of Mar Saba*, the twin rediscoveries of Q and *Thomas* have been hailed as exposing the true Jesus concealed behind the clerical complexities of the churches. Modern interpretations of these documents represent in their starkest form the whole mythology of the hidden gospels, the idea that a lost truth has been rediscovered—resurrected, even—with incalculable impact on modern thought. *Thomas* also serves as the thin end of a substantial wedge: if indeed so valuable a text has been excluded from the canon, then surely the process of revising that canon needs to begin forthwith, and who knows what other works might be added or deleted?

This whole interpretation is, however, built upon shaky foundations and a misunderstanding of how gospels would actually have been used in the ancient church. Some of the scholarship surrounding these supposed "first gospels" is by no means as conclusive as is sometimes claimed. Much of what seems important about these texts concerns what they do not say, and these mysterious absences can be filled up from a variety of other sources. Even these primitive lost gospels, by far the most important of their kind, are nothing like so eye-opening as sometimes appears. The fact that so much has been made of them says much about the theological and political messages that scholars hope to draw from them.

Discovering Q

The impact of *Thomas* can be understood only in the context of Q, that other lost document, which has in turn inspired some of the most remarkable recent work on Christian origins. Technically, this "lost gospel" was never truly lost, in that many millions of people already had it on their shelves without recognizing its true significance. Nineteenth-century German scholars discovered Q within the canonical text of the New Testament by exploring the detailed similarities and differences between the four gospels, conventionally named for Matthew, Mark, Luke, and John. Many ordinary believers tend to merge these four into virtually a single gospel narrative: this process of harmonization is easily observed at Christmas, when we encounter the crowded scene in which wise men, shepherds, angels, and farm animals jostle each other for a glimpse of the baby Jesus, who lies under the familiar star shining in the Bethlehem sky. All these elements are indeed found in the New Testament, but neither Mark nor John says a word about the circumstances of Jesus' birth, or suggests anything out of the ordinary about the event. Mark does not refer to Bethlehem at all, John only obliquely. The shepherds are found only in Luke, who never mentions the star or the magi, elements which appear only in Matthew; Matthew in turn knows nothing of shepherds and angelic hosts. Matthew tells the story chiefly from the perspective of Joseph, Luke from Mary's vantage point: combining the two accounts of Matthew and Luke we have the dramatic scenes that have been retold through the centuries.

Once we separate the different gospels, each not only has its distinctive character, but draws on different sources. Of the four gospels, John stands out as the most individual, throughout which Jesus speaks in the most mystical and divine language. The remaining three texts present a more or less common view of Jesus, recounting similar stories and speeches, and the three can be printed in parallel form to create a synopsis: hence the term "synoptic gospels." Examining the three synoptics together, we find large areas of similarity, and already by the 1830s, German scholars had proposed that both Matthew and Luke used Mark as a source, indicating that this work was written first. In addition, Matthew and Luke each used some materials distinctive to them, which appeared in no other Gospel, such as Luke's shepherds and Matthew's wise men. But once we have separated out these various elements, we are left with a fascinating body of material common to Matthew and Luke, but not found in Mark.[2]

The suggestion was soon made that this overlapping material all derived from a common source (not necessarily a written text) used by both evangelists. This would have been a collection of sayings without narrative structure, which was perhaps the same as the collection of logia (sayings) of Jesus referred to by the author Papias around 150: allegedly, this compilation was the work of the evangelist Matthew.[3] The work in its latest form can be dated quite reliably: since Matthew and Luke were both using it in the 80s, the collection cannot have been put together later than about 70 or 75. A scholarly consensus accepts that core material may date back still further, to the 40s or 50s, perhaps twenty years after the death of Jesus. John Dominic Crossan describes the collection as "composed by the fifties, and possibly at Tiberias in Galilee."[4] While different scholars had their own opinions about what this earlier source might be, the hypothetical material came to be known by the uncontroversial term *Quelle*, German for "source," and from the 1890s this was usually abbreviated to Q. Matthew thus drew on Mark and Q as well as his own particular sources; Luke likewise combined Mark and Q, in addition to his own materials. Both Matthew and Luke made free use of the Q materials, chopping, editing and rearranging their materials to fit their narrative purposes, though Luke was generally more faithful to the original arrangement.

The Q theory was well known in Germany by the end of the nineteenth century, and it received strong confirmation from the finding of the Oxyrhynchus papyri, which showed that such a sayings collection had indeed existed.[5] Already in these years, the great New Testament critic Adolf von Harnack was arguing that the authentic core of Jesus' message was to be found in the sayings and parables found in Q, which should be examined without the theological baggage added by the later church. In 1908, von Harnack's translation of the Q document was translated into English as *The Sayings of Jesus*.[6]

This neat analysis of the composition of the gospels is generally accepted, though some scholarly heretics have made a remarkably convincing case that eliminates Q altogether. According to one minority position, Matthew was the first gospel to be written, and his work was then used in edited form by Luke, who added his own distinctive materials in the process. Mark represented a summary or digest of the two. Alternatively, perhaps Luke copied from both Matthew and Mark. Other conservative scholars agree with the general idea that Q exists, but are skeptical whether it ever constituted a well-defined or unified body of material, and strongly doubt whether it can be reconstructed in any useful form.[7] The resistance to reconstruction efforts is particularly strong among European scholars, for whom the fascination with Q is sometimes dismissed as a North American fad.

Assuming, though, that Q was correctly identified, the source was so important because it included many of the best-known and most familiar tales and sayings in the whole of Christian thought, including Jesus' temptation in the desert, the Lord's Prayer, and the Sermon on the Mount.[8] Originally, Q would have chiefly comprised sayings, to which the later evangelists added a

narrative framework. By comparing Matthew and Luke's treatment of identical Q sayings, we might be able to reconstruct older
passages, which perhaps derived from Jesus himself. This analysis
can have quite dramatic effects on some of the best-known passages: in the Lord's Prayer, for example, Luke omits "Thy will be
done on earth as it is in heaven" as well as the line about deliver-
ing us from evil (or "from the evil one"). The longer and more
familiar version found in Matthew might be a closer rendering of
Jesus' actual words, but if so, it is puzzling that Luke would have
felt free to jettison lines which came straight from the mouth of
Jesus, had he found them in the source he used.[9]

To see how the evangelists edited their materials, we can look
at the passage in which Jesus informs his listeners that they will
receive no sign "except the sign of Jonah the Prophet."[10] But
what is this mysterious sign? In Luke, the next verse reads, "For
as Jonah became a sign to the Ninevites, so will the Son of Man be
to this generation," so that Jesus will be like Jonah, a prophet call-
ing to repentance. At the corresponding place in Matthew, however, we read "For as Jonah was three days and three nights in the
belly of the sea monster, *so will the Son of Man be three days and three
nights in the heart of the earth*": Jesus will thus be made a prophetic
sign by means of his death and resurrection.[11] It is unlikely that
Luke would have omitted such a stark prophecy of Jesus' death
and resurrection, had he known of its existence: on the other
hand, Matthew, or some intervening source, might well have
added this retroactive prophecy to a preexisting Q saying.

Thomas

The widespread acceptance of the Q theory helps explain the
excitement caused by the discovery of *Thomas*, which in so many
ways resembled that hypothetical document. If indeed *Thomas* too
dates back to the decades before the composition of the canonical
gospels, then it would provide an important lens for examining
the very oldest stages of the Jesus tradition.

Thomas has a close relationship with Q, and scholars commonly speak of "Q–*Thomas*" as a field of investigation. *Thomas* is
not identical with Q, and the version that we have from Nag
Hammadi was not collected until the mid-second century; nevertheless, about a third of the *Thomas* sayings have parallels in Q.
Moreover, *Thomas* lacks the kind of narrative and miracle stories
that we would expect from the familiar four gospels: it comprises
a series of 114 sayings of varying lengths, each introduced by the

phrase "Jesus said," and loosely connected by themes and key words. This pattern might suggest a primitive origin, as it so closely resembles reconstructions of Q. Supporting the suggestion that *Thomas* was composed independently of the canonical gospels, the order of sayings in *Thomas* does not appear to rely on the structure of those works. In some cases, too, the forms of the stories presented in *Thomas* arguably (but not definitely) look more primitive than the better-known forms we find in Q.[12]

Other evidence suggests an early date for *Thomas*. Patristic writings show that some of these sayings, though not necessarily the whole gospel, were regarded as authoritative very early within the mainstream catholic tradition. In the orthodox mid-second-century document known as 2 Clement, we read that "the Lord Himself, being asked by a certain person when his kingdom would come, said, 'When the two shall be one, and the outside as the inside, and the male with the female, neither male or female.'" Jesus here is quoted from *Thomas,* saying 22. Around 230, Origen recalls, more dubiously, that "I have read somewhere an alleged word of the Savior, and I ask whether someone imagined the figure of the Savior, or called the words to mind, or whether the saying is true. The Savior at any rate said, 'He who is near me is near the fire; he who is far from me is far from the kingdom.'" Origen is quoting *Thomas*, 82.[13] *Thomas* is at least drawing on ancient traditions.

The Deepest Levels?

Parts of *Thomas* might conceivably be as old as Q, though this is hotly contested; but might they even be older? Evidence for this surprising idea came from noting the differences between the two texts, since the *Thomas* sayings have parallels with a certain type of Q passage, but not with others. Specifically, *Thomas* resembles those portions of Q in which Jesus teaches an inner-oriented mysticism, but not those in which his message is prophetic or apocalyptic. Comparing the two gospels has led some writers to argue that *Thomas* might indicate the existence of an earlier core version of Q, which included the mystical sayings (the kingdom is within you) but not the doomsday prophecies (the day of the lord is at hand). These "inner" sayings, it is claimed, were collected at a very early stage of the Jesus movement, and might reflect the authentic words of Jesus. It is this perception which has given rise to much of the recent research into the "historical Jesus," and which now seems to be substantiated by documents much closer to the actual events than any of the four gospels.

The nature of the "kingdom of God" proclaimed by Jesus has been debated by scholars for centuries, as they wrestle with what appear to be two contradictory strands in the gospels: is the kingdom of God something that will come in the future, or is it already present? In parts of Q, the kingdom will come in a day of divine wrath and judgment, which will end the earthly order. This is what might be called an apocalyptic or eschatological teaching, referring to the last days, or the times of the End (Greek, *eschatos*). Jesus warns of the day of doom in sayings that draw heavily on traditional Jewish prophecy: "Just as lightning flashes and lights up the sky from one side to the other, so it will be on the day when the son of man appears", . . . "there will be two in the field. One will be seized and the other left."[14] Elsewhere in Q, though, Jesus refers to the kingdom as a state which can be achieved here and now, and is really or potentially within each individual: "Behold, the kingdom of God is among you" (or "within you"). "Ask and it will be given to you; seek and you will find; knock and the door will be opened for you."[15] These are what I call inner or mystical teachings.

The Q comments that find parallels in *Thomas* are those which speak of the kingdom as already existing within the believer. In *Thomas*, Jesus declares that "the Kingdom of the Father is spread out upon the earth, and men do not see it."[16] *Thomas*'s kingdom is something to which one returns through an inner pilgrimage, not a revelation that will descend from on high. It is a primordial reality, the state of the world in the original innocence described in Genesis, a kind of cosmic childhood: "Jesus said, 'Blessed are the solitary and elect, for you will find the Kingdom. For you are from it, and to it you will return.'"[17] Conversely, the Jesus of *Thomas* ignores or even mocks notions of the future coming of the kingdom: "If those who lead you say, 'See, the Kingdom is in the sky,' then the birds of the sky will precede you. If they say to you, 'It is in the sea,' then the fish will precede you. Rather, the Kingdom is inside of you, and it is outside of you. When you come to know yourselves, then you will become known, and you will realize that it is you who are the sons of the living Father."[18]

A kingdom within, or a kingdom to come? These different proclamations might be better understood if we assume that they come from different phases of the tradition, and were composed at different times. One of the most important scholars currently working on Q is John Kloppenborg, who argues that the text is made up of several strata: in the earliest layer of composition, which has been named "Q1," are preserved statements about the kingdom as an inner reality. At these levels, we find a Jesus who speaks as a radical social prophet, whose pithy sayings are intended to challenge conventional thinking and social structures, much like that other gadfly Socrates had done several centuries before him. We find here laconic, proverbial statements such as "Salt is good, but if the salt has lost its taste, how can its saltiness be restored?"[19] In contrast, the doomsday sayings belong to later editorial stages, composed or collected twenty or thirty years later, and summoned forth in polemical debates with Pharisees and other mainstream Jewish factions.

While scholars such as Albert Schweitzer once argued that the imminent apocalypse was at the core of Jesus' doctrine, many modern students of Q and *Thomas* insist to the contrary that doomsday formed no part whatsoever of the original message. In this view, the apocalyptic or future-oriented sayings found throughout the canonical gospels were added by later followers who found themselves in an increasingly desperate position as they were persecuted, and saw the ever-growing signs of war and social catastrophe as signs of approaching doomsday. These omens would have become all the more acute with the catastrophic Jewish revolt that raged between 66 and 73, culminating with the sack of Jerusalem in 70, and the destruction of the Temple. For these contemporary scholars, the idea of Jesus as doomsday prophet is an invention of these later years, and was retroactively projected onto the historical figure.

Dating Thomas

The effort to find layers of composition within Q may sound like a curious technical exercise, but at least according to some critics, this approach provides startling clues to dating *Thomas*, and thereby establishing its authority as a source for the earliest Christianity.[20] The task of dating is difficult because *Thomas* has obviously gone through several stages of composition and editing, but the logic proceeds as follows:

> Q in its final form can be no later than 70 or 75.
> Q1, the core collection, must be earlier still, perhaps as early as 45 or 50.
> *Thomas* closely resembles the hypothetical Q1, and at least in its original version, probably stems from the same period.
> Therefore a core of *Thomas* may date from the 50s, which

would make it actually older than any of our existing four gospels, and close to Jesus himself.

As we see below, the whole attempt to dissect Q is very controversial, and so is the related effort to prove the antiquity of *Thomas*. Still, these ideas have enjoyed great influence through the writings of several members of the Jesus Seminar, including Robert W. Funk, John Dominic Crossan, Burton Mack, Stevan L. Davies, Stephen J. Patterson, and Kloppenborg himself. Davies is a principal advocate of the crucial importance of *Thomas*: he writes that the work "is wholly independent of the New Testament gospels; most probably it was in existence before they were written. It should be dated AD 50-70."[21] This was also the view argued by Stephen J. Patterson; indeed, the editors of the Jesus Seminar's *Five Gospels* write that Patterson's study "has helped break the privileged position of the canonical gospels on the Jesus question."[22]

Extreme estimates about the dating and independence of *Thomas* underlie recent attempts to challenge or verify other passages in the New Testament. For the Jesus Seminar, a primary criterion of an authentic Jesus saying is multiple attestation, that the saying is cited in at least two independent sources. If in fact Q and Thomas are independent witnesses, then a saying which occurs in both is ipso facto likely to be "original Jesus." But, of course, this judgment depends entirely on the fact that the two sources are in fact independent of each other. As L. Michael White observes, the early dating of *Thomas* "is in fact, without most people realizing it, actually the lynchpin for most of the arguments of the Jesus Seminar. It's the crucial issue that they don't talk about—that dating—because what they do is, they take a layer of Q prior to what we now call Q—say that that's what's preserved in the *Gospel of Thomas*—use the Q–Thomas connection in a pre-70 state, and say that's the earliest collection of sayings of Jesus. And that's what they use to authenticate sayings." Two hypothetical documents—Q and original *Thomas*—are thus given priority over all known written sources, including the indisputably early Mark.[23]

The high status accorded to *Thomas* is apparent from a subtle but misleading usage in the *Five Gospels*, in which passages are cited with their supposed sources. In Luke 6:39, for example, we read the familiar phrase, "Can the blind lead the blind? Won't they both fall into some ditch?"[24] As this passage occurs in very similar form in both Luke and Matthew, but is not found in Mark, we can identify it as a Q passage, and the editors properly cite it as such. The saying is, however, also found as saying 34 of *Thomas*. Many commentators would say that *Thomas* is quoting the phrase from Q, but to admit this would challenge the doctrinaire belief in Thomas's independence and authority. In the *Five Gospels*, therefore, we read that the source of the phrase is "Q, *Thomas*," which presumes that *Thomas* is indeed a truly ancient document, and served as an independent source for the evangelists. A similar editorial practice results in many Q passages being sourced as "Q, *Thomas*," with the result that almost every page cites *Thomas* as authoritative. A casual reader of this text is left with the tendentious impression that *Thomas* is a critical source for virtually every part of the canonical gospels, an assumption which begs a great many questions.

Curious Absences

Though the Q theory is long established, it was only in the last quarter of the twentieth century that scholars began to make sweeping claims about the full implications of the document and, particularly, the significance of what the work did not include. When supported by the additional evidence from *Thomas*, these claims became all the more ambitious. Let us assume that Q originally existed as a free-standing source, whether oral or written, and served as *the* gospel or primary authority for some very early Christian community: what can we learn about the ideas of the people who wrote and used it? The work has a clear beginning with the career of John the Baptist and the baptism of Jesus, and it ends neatly when Jesus tells his apostles of a time to come when they will each receive a kingdom, "and sit on thrones, judging the twelve tribes of Israel."[25] The work includes no hint of a miraculous birth, nor do we hear of those episodes which to us seem so basic to Jesus' career: there is nothing about a challenge to the accepted structures of Judaism, no conflict with the powers of this world, either the priests and Pharisees, or the Roman empire.

More disturbing, Q contains no certain reference to Jesus' crucifixion, death, or resurrection. The only likely reference is the famous line that "Whoever does not bear his own cross and come after me, cannot be my disciple," which probably indicates knowledge of the crucifixion.[26] As this death holds no significance, neither do ideas such as atonement, vicarious sacrifice, or Christ dying for sinners. As we have seen in the passages about the "sign of Jonah," some such interpretations have been added retroactively to the original text, but comparing Matthew and Luke makes it possible to see where such scissors-and-paste revisions have occurred. Furthermore, all these curious absences are reflected in *Thomas*, which likewise omits virtually the whole of what later generations would consider Christian doctrine. A little external evidence suggests that earlier generations of Christians noticed these omissions, and were duly troubled by them. In the mid-second century, the Christian leader Polycarp attacked those who denied the cross and resurrection by "perverting the logia of the Lord": apparently, they were already citing the lack of reference to these phenomena in the sayings collections which circulated in his day, probably collections such as Q itself.[27]

What kind of Christian communities existed without the tenets of orthodox belief? Just what did Jesus mean to them? Superficially, it appears that these first followers of Jesus treasured his words, but saw his death as merely the untimely end to a career spent spreading enlightenment. As Burton Mack writes of the community which produced Q, "they did not regard [Jesus'] death as a divine, tragic or saving event." Helmut Koester argues that "both documents [Q and *Thomas*] presuppose that Jesus' significance lay in his words, and in his words alone." From this perspective, Q and *Thomas* might be survivals from a Jesus community that saw little significance in the idea of Resurrection, or had not yet felt the need to invent the story. For many recent writers, the evidence of the ancient gospels suggests that Jesus' disciples were far less supernaturally oriented than might be expected from the standard histories written over the next 1900 years. In the revisionist view, the disciples believed that Jesus survived his death in the form of his message and his community, rather than in any literal form. He survived in the same purely metaphorical sense as twentieth-century subversive heroes such as Che Guevara and Joe Hill:

> I dreamed I saw Joe Hill last night alive as you and me.
> Said I, "But Joe, you're ten years dead," "I never died," said
>   he.
> . . . "Joe Hill ain't dead," he says to me, "Joe Hill ain't never
>   died,
> When workers strike and organize, Joe Hill is by their side."

Or to take a well-known literary parallel, Jesus carried on much as Tom Joad envisaged his own pantheistic continuation, in Steinbeck's *The Grapes of Wrath*: "Then I'll be all aroun' in the dark. I'll be ever'where—wherever you look. Wherever they's a fight so hungry people can eat, I'll be there. Wherever they's a cop beatin' up a guy, I'll be there. . . . An' when our folk eat the stuff they raise and live in the houses they build—why, I'll be there." According to the radical reconstruction of Christian origins, Jesus lived on in much the same symbolic way for his followers in the first century as Joe Hill would for his in the twentieth.[28]

Did the early Jesus Way really know no cross, no tomb, no Easter? It is appropriate that the gospel with such far-reaching implications was named for that Thomas who has become a byword for doubt and disbelief. Neither Q nor *Thomas* offers any hint that his first followers saw Jesus as the Son of God or Messiah. Neither work uses the term "Christ": as Stevan Davies writes, "perhaps *Thomas* was written in a time when such words as Christ, Son of Man, Savior etc. were not yet universally used of Jesus." Jack Miles describes the discovery of Q as "the critical triumph that broke open the story of Jesus and the non-Christians who were his first followers." In that case, Q might indeed be a "pre-Christian gospel." For Robert Funk, work on Q–*Thomas* raises the possibility "that the Christian overlay found in the New Testament gospels may be just that—an overlay."[29]

Instead of a messianic figure, it is claimed, Jesus was a "traveling sage and wonder-worker," a teacher seeking to reform the present world, rather than to usher in a new divine order.[30] Jesus taught not a new religion, still less a supernatural doctrine with himself as its center. According to Crossan, the most radical life changes introduced by Jesus involved a frontal assault on the etiquette rules of whom one can acceptably eat with, and his "healings" are basically a refusal to accept the stigma of sickness. Jesus was "a peasant Jewish Cynic," whose key beliefs were "free healing and common eating."[31] There is nothing vaguely approaching the miraculous here. His followers had no interest in the coming of a future kingdom of God or an apocalypse, nor indeed of God in anything like the traditional sense found in the Hebrew Bible. In addition to being dechristianized, the Jesus of this interpretation also strays far from any obvious Jewish roots. All the Q references to Old Testament figures (Jonah, Solomon, Noah, Moses, the patriarchs) belong to what are regarded as the later levels of the tradition, while *Thomas* never once refers to the figures of Hebrew antiquity, beyond a couple of general references to "the prophets."[32]

In trying to comprehend the bizarre Jesus they find in Q and *Thomas*, scholars focus not on the image of Christ or Son of God but on the concept of Wisdom, *Sophia*. The sayings attributed to Jesus in *Thomas* and the supposed oldest levels of Q resemble the Wisdom teachings found across the Mediterranean world, in both Jewish and non-Jewish contexts.[33] Wisdom teachers offered lessons in the form of proverbs, anecdotes, and maxims, which were collected under titles such as the "sayings of the sages." This approach to Jesus suggests that his early followers had a great deal in common with other philosophical and mystical schools of the Roman empire and indeed beyond, and there are parallels with the teachings of Eastern masters, notably in Buddhism. The Jesus imagined by modern scholarship would have felt quite comfortable uttering the last words attributed to the Buddha, namely, that all is transient, that his followers must work out their own liberation, and that no reliance should be placed on external saviors, including himself. If Jesus did indeed claim supernatural significance, it was not as Christ but as a manifestation of divine Wisdom. We might conceivably see evidence for such ideas from St. Paul's correspondence with the faction-ridden church in Corinth in the early 50s where some of Paul's opponents claimed to be followers of Wisdom. In this scenario, perhaps Paul was attacking mystical ideas related to those of *Thomas*, which stood in such sharp contrast to his own doctrines, which focused on the sacrificial death of Christ. In his refutation, Paul even quotes a saying which looks somewhat like one found in *Thomas*.[34]

The portrait of Jesus as sage and Wisdom teacher can be carried to extreme lengths. Burton Mack argues from Q that the earliest Jesus movement was very much like the Greek Cynics, who challenged all the values of customary decency and common sense. It is in this context that we should read the Cynic-sounding sayings about believers selling all, taking no thought for the morrow, possessing only one cloak, and carrying neither money nor bag, sandals nor staff, while hating their parents and siblings.[35] Jesus' aphorisms and parables were deliberately intended to snap listeners out of conventionality and commonsense approaches: the meaning of these texts is found only "by abandoning sense."[36] According to this radical interpretation, which all but denies Jesus any Jewish context, Jesus' first followers were groups of (hypothetical) wandering charismatics, who find their closest modern equivalents among homeless street people. Charlotte Allen's wry summary of this view is that "[Jesus'] original acolytes, who later became the Q community, were proto-beatniks encamped along the Sea of Galilee, who recorded his teachings during spare moments in their wanderings." To quote Crossan, "Jesus and his first followers . . . were hippies in a world of Augustan yuppies."[37] In contemporary scholarship,"the people of the Q Gospel," the "Q community," that held such outré views has become the earliest example of an authentic manifestation of Jesus' Way which found itself silenced and consigned to historical oblivion. Hidden Christians were commemorated only in a hidden gospel.

Without having to invoke the existence of "proto-beatniks" or Jesus hippies, the new views of Jesus and his milieu raise devastating questions about the origins of Christianity. If in fact these first gospels accurately reflect the apostolic thought-world, so apparently untroubled by concepts like the resurrection or atonement, to say nothing of sacraments or ecclesiastical structures, how did these later complexities emerge? The implication is that the whole religious edifice of Christianity was a later accretion to the primitive doctrines of the skeptical Jesus followers, and that Christians have since early times been cut off from their subversive mystical roots. Historical Christianity was a gigantic mistake, or a collective delusion. This would be very bad news for traditionally minded believers, though it has an obvious appeal for modern-day liberals or skeptics who wish to take the doctrines of the faith in a symbolic way. For these latter, *Thomas* and reconstructed Q provide a vehicle for finding a way back to the pristine teaching of Jesus.

Some scholars have suggested how the authentic Jesus movement reflected in Q–*Thomas* might have evolved into Christianity, usually with a sense of tracing a process of decline or betrayal. According to Mack, the followers of Jesus followed a trajectory that involved them in ever more complex supernatural beliefs. For the first followers, the meaning of Jesus' life was contained in his teachings and sayings, but as time went on and the movement spread, new supporters focused on other images, seeing Jesus as a sage, prophet, or exorcist. Later still, "the mythology that is most familiar to Christians of today developed in groups that formed in northern Syria and Asia Minor" where, under Hellenistic influences, Jesus' death was seen first as a martyrdom, "and then embellished as a miraculous event of crucifixion and resurrection."[38] It is almost as if twentieth-century American radicals came to believe that Joe Hill was literally appearing to them from beyond the grave, and evolved a story that his grave had been found empty. In the eyes of the Hellenized believers which emerge from the letters of Paul, Jesus was transformed into Christ, Lord, and Son of God. As a later generation of believers claimed to see meaning in the events of Jesus' life and death, this perception was reflected in the composition of the narrative gospels in the 70s and 80s. A quite human Jesus, who confronted worldly prejudices and hypocrisy, was transformed into a cosmic overlord.

In describing the rise of otherworld-oriented Christianity, authors use loaded terms that have a correct technical meaning, but which in popular parlance sound distinctly sinister. Mack repeatedly speaks of the "Christ myth" or "Christ cult." Both myth and cult are proper anthropological terms, and I have myself used "myth" and "mythology" in the present argument; but for the general reader, a "myth" is a lie or a fiction, and a "cult" is a gullible group of believers who accept the absurd doctrines of a fanatical leader. Linked with the growing emphasis on apocalyptic ideas, a modern reader might even speak of a "doomsday cult" of the sort that have attracted such notoriety over the last decade or two: for modern Americans, the phrase calls to mind the cult massacres at Waco and Jonestown. These popular meanings run through contemporary writings, usually with Paul as the inventive cult leader who egregiously perverts the pure doctrine.

Doubting *Thomas*, Doubting Q

Though these ideas have become so influential among scholars, the proposed evolutionary sequence from Jesus the sage to Christ the Son of God is by no means as clear as it first appears. At every stage of the critique, there are dubious assumptions that must be confronted, and most concern the nature and authority of the two supposed proto-gospels.

To begin with Q, while the existence of that document is very likely, it is far from clear that the supposed layers can be reconstructed, since so much depends upon subjective interpretations and individual opinions about the likely stages of the text's internal evolution. Scholars disagree on many issues about the reconstruction of Q, arguing whether particular passages should in fact be assigned to that document, so obviously there is still more intense debate about which sayings should be placed in particular levels. The view that Wisdom sayings stand at the earliest stage of the tradition, with prophetic remarks evolving much later, looks very much like an a priori assumption. Q existed, but a core "Wisdom" level of Q (sapiential Q, or Q1) is a much more speculative animal.[39]

Similarly, it is very dubious that all the remarks about the imminent end of the world date from a later stage of composition, presumably during the terrifying social upheavals that the Jesus community faced in the 60s and 70s. Though it has become an article of faith among radical New Testament critics that the "doomsday" remarks are retroactive, a substantial body of evidence demonstrates that such thinking was deeply embedded in early Christianity, and indeed in the sectarian Judaism of Jesus' own day. On the Jewish side, messianic fantasies and apocalyptic nightmares pervade the Dead Sea Scrolls, which were written over a lengthy period between perhaps 150 B.C. and 70 A.D. We also know that John the Baptist was a doomsday preacher, and even the most skeptical historians accept that Jesus was connected to John's movement, perhaps as a disciple.

The power of doomsday thinking is evident in the very earliest Christian documents that we possess, particularly the letters of St. Paul. Though there is debate about which of these texts may actually be the work of the apostle to the Gentiles, most scholars accept that the letters to the Thessalonians are Paul's work, and must be dated around 50. In First Thessalonians, Paul writes to a congregation who have taken too literally his message about the end of the world, and refuse to carry on their daily lives in the face of looming catastrophe. Long before the Jewish revolt, and outside Palestine, at least some Jesus followers had a profoundly eschatological bent. It is only natural that such ideas would be expressed in detail in any gospel record that Jesus followers would have composed in these years. The idea of Jesus as apocalyptic prophet assuredly goes back to the very earliest stages of the tradition, and any attempt to purge the doomsday sayings from reconstructions of Q is arbitrary and unacceptable.[40]

There are at least as many difficulties in accepting the standard modern view of *Thomas* and, above all, its early dating.[41] Though *Thomas* looks primitive in its format and organization, neither characteristic can be used as conclusive proof of a very early date. Generally, texts like Q that offer sayings without narrative belong to an early stage of the tradition, but the same format also appears in much later documents. One example is a Gnostic text known as the *Gospel of Philip*, which probably dates from the later third century. Though lacking the recurrent "Jesus said" formula, *Philip* is an anthology of seemingly unconnected sayings and statements, without any narrative or biographical structure. And some statements in *Philip* are quite as brief and cryptic as those in *Thomas*.[42] Despite this superficial resemblance to *Thomas*'s format, no scholar has suggested a comparably early date for *Philip*.

The most important reason to argue a late date for much of *Thomas* is that the text as we have it contains many sayings which unmistakably suggest Gnosticism and other heresies which developed during the mid- and late second century.[43] *Thomas* includes dialogues featuring Mary Magdalen or Salome, of the sort which are very characteristic of *Pistis Sophia* and other Gnostic texts of the late second and third centuries.[44] Some of Thomas' advocates play down these Gnostic elements, since they are so inconvenient for any attempt to date the whole text to the mid-first century, but in fact perhaps a third of the sayings are suffused with Gnostic ideas and phraseology. Saying 50 is a classic example: "Jesus said, 'If they say to you, "Where did you come from?," say to them, "We came from the light, the place where the light came into being on its own accord and established [itself] and became manifest through their image." If they say to you, "Is it you?," say, "We are its children, we are the elect of the Living Father." If they ask you, "What is the sign of your father in you?," say to them, "It is movement and repose."'" "They" in this saying must refer to the archons, the rulers of the material world in Gnostic mythology, and the saying fits perfectly into the Gnostic literature described by Irenaeus in the 170s.

This mythology also provides the setting for another cryptic passage in which Jesus declares, "Blessed is the lion that a man will eat, and the lion will become man." Lion imagery was commonly used for the rulers of the heavens, the cosmic gate-keepers, in the Gnostic systems of the mid- and late second century. Commonly, the lion-headed figure was Ialdabaoth, who appears thus in Gnostic texts such as the *Pistis Sophia* and the *Apocryphon of John*.[45] In saying 77, Jesus speaks as the Gnostic Redeemer from the spiritual realms when he announces that "I am the Light that is above everything, I am All. . . . Split the wood and I am there. Lift up the stone and you will find me there." This saying was immediately recognized as proclaiming a Gnostic origin when the original Oxyrhynchus fragments were discovered in the 1890s.[46] These Gnostic-looking elements presumably explain why *Thomas* was a favorite of heterodox movements like the Naassenes and the Manichaeans, and why individual sayings are quoted in so many diverse heretical sources.[47]

An original text of *Thomas* has been heavily edited and amended under Gnostic influence, at the earliest in the mid-second century. *Thomas* thus includes some early sayings that may be linked to the time of Jesus, some from perhaps 150 years later, and a number which cannot certainly be placed in either category (the Nag Hammadi manuscript itself dates only from 350, though some Greek versions of the gospel are much earlier). The question then is how extensive were the changes that occurred at a late editorial stage, and whether these revisions might have distorted the original substance of *Thomas*. In addition to inserting sayings that appealed to Gnostic sentiment, the editors might well have removed passages which the likely readership would have found incomprehensible or unpalatable. That could conceivably have meant removing all apocalyptic or prophetic elements, as well as references to concepts like crucifixion or messiahship, or anything that was conspicuously Jewish. This revision might also have involved interpolating passages which reflected the Gnostic view at the time. When, for instance, we read the saying quoted above in which Jesus denies the literal coming of a day of judgment, it is impossible to know whether this truly reflects the Jesus movement's early doctrine, or whether it represented the views of heretical editors a century or so later.

Is *Thomas* an independent source? If the text did not receive its final reworking until perhaps 140, then all three synoptic gospels were in existence by this point, and in fact were so well established that many Christians would have grown up intimately familiar with these sayings. This fact prompts some scholars to argue that *Thomas* passages which resemble the synoptics might have been derived from them, in whole or in part. This was the argument of many of the critics who first discussed the work when it became available in the late 1950s. The issue can be illustrated from the complicated logion 33, in which Jesus declares, "Preach from your housetops that which you will hear in your ear. . . . For no one lights a lamp and puts it under a bushel, nor does he put it in a hidden place, but rather he sets it on a lampstand so that everyone who enters and leaves will see its light." This is reminiscent of a number of Q passages, but the author or editor of *Thomas* seems to have combined at least two separate Q verses, possibly because he was using the order in which materials were already arranged in the Gospel of Matthew.[48] John P. Meier argues strongly for *Thomas'* reliance on all the canonical gospels, especially Matthew and Luke, but also including John, which is commonly agreed to be the latest of the four.[49]

If *Thomas* is later than the already existing canonical gospels, and is indeed using them, then its value as an independent source shrinks dramatically. As Ben Witherington observes, "there are clear traces of Jesus' sayings material both in Paul's letters . . . and in the homily attributed to James . . . but there are *not* clear traces in the canonical gospels of the *Thomas* forms of synoptic sayings, nor any traces of the sayings found only in *Thomas*." Witherington concludes that "*Thomas* can be shown again and again to be a later Gnosticizing reappropriation of the Jesus tradition found in the synoptics."[50] Elaine Pagels suggests that *Thomas*'s readers would already have been expected to know the standard teachings of Jesus of the sort found in the synoptics: *Thomas* "claims to give teachings that Jesus *didn't* give in public. It would be incomprehensible if the reader didn't know something about the teaching Jesus gave in public." Without already knowing something about Jesus and his teachings, "it would make absolutely no sense at all."[51]

The First Followers

At many points, too, there are serious difficulties with the vision of the earliest Jesus movement as reconstructed from Q and *Thomas*.[52] Contradicting the picture of Jesus as a misplaced Greek rationalist is the evidence we have of the earliest Jesus followers in Palestine and Syria, who looked to the leadership of the Jerusalem church under James the Just, reportedly the brother of Jesus. If in fact Q (and *Thomas*?) arose from that first generation of followers, then presumably these documents came from communities which accepted the exalted position of James: in one striking *Thomas* passage, Jesus commands his followers to "go to James the Just, for whose sake heaven and earth came into being."[53] We would expect Q and *Thomas* to reflect the ideas of the Jerusalem church, in contrast to the deviant Gentile Christianity spread by Paul. But one thing we know for certain about that early Jerusalem church and its leaders in the 40s and 50s is that they were diehard defenders of Jewish practices such as circumcision and food laws, which they condemned Paul for flouting. It is extremely unlikely that a strictly observant Jewish community like that could have put together anything like *Thomas* or the reconstructed oldest levels of Q, both of which stray so far from distinctively Jewish teaching or belief.

Furthermore, as the truism holds, absence of evidence is not evidence of absence, and the fact that some Jesus followers preserved a work which failed to mention messiahship, resurrection, or divine status does not mean that these doctrines were not held. Perhaps they were so thoroughly known that they were too obvious to be stated. As Pagels remarks, *Thomas* "never says Jesus is the son of God. It never says he dies for our sins. There's no crucifixion. Of course, the author may just have assumed that we know all that."[54] The familiar theological interpretations about Jesus' death may have been known, and preserved in some other source not now known to us. The existing synoptic gospels were written by combining sayings materials with originally separate Passion texts. In addition to their sayings gospel, did the Q people (whoever and wherever they were) have a distinct passion/resurrection account, whether written or oral?

Nor can we simply accept that the Q–*Thomas* tradition failed to ascribe some very special status to the death of Jesus. Twenty or so years after that event, Jesus was sufficiently important to record and collect his teachings and prophecies, however cryptic, suggesting that in some sense, he lived on. It is incomprehensible that such a lofty reputation should surround the cracker-barrel peasant philosopher posited by recent readings of the sayings recorded in Q or *Thomas*. Nor, if Jesus represented such a supposedly commonplace type as the itinerant sage, is it apparent why this individual rather than any other should have been chosen for elevation to messiahship, and later godhood. While some early Jesus communities might have been fascinated by the picture of Jesus as sage and moral teacher, they collected sayings and stories so avidly because they believed there had been something very special about his life and, particularly, his death. In the very first verse of *Thomas*, Jesus promises the reader that "whoever finds the interpretation of these sayings will not experience death." This surely implies a belief that Jesus himself was already celebrated for having cheated the grave, and that this special status gave authority to his teachings and parables.

Mysteries of Faith

A reluctance to put key ideas in writing may explain some of the puzzling absences from sayings documents such as Q and *Thomas*. Perhaps these collections were intended as an instructional or evangelistic device, for proselytes who would later be instructed into the deeper mysteries of the emerging faith: they were intended to intrigue rather than explain. These texts might even have been intended to be as cryptic and superficially nonthreatening as possible in order to disarm the suspicions of potential persecutors. Anyone who reads the New Testament book of Acts finds first-century Christians portrayed as evangelizing openly in the streets, but there was a fundamental difference between such preaching and the fact of writing down the core doctrines of the faith.

To a modern audience, it is incredible that a gospel or any writing about Jesus would fail to mention the essential doctrines of the religion, even an idea as basic as the Resurrection, but such a gap would not have surprised an ancient reader. Religious scriptures of all types had a very different role in ancient times from what we consider normal today. The notion that the essential doctrines of a religion can or should be plainly laid out for everyone in scriptural form, as opposed to liturgy or oral teaching, is a distinctly modern and Protestant view. The idea that cheap editions of such a precious text as the Bible could be freely distributed on the streets, or left in hotel bedrooms, would have seemed quite bizarre, not to say blasphemous, to early Christians. Jesus' followers lived in a world when the most ambitious and successful religions only gradually revealed their innermost secrets to believers, after a lengthy process of initiation: these were the mystery religions, formed by devotees of Mithras, Isis, and other divine figures, usually movements from the East.

Patristic writers show that some Christians shared this reluctance to broadcast the great truths of the faith. Around 200, Clement of Alexandria wrote that "it is requisite, therefore, to hide in a mystery the wisdom spoken, which the Son of God taught. . . . And even now I fear, as it is said, 'to cast the pearls before swine, lest they tread them under foot, and turn and rend us.' For it is difficult to exhibit the really pure and transparent words respecting the true light, to swinish and untrained hearers." Believers were to "receive the secret traditions of the true knowledge, and expound them aloft and conspicuously; and as we have heard in the ear, so to deliver them to whom it is requisite; but not enjoining us to communicate to all without distinction, what is said to them in parables."[55] For Origen, as for other Alexandrians, Jesus' parables were laden with secret meanings that were only gradually to be released to the multitudes: Jesus himself had told his apostles that to them alone was it "given to know the *mysteria* of the kingdom of God," the mysteries contained in the parables. Origen defended the church's right to restrict the release of "gospel truths": "But that there should be certain doctrines, not made known to the multitude, which are (revealed) after the exoteric ones have been taught, is not a peculiarity of Christianity alone, but also of philosophic systems, in which certain truths are exoteric and others esoteric." The evangelists, he argued, had been cautious about which of Jesus' teachings "were to be committed to writing, and how this was to be done, and what was by no means to be written to the multitude, and what was to be expressed in words, and what was not to be so conveyed."[56]

Alexandrians were notoriously fascinated by the idea that Christianity was a religion of "mysteries," but other Christians demonstrated a taste for presenting doctrines in cryptic form, to the extent that modern scholars can debate whether a given text is indeed Christian. We can illustrate this with the famous tombstone inscription of one Avircius Marcellus, "a disciple of the pure shepherd" who died in Phrygia (in modern Turkey) around 180. This allusive text records how Avircius had traveled "with Paul before me . . . and Faith everywhere led the way and served food everywhere, the Fish from the Spring—immense, pure, which the pure virgin caught and gave to her friends to eat for ever, with good wine, giving the cup with the loaf."[57] Like any text from a mystery religion, the inscription is intended to baffle outsiders, while preaching to the initiated. But even in this disguised format, there are no references to some of the most potent doctrines of the faith, including the incarnation, death, or resurrection of Christ, absences of a sort we repeatedly note in written texts.

Gospels played a critical role in the process of revealing the "mysteries" of Christianity. These scriptures contained the most cherished treasures of the faith, namely, the words of Jesus and an explanation of the significance of his death and resurrection. These holy truths were not to be lightly shared, and at least some churches prevented converts to Christianity from hearing the gospels and their mysteries until after they had been formally initiated into the new religion, by means of baptism. Prior to this, they held the probationary status of catechumens, and in the early centuries, catechumens were barred from participating in many parts of the service, including, it seems, the reading of the gospel. Even today, Orthodox church services still admonish catechumens to depart before the saying of the creed and the beginning of the sacred eucharistic mysteries.

In various third- and fourth-century texts concerning church order, we hear that prospective Christians were required to fulfill lengthy periods of candidacy and teaching before they were finally permitted to hear "the word," "the gospel," whatever that may have meant exactly. While undergoing instruction, most of their scriptural lessons apparently came from the Old Testament, not the New. Paul Bradshaw notes that the fourth-century document known as the *Apostolic Constitutions* may "reflect the two stages of teaching, since it indicates that the catechumens first learn about creation, the Old Testament saints, etc., and only after baptism do they learn about Christ's incarnation, death, resurrection and ascension."[58] As late as the fifth century, church councils had to specify "that catechumens are to hear the reading of the gospel," showing that this practice was new, and perhaps controversial. It is a matter of debate how much of those inner secrets had spread to become public knowledge, at least in general form, yet the church remained cautious about exactly how these "mysteries" were presented at large.[59]

The Sayings in Which You Have Been Instructed

With these church practices in mind, it is useful to look again at Q and *Thomas*, with a view to the religious mysteries that they do not mention, which conspicuously included "Christ's incarnation, death, resurrection and ascension." The common explanation for these lacunae is that the early communities either did not know these doctrines or else set no store by them, but we can now see that a quite different explanation is possible. Perhaps Q and *Thomas* reflect a time in the early church when evangelists aroused the interest of potential recruits, especially gentiles, by promoting the image of Jesus as a provocative teacher, who in some infuriatingly unspecified way could promise victory over the grave. In modern terms, these texts could be seen as teasers or recruitment brochures. New seekers would gradually be taught the fuller version of the truth, and ultimately the core doctrines of Jesus' saving death and resurrection.

This gradual method has implications for the process of committing Christian ideas to writing. Initially, the community might write the actual words of Jesus, which were too enigmatic to reveal much to the casual observer, but it would be some years or decades more before they would venture to write down the still more sensitive doctrines of the new faith. (Paul and others did write such doctrines, but only when communicating with fellow initiates.) A record of sayings like Q could have circulated for years independently of the more theologically elaborate materials, without this meaning that these latter doctrines were unknown or undeveloped. Matters would have changed after the 60s, with the death of important early leaders such as James and Peter, and the disasters of the Jewish revolt, which cumulatively threatened to cut the community off from its roots and to obliterate native traditions about Jesus. This apparently provoked a decision to write the community's beliefs and history more fully. By the end of the first century, the canonical gospels supplied the complete instruction and enlightenment promised to those converts who had originally been intrigued by something like Q.

In this context, we find special significance in the opening passage of Luke, the gospel which includes Q in the form closest to the original. Writing to a certain Theophilus, Luke describes how he had decided to "write an orderly account . . . that you may know the truth concerning the things (*logoi*) of which you have been informed."[60] But *logoi* can also mean words or sayings rather than things, and the fourth-century Latin translation in the Vulgate renders *logoi* as *verborum*, "words." The word *logoi* also appears in the opening of the Greek text of *Thomas*, "these are the secret *sayings* which the living Jesus spoke." If *logoi* has this meaning in Luke, then the passage might be translated rather differently. Luke is actually promising to write the full truth about the *sayings* in which Theophilus has been *katechethes*, "instructed," a word related to catechumen. A century ago, Kirsopp Lake made the ingenious suggestion that the *logoi* referred to here might have been "a series of sayings used for the instruction of converts, which Luke is providing with a historical framework."[61] Perhaps Theophilus, like other converts of the late first century, had received his instruction by means of the sayings in Q, but now he had been fully initiated, he had earned the right to know the full story, of which Q formed only a suggestive component.

Once narrative gospels like Luke were in existence, Q had entirely lost its original function, and it is not surprising that the text ceased to exist as a separate document. (Some years later still, at least some churches decided that even the words of Jesus were too sacred to be wantonly displayed before the uninitiated, and began to exclude catechumens altogether from hearing any part of the gospel.) Related sayings gospels survived in various forms, and were adapted by Gnostic and other groups for their own purposes. Perhaps around 140, one of these became our present version of *Thomas*. Q and *Thomas* did not become hidden gospels because they exemplified an alternate tradition of early Christianity, but rather vanished because they represented an outmoded literary genre. There never was a "Q community" or a group of "Thomas people" distinct from the mainstream Jesus Way, that is, the incipient Christian Church.

These documents look as strange as they do to us because they were never intended to offer anything more than a partial or suggestive introduction to the faith. The communities which created these texts would have been appalled to find that anyone, whether contemporary heretic or later scholar, could have taken these documents as entire or rounded statements of the Jesus movement, which stood or fell on the truth of those core ideas, the Cross and the Resurrection. Alternatively, they might have been pleased that their subterfuge had been so effective.

Resurrection

Influenced by modern interpretations of Q–*Thomas*, a remarkable number of New Testament scholars accept that Jesus' supernatural status was a later addition to a primitive system of Wisdom teachings. It should be stressed, though, how very early such exalted ideas really are. This is obviously true of the concept of the Resurrection: though this idea is not referred to explicitly in either Q or *Thomas*, it is inconceivable that their authors did not know of it. We have overwhelming evidence for a very early belief in Jesus' resurrection—which is of course quite different from proving this as an objective historical event. Nor can we be sure of exactly how the faithful understood this phenomenon, and early groups may or may not have known the idea of literal bodily resurrection, in the sense that later became Christian orthodoxy. Some did, but others saw the event in nonmaterial terms: the famous scene in the Gospel of John in which the risen Jesus lets Thomas touch his wounds must be intended to refute this latter school of thought. Elisabeth Schüssler Fiorenza offers a nice phrase here, imagining the early Christians working, living and preaching in the "force-field," the life-giving spirit that Jesus had become following his death.

The best evidence for very early belief in Jesus' resurrection comes from a passage included in St. Paul's first letter to the Corinthians no later than 55, and almost certainly including much older materials, perhaps a kind of creed. Paul reports the tradition he had received, which declared that Jesus appeared "to

Cephas, then to the twelve. Then he appeared to more than five hundred brothers and sisters at one time, most of whom are still alive, though some have died. Then he appeared to James, then to all the apostles."[62] This was the tradition which Paul received from James, Peter, and the other leaders of the Jesus community, presumably during his visit to Jerusalem around 40.[63] That is before the earliest date at which Q could plausibly have been composed, and long antedates the oldest possible date for *Thomas*. Also, this description of Resurrection appearances comes not from any supposed gentile converts who were introducing their Hellenistic mysteries into the church, but from the core of the original Galilean disciples, from Jesus' immediate disciples and family. The reports come from exactly the sort of people who should, according to theory, have at just this time been recording the resolutely antisupernatural ideas found in Q, in which the Resurrection is supposedly an unknown concept.

The evidence from Paul's epistles long predates the famous resurrection accounts in the four gospels, but in those documents, too, we find clear early evidence of resurrection belief. This needs to be emphasized because it has become common in recent years to read the gospels, particularly Mark, in a way that minimizes the centrality of the resurrection for the first Christian generations. In particular, it is often argued, misleadingly, that the idea of Jesus' postresurrection appearances was a literary invention dating from decades after the supposed events.

Certainly, the four gospels were written decades after the events they describe, and the evangelists may well have interpreted or invented stories with the aim of being more relevant to their audience. In some cases too, we can see ideas about Jesus developing as time went by, and mythological and supernatural elements accumulated. The birth stories developed over the course of the first century, and many modern critics suggest that something similar has happened to the story of the Resurrection.[64] Virtually every scholar agrees that the earliest texts of Mark, written around 75, end at the present chapter 16, verse 8, with the remainder of this chapter being a later addition. In the oldest version, the women find the tomb of Jesus empty and are told by a figure in white that he had risen: they then run away in terror, and the gospel ends abruptly. John Dominic Crossan stresses, simply, that "Mark ends with an empty tomb."[65] Twenty or thirty years later, Matthew and Luke offer the familiar Easter stories we know today, as Jesus meets Mary Magdalen and appears to the incredulous disciples. At first sight, it looks as if a largely symbolic or perhaps psychological resurrection in Mark has become a painfully literal event for later writers, who feel the need to spell out to their congregations that Jesus really did rise and reappear.[66]

There are two difficulties with this approach. First, we know from 1 Corinthians that ideas of multiple Resurrection appearances were very well known decades before Mark wrote. Second, though the idea is now commonly accepted, the notion that Mark originally intended his story to end with the women fleeing is just untenable. In literary terms, a carefully crafted work like Mark could not have ended on such a note, however appealing the idea seems to postmodern readers. Also, this interpretation would mean that the whole text ends with a Greek grammatical form called an enclitic which is inappropriate for the ending of a paragraph, never mind a whole book. In English, it would be roughly equivalent to ending a book in mid-sentence: we may be happy to do such a thing today, but the idea would have been unthinkable for most previous generations. Mark surely did not mean his book to end in this curtailed way, although this was the form in which the text became available to Matthew and Luke. We have no way of knowing what happened in the interim; the author may have been unable to complete the work, or perhaps the original ending was lost in a time of persecution or neglect. But whatever the reason, it is remarkable to see how many modern scholars accept that the impossibly abrupt ending represents the author's intent. Some apparently do so from an ideological motivation, namely, to show that the Resurrection idea is a late accretion to proto-Christian thought.

Jesus' followers believed in his resurrection and his appearances from beyond the grave, and from very early on, granted him a high supernatural status. The evidence of the Dead Sea Scrolls shows that at least some Jews had a highly developed concept of the Messiah in the century before Jesus' career, seeing a figure who healed the sick and raised the dead; arguably, they even believed that the coming redeemer would be "fathered" by God himself (though the "fathering" terminology is controversial).[67] Already by the 40s, before the compilation of Q, these Jewish images of messiah and Son of God were being applied to Jesus. In Paul's letters to the Thessalonians, written around 50, the term "Lord Jesus Christ" has become a standard title, as has "Christ Jesus," which is to say, Messiah Jesus. Over the next decade, Paul repeatedly uses the standard credal declarations that "Jesus died and rose again," and "the dead in Christ will rise first" at the general resurrection.

We might conceivably see these remarks as products of the fertile theological imagination of Paul, the creative cult leader, but Paul's letters also draw on the works of others who were thinking similarly, and who illustrate the existence of a much wider culture. Scattered through the letters, we find traces of very early texts that seem to be hymns or creeds, which are already constructing an elaborate theology. One of the most famous occurs in Philippians, which describes Christ abandoning his divine status in order to become incarnate as a man. "Therefore God highly exalted him and gave him the name that is above every name so that at the name of Jesus every knee should bend . . . and every tongue should confess that Jesus Christ is Lord." A similar statement in Colossians speaks of Christ as "the image of the invisible God, the first born of all creation . . . he is before all things and in him all things hold together."[68] In 1 Corinthians, Paul can write that the powers of this age have "crucified the Lord of Glory." It is difficult to imagine such a process of glorification unless there was thought to have been something from the first which marked out Jesus very sharply from the common run of sages and wonderworkers.

Jesus' first followers may have disagreed widely on the exact nature of the Resurrection, as on the particular role which Jesus had been destined to play: was he Wisdom personified, Son of Man, messiah, or Son of God? But these followers undoubtedly viewed Jesus as far from the common run of humanity. They also understood Jesus' importance in terms of some special role or relationship with God, and that that position was confirmed or declared by the Resurrection. Whenever Q and *Thomas* were collected, these documents must have been composed by people who knew and valued doctrines such as the Resurrection and possibly messiahship, but chose not to include them in these particular texts. It is not legitimate to use the absences in these gospels as evidence of any belief or lack of belief in the earliest church. For all their apparent oddness, Q and *Thomas* provide a poor foundation upon which to build a whole alternate history of the first Christians.

4

Gospel Truth

The remaining writings which have been compiled or been recognized by heretics or schismatics, the catholic and apostolic Roman church does not in any way receive; of these we have thought it right to cite . . . some which have been handed down, and which are to be avoided by catholics.

DECRETUM GELASIANUM (SIXTH CENTURY)

THOUGH DOUBTS CAN BE RAISED about the importance of *Thomas*, the high claims made for this text have raised challenging questions about the whole nature of the Christian canon, and why Christians possess the New Testament in its current form. If so much of value is found in "apocryphal" gospels, just why are they apocryphal, rather than being included in the canon? This question is all the more relevant for modern readers who have learned to be suspicious of all literary canons, of any approved lists of favored texts, because such choices are believed to reflect the interests of particular ideologies and interest groups. To canonize some texts is to exclude others, and according to contemporary theories, the excluded voices generally belong to the powerless and disinherited.

The idea that the books included in the New Testament possess a peculiar sanctity is so deeply embedded in our culture that we rarely ask how and why this particular canon came to exist, and why it closed when it did. The writers of the New Testament books themselves had no sense that they were writing components of a closed work, like chapters in a modern collection of scholarly essays; nor was there any sense that gospel writers were competing for inclusion in a field limited to four possible winners. There was a long period of flux in determining exactly what texts should be included as Christian scriptures: several works came close but are now forgotten, while some documents now found in Christian Bibles very nearly failed to meet the standard. And why did the new religion have a fixed canon at all? Other religions are unperturbed by a lack of precise definition of what is and is not scriptural. Hindus venerate the mystical tracts known as the *Upanishads*, which mainly date from the first millennium B.C., but teachers of the nineteenth and twentieth centuries presented their own writings as new *Upanishads*, and there is no theoretical reason why this should not be done again in future. Why, then, is it unthinkable for Christians to write a new gospel? What, exactly, gives a gospel its particular status and authority?

Many different gospels once existed. At the end of the first century, St. Luke begins his own work by noting that "many have undertaken to compile a narrative of the things which have been accomplished among us," and some of these early efforts are represented by manuscript fragments which emerge occasionally from Egyptian excavations, such as the Egerton Gospel. But why does our New Testament not include the gospels of *Mary*, *Peter*, or *Philip*, the gospels of the *Hebrews* or the *Egyptians*? Why had these other gospels been lost or, rather, hidden? The traditional or orthodox view was that the canonical texts gained this status because they were earlier and authentically reflected the historical reality of Jesus and the first-century church, while their competitors were later, and were created by flagrant heretics who stood at best on the fringes of Christianity. Some gospels have more value than others, and the four best are Matthew, Mark, Luke and John. In recent decades, though, a more suspicious alternative view has gained widespread credence, which views the selection of the canon as a capricious process, in which the heavy hand of church orthodoxy excluded anything which failed to serve its dogmatic purposes. As Helmut Koester writes, "only dogmatic prejudice can assert that the canonical writings have an exclusive claim to apostolic origin, and thus to historical priority."[1]

This view of the canon as a political artifact has a natural appeal for modern Western audiences, who have a natural antipathy for canons, for dogmatic authority in religion, and still more for book-burning, but the idea that the various noncanonical gospels are equally valid witnesses to Christian antiquity is deeply flawed. In terms of their dating, as much as their access to independent traditions and sources, some gospels really do carry more weight than others, and to use a term that has become controversial in

the modern intellectual climate, some genuinely are more historical. If we consider the different texts that purport to record the
words and deeds of Jesus, then the canonical gospels simply have
vastly more credibility than their rivals, and the claims advanced
for these other gospels are exaggerated and tendentious: all
gospels are not created equal. Overall, the choice of the canon was
a much more rational process than is often alleged.

Making the Canon

The shape of the Christian canon was laboriously hammered out
over a lengthy period, roughly between the second century and
the fifth, but the most intense activity occurred in the early part of
that time span.[2] This deserves emphasis because recent popular
presentations of Christian history imply that the canon was much
slower to emerge, and was largely decided by the whims of the
Roman state. In this view, most of the credit or blame for the
shape of the New Testament falls to the Emperor Constantine,
who adopted Christianity about 312, and the great bishop
Athanasius, staunch advocate of strict doctrinal orthodoxy. In
1998, for example, television's Arts and Entertainment network
offered a major documentary series entitled *Christianity: The First
Thousand Years*, for which John Dominic Crossan served as historical consultant. In this program, it was claimed that the decisive
event in determining the New Testament canon was Constantine's
commissioning of fifty great Bibles for the major churches of his
empire, as the bishops were too embarrassed to admit that there
simply was no consensus about what books were and were not
included in that collection.

The implication is that prior to about 320, the churches read an
almost limitless range of works, including the most bizarre Gnostic texts, which now, tragically, found themselves condemned.
This idea has become widespread in recent years. To quote a journalistic account of hidden Gospels like *Thomas*, "these days, scholarly research and mass market publishing are bringing to the public ancient texts that Athanasius and other early church leaders
excluded."[3] In presenting his own modern pseudogospel, James
Carse explicitly says that the exclusion of all gospels beyond the
famous four was a direct outcome of the council which Constantine convened at Nicaea in 325.[4] If the canon was imposed by
imperial power, then there is all the more reason to expand it, or
to supplant it altogether. This notion of the highly fluid nature of
the New Testament has grave ramifications for contemporary

debates over scriptural authority: if confronted with a statement based on what "the Bible says," the obvious riposte is, which Bible?

Despite these statements, the process of determining the canon was well under way long before Constantine became emperor, and before the church had the slightest prospect of political power. The crucial phase occurred in the mid-second century, as the orthodox engaged in ever more acrimonious debate with their rivals, particularly the Gnostics, so that any text favored by those enemies was likely to be condemned. The list of approved gospels was the first to be determined. Already by 150, Justin Martyr's Roman school was using a fourfold gospel collection, namely, Matthew, Mark, Luke, and John. About 170, the Syrian Tatian composed his *Diatessaron* (literally, "through four"), a harmony or synthesis of the texts of the four gospels, again showing that four was the full and appropriate complement of gospel texts.[5] A few years later, in Gaul, Irenaeus argued that the only correct number of gospels was four, on the mystical analogy of the four winds, four directions, and so on: "it is not possible that the gospels can be either more or fewer in number than they are."[6] Accordingly, the four strongest and most celebrated candidates drove out their competitors, and in terms of gospels at least, if not of other scriptures, this policy very soon became the norm across the Empire.

By the third century, there was a lively debate about what texts were included within the canon, but not, generally, about the approved list of gospels. In the churches of which we have any knowledge, this list had largely been fixed by about 200, long before the supposed machinations of Athanasius and Constantine. Some marginal difficulty concerned the Gospel of John, which some disliked because heretics found it so congenial; some even attributed it to the Gnostic thinker Cerinthus. Otherwise, there are only a few marginal cases where gospels other than the big four gained any degree of acceptance, however tentative, from the orthodox anywhere. One local instance occurred around 200, when a bishop in Syria was induced to permit the reading of the *Gospel of Peter* in a local church, but he soon repented when he examined its contents. About the same time, Clement of Alexandria seems to cite the *Gospel of the Egyptians* as authoritative, which none of his successors would do.[7]

Even this limited tolerance dried up soon afterward. In the mid-third century, the great Origen declared, "I accept the traditional view of the four gospels, which alone are undeniably authentic in the Church of God on earth."[8] In contrast, he utterly rejected gospels such as those of the *Egyptians*, of *Matthias*, and of *Thomas*, which were not remotely comparable in authority with the canonical four. As we have seen, orthodox writers of the third and fourth centuries cite a wide range of alternative gospels, usually for the extra detail which they might cast on the canonical texts, but there is never the sense that these rival gospels should be read in churches, or treated comparably to the "holy quaternion"; these other texts are rather treated as dead reference materials.

By the fourth century, the canon of gospels was long known and (apparently) thoroughly accepted. The chief deviant gospel which the church authorities actually had to combat with any frequency was nothing so bizarre as *Thomas*, *Mary*, or *Matthias*, it was the *Diatessaron* itself, a compilation based solidly on the standard four gospels. The only remaining area of uncertainty involved the *Gospel According to the Hebrews*, which according to Eusebius was highly esteemed by Jewish Christians, "the Hebrews which have accepted Christ." Eusebius never comes close to endorsing it: the book was no candidate for canonical status alongside Mark or Luke, nor could it even be considered a "disputed" text, like some of the lesser epistles. Even so, he was aware that at least some authorities placed it in a category that, while somewhat inferior, remained barely on the fringes of approved reading. It was several steps above the blatantly heretical works that should be condemned out of hand, works such as the *Gospel of Thomas*. The *Gospel According to the Hebrews* might just squeeze into the list of "spurious" books. Although this sounds like faint praise, this meant that the gospel was on a par with some ancient and still popular writings like the *Didache* and the *Shepherd of Hermas*. Beyond the big four, the best that could be said of an alternative gospel by this time was that it did not necessarily deserve to be burnt.[9]

Though the limits of the canon were not absolutely fixed, the range of disagreement was not large. Debate focused on a few books which were widely read in some orthodox communities, such as *Hermas*, the *Didache*, the *Epistle of Barnabas*, the *Acts of Paul*, and the *Revelation of Peter*, while there were doubts about other documents that later churches accepted as orthodox, such as the *Revelation of John*. The exact number of epistles thought worthy of acceptance also fluctuated dramatically, particularly among the so-called Catholic epistles attributed to figures like Peter, James and John.[10] Probably in the early third century, the list of approved texts in the Muratorian Fragment included most of the works familiar from the later New Testament, though it makes no mention of the Epistle to the Hebrews or the Epistles of Peter and James, and it accepted as canonical the *Wisdom of Solomon* and the *Revelation of Peter.* Even so, contrary to recent popularizations, texts like those from Nag Hammadi never made it as far as the gray areas of debate over the canon; they were always far beyond the pale (though the Nag Hammadi collection did produce a *Revelation of Peter,* which has no connection with the work accepted in some orthodox churches). The New Testament as we know it today was not finally settled in the West until perhaps 400, and eastern communities continued to differ in the selection of some texts. Nevertheless, the Great Church had substantially decided its canon of approved gospels no later than the early third century. Neither Constantine nor Athanasius had anything to do with these decisions.

But what about the gospels that were excluded from the canon, and found themselves suppressed once orthodoxy gained the support of the secular state? As more of these texts have come to light since the late nineteenth century, some scholars have sought to vindicate the lost gospels, and even to reinstate them them in a new Biblical canon. As we have seen, the Jesus Seminar group has produced a collection of twenty texts labeled *The Complete Gospels,* which includes not just the inevitable *Thomas* but also the gospels of *Mary* and *Peter,* the *Apocryphon* ("Secret Book") of James, the *Dialogue of the Savior,* the Infancy Gospels of *Thomas* and *James,* and several fragmentary gospel texts such as the Egerton Papyrus.[11] To quote the Seminar's cochair, John Dominic Crossan, the collection contains "everything you need to empower your own search for the historical Jesus."[12] It is easy to imagine the excitement that such a volume causes, especially when it comes from a major publisher, with the texts vouched for by accredited scholars from major universities. The idea of a new canon has already had its impact, as journalists referring to an apocryphal gospel note that it is among those included in this collection. At a stroke, it seems, we have leapt from four gospels to twenty.

Inclusion in this collection implies that these other gospels are equal to the canonical texts in historical and spiritual value, and their obscurity is a consequence of their persecution by a bigoted church. Because this view is at least implicit in much contemporary writing about the New Testament, it deserves careful examination. So do the four gospels merit their privileged position? As historical sources—not necessarily as spiritual documents—how do they compare with the countless texts described as gospels but which are not recognized by the churches? The whole debate about hidden gospels raises fundamental questions about the nature of historical truth in an era of postmodernism, particularly when that history relates to matters of religion.

Before assessing the truthfulness of a particular source, we have to define what truth means in this context, and how it can be determined. The issues involved are illustrated by a book published in 1993 by Miriam T. Winter as *The Gospel According to Mary: A New Testament for Women*. Despite the title, the work has no relation to the apocryphal *Gospel of Mary*, but is rather a feminist rewriting of the four canonical gospels, emphasizing female characters and perspectives throughout, with some incidents purely of the author's invention. Though God is depicted throughout as female, Winter presents a pretty conservative rendering of the text, with far more willingness to accept the canonical sayings of Jesus than would be favored by many critical scholars. Avowedly a modern imaginative creation, the story is attributed to a fictional Mary, "the grand-daughter of Mary the mother of John Mark, who led a house church in Jerusalem."[13] But this is more than a novel; it is, rather, "an imaginative work. Imaginative, but not ahistoric, for this text, which is not entirely factual, is not exactly fiction. . . . This gospel makes explicit what might have been and still is of primary interest to women and hints at the development of a women's tradition which differed from that of the men." Winter's project is thus in keeping with the pedagogy of feminist scholars such as Elisabeth Schüssler Fiorenza, who advocate the exercise of writing pseudo-ancient texts as a valuable tool for students who can situate themselves in the debates of the time, as part of a "hermeneutics of imagination."[14]

Though it is "imaginative," Winter speaks of her work as a "gospel," which is "not ahistoric." But what does history mean in this context? Though she never pretends that this is an actual first-century text, Winter's work does lay claim to gospel status, just like that of Mark or Luke. In some ways, it is hard to dispute this, any more than with other modern attempts at gospel-writing by Reynolds Price, James Carse, and others. From a postmodern view, texts in themselves lack authority, and have value only insofar as they speak to their readers; and while postmodern theory dethrones the notion of privileged texts or canons, there is a strong preference for works that reflect the experience of the excluded or the traditionally powerless. As Karen King remarks, the central issue in understanding scriptures is "not what they say, but who is authorized to interpret them."[15] If a recently composed gospel speaks to the experience of women and conveys spiritual truth, then it is in some sense valid. If it claims to announce "good news," then by definition, it is a gospel. And if a modern "imaginative" work like Winter's *Mary* can claim to be a legitimate gospel, then these claims apply with still greater force to a second- or third-century account of Jesus stemming from a community later dismissed as heretical. If the rediscovered gospel in question appeals to the tastes and interests of modern readers, then that is all the authority the text requires.

In a universe of extreme subjectivity, the whole question of "but is it true?" is not only irrelevant, it is almost offensively naive. In what sense can we say that one gospel might be truer than another? Perhaps a spiritual text is neither more nor less "true" than a poem or a symphony, that *Luke, Thomas,* or *Philip* is precisely as true as the *Ode to a Nightingale.* Or as one member of the Jesus seminar has asked, "Are the infancy narratives [of Christ] true? Is Mozart's Twentieth Piano Concerto true? They are both true transformatively, in my experience."[16] If we carry the argument to an absurd extreme, we might suggest that Winter's modern *Gospel of Mary* is just as valid a candidate for inclusion in a collection of *Complete Gospels* as any other text. It is admittedly different from the apocryphal gospels which have attracted so much attention recently in that it is separated from the other competitors by some eighteen centuries, but still, it lays claim to be a gospel. Why should it not be included? Why indeed should one's search for the historical Jesus not be empowered by still other works claiming to be gospels, like the nineteenth-century *Book of Mormon,* or by twentieth-century works like the *Aquarian Gospel of Jesus the Christ* or the *Course in Miracles*? The Christian Science church has taken the logical step by recognizing as canonical the revelations of Mary Baker Eddy's *Science and Health.*

Phrased in this way, the question of inclusion answers itself: even an age accustomed to postmodern approaches recognizes that some statements have a greater claim to historical truth than others, and some documents are more rewarding as potential historical sources. This is acknowledged by the Jesus Seminar scholars themselves, as their *Complete Gospels* include only texts which can be claimed as "early," namely, belonging to the first two centuries or so after the time of Jesus. The fact that they do not include much later works indicates that they are attempting to apply at least some traditional criteria about historical sources, in which factors such as date of composition are crucially significant.

There are different kinds of truth, some of which can be dealt with by historians, and some not. The claim that "Jesus descended to Hell" may or may not be theologically true, but it has no place in any objective historical account, as its validity cannot be determined. At the other extreme, the statement that Pontius Pilate was Prefect of Judea can be tested, proven, and found to be objectively accurate. Between these two extremes we have the claim that Jesus took cords and made a whip in order to drive the money-changers from the Jerusalem Temple. The statement may be historically true, and many scholars believe that the event actually occurred, though we cannot be absolutely certain. Something like this might or might not have occurred, and historians can analyze the sources to determine whether in fact it did. Disagreement is possible, but we can at least claim that this is a statement about Jesus which is historically true, however much the events described are adorned with scriptural significance. If we are convinced that the sources warrant this statement, then the cleansing of the Temple is just as historical as the D-Day landings of 1944. Some texts, some gospels, can provide information about the life and times of Jesus because they use traditions and sources which stem from that era; others do not. In that sense, we can legitimately say that the Gospel of Mark is a historical source for the time of Jesus, but twentieth-century texts such as the *Gospel of Mary* or the *Aquarian Gospel* are not, because these latter were written with no direct sources linking them to the events described, and were composed very much later. And exactly the same criteria count against the reliability of the vast majority of the apocryphal works included in the *Complete Gospels,* and cited so widely as authoritative in much contemporary writing on the New Testament.

The Dating Game

If we want to use a text to cast light on first-century conditions then we have to know something about the date of that document, that gospel, and especially the sources on which it relies. By both standards, date of composition and value of sources used, we can confidently say that the four gospels are far earlier than the vast majority of their heretical or apocryphal competitors. They are older in terms of their oldest identifiable layers of composition, and earlier in terms of achieving their final edited form. Also, it is far easier to establish a plausible chain of traditions from the canonical gospels back to the events described than it is for their noncanonical rivals. This does not necessarily mean that the four gospels are accurately describing all or any of the events or sayings in the life of Jesus, but that they have a far better claim to be taken seriously than their rivals.

In terms of chronology, we are on solid ground in dating many of the documents in the New Testament. By far the earliest surviving Christian documents are some of Paul's letters, particularly those to the Thessalonians, which come from around 49-50, and to the Corinthians, from a few years later. We are on shakier ground with the canonical gospels, but it is helpful that they are so widely quoted by other authorities who can themselves be situated in relation to known historical events. Particularly useful here are the writings of second-century church leaders, the so-called apostolic fathers such as Ignatius and Polycarp, and also a host of theologians and controversialists such as Justin Martyr. A scholarly consensus indicates that the four canonical gospels should be dated roughly as follows, though with plenty of room for debate: Mark was the first gospel, written sometime in the early 70s, not too long after the destruction of the Jerusalem Temple; Matthew and Luke followed between about 85 and 95. Establishing a date for John is more difficult, but at least parts of the gospel are not much later than Mark: the final recension might have been completed around 100, perhaps a little later. The earliest existing papyrus fragment of any gospel (P^{52}) is a tiny portion of John, probably from around 125. The four canonical gospels all achieved substantially their present form within the first century, or perhaps a few years into the second. All were written within living memory of the time of Jesus and, conceivably, within the lifetimes of his apostles and early followers.

In contrast, it is far harder to date the noncanonical gospels with any confidence, precisely because they and their readers fell into historical disfavor, and remarks and quotations concerning them were less likely to have been preserved. All we can say with certainty is that the Nag Hammadi texts must have reached their final form before those particular manuscripts disappeared into the ground sometime in the later fourth century. Even so, there are some important indications about dating, which generally point to origins no earlier than the mid-second or third century, in most cases fifty or a hundred years after the canonical gospels, and often later. It is in the areas of dating and independent authority that all subsequent assertions about the hidden gospels stand on their weakest foundations.

Much of the evidence for chronology depends on the fringe gospels' powerful associations with Gnosticism, and the fact that they are so obviously permeated by highly developed Gnostic thought: Elaine Pagels's influential book on the Nag Hammadi library is titled, simply, *The Gnostic Gospels*. Although Gnostic thinkers were active in the first century, the movement's golden age began only about 135, and most of the apocryphal gospels show evidence of ideas and technical phrases which are unlikely to have arisen before the mid-second century. Some can be associated with heresies of the third century, or even later.

Just how late some of the Nag Hammadi texts might be is open to debate, since Gnosticism survived and continued to produce new thinkers and sects through the end of antiquity and beyond: as late as the eighth and ninth centuries, the Arab conquerors of Mesopotamia and Syria still had to deal with Gnostic groups who traced their roots to Roman times. One of the most extensive polemics against the Gnostics was written by Bishop Epiphanius of Salamis, in Cyprus, as late as the mid-370s, at a time when we might think that the church's interests had moved on to other things. Though Epiphanius's work recycles older materials, some dating back 200 years, he is deeply concerned about new sects that had emerged in his own age, and who had only recently created their own particular scriptures.[17] This evidence shows that fresh Gnostic texts, and perhaps gospels, were still being written in 350, or later. It is useful to remember these much later activities when we read confident assertions that a given Gnostic text, which contains virtually no internal indicators of dating or provenance, might date from the first or second centuries. In most cases, all that can be known for certain about a given Nag Hammadi document is that the particular manuscript was written before the late fourth century, when it was concealed: the date of composition remains highly uncertain. Conceivably, even at this very late date, the ink might not have been too dry on some of these writings.

While the canonical gospels were completed by 100 or so, it is unlikely that any of the Nag Hammadi materials date from much before 150, and most were probably written between about 150 and 250, or later. Indeed, the fact that we find so many efforts in the late second and early third century to specify the orthodox canon may indicate that it was in exactly these years that spurious and heterodox works were pouring forth from their creators in unprecedented numbers.

Though no one doubts that the Nag Hammadi documents are authentic ancient texts, there is ancient and there is ancient. This does not mean that apocryphal texts such as the gospels of *Mary* or *Philip* have no historical value. A text written in, say, 225 can be priceless for what it tells us about the intellectual, cultural, and social world of the early third century, and particularly for the history of the churches or communities which created that work. But it is as far removed from the world of Jesus as we today are from the time of Thomas Jefferson or Napoleon, and a third-century gospel stems from a cultural and political environment utterly different from that of Palestine in 30. It can tell us nothing whatsoever about the life or sayings of Jesus, or the environment of his earliest followers, unless it can claim independent sources or traditions. This is not to say that such independent traditions might not be preserved, but that proposition cannot be accepted without proof. In the same way, the novel *Ben-Hur* (1880) tells us much about the world-view of nineteenth-century American Christians and antiquarians, but nothing of original value about the first-century events which it describes.

An earlier document is not necessarily more historically reliable than a later one. A report of the battle of Gettysburg published days after the event might be inaccurate or fictitious, while a memoir written thirty years later by a participant might contain invaluable information. Nevertheless, sources written nearer the time of the events they describe generally tend to be more useful and reliable, and this explains the powerful tendency of radical New Testament critics to place the earliest possible dates on the heterodox materials they are using. Since none of the texts bears any precise date, scholars must use their expert judgment to decide whether any given piece dates from, say, 50 or 350. This leaves enormous scope for disagreement, particularly since such documents have generally gone through various stages and editions. It is tempting to interpret ranges of possible dates in a way that best suits one's ideological or rhetorical purposes.

Overclaiming

We can often see a redating process at work in some writings of the Jesus Seminar group, in which accounts of early Christian documents systematically give improbably early estimates for noncanonical or heretical texts. The *Complete Gospels* offers a table of sources with their dates, as shown in Table 4.1. For the typical reader without a detailed knowledge of the literature, the implications of such a list are disturbing. The four gospels seem to be later than some other sources which most people have never heard of, such as the *Dialogue of the Savior* and the *Gospel of Peter*. Moreover, the canonical gospels appear to belong to the same generation as a great many other writings, so that they become quite unexceptional, and it is tempting to believe that they achieved their exalted status through political factors. Perhaps they even acquired their position through misguided or primitive-seeming concepts like Irenaeus' notion of the four winds and four compass points: there had to be four gospels, and these were just the lucky winners. In terms of historical or religious authority, the four gospels are nothing special. Why should we pay any more attention to the Gospel of Mark than to that of *Mary*?

TABLE 4.1.
Dating the Gospels: The Jesus Seminar's View

Period	Text
30–60	Q (first edition, c. 50)
	Thomas (first edition, c. 50)
60–80	Gospel of Signs (60-70)
	Gospel of Mark (c. 70)
80–100	Gospel of Matthew ("about 80 C.E.")
	Gospel of Luke ("about 90 C.E.")
	Gospel in Egerton Papyrus
	Gospel of John, incorporating Gospel of Signs ("about 90 C.E.")
	Dialogue of the Savior ("first edition, probably c. 50-100 C.E.")
	Gospel of Peter ("first edition, probably c. 50-100 C.E.")
	Gospel of Mark, "canonical edition" ("about 100 C.E.")
100–150	Gospel of John "third edition"
	Apocryphon of James, first edition
	Gospel of Mary
	Jewish Christian Gospels (e.g. *Gospel of the Hebrews*)

Source: Adapted from *Complete Gospels* 6; *Five Gospels* 128; Funk, *Honest to Jesus*, 125.

The problem is that the dates given here for the noncanonical texts are improbably early, and most scholars believe that apocryphal works such as the *Dialogue of the Savior* and the *Apocryphon of James* come down to us in the form they reached in the mid-second century or later. To achieve the datings offered here, scholars are speculating on the existence of older "first editions" or cores of material within the existing works, in the way we have already described with Q. In itself, this kind of literary dissection is a defensible practice which was originally designed to analyze ancient or medieval texts, and it has often been applied to scriptural works. There is a long and respectable tradition of using internal evidence to trace the stages by which a work is composed, and layers of this kind can sometimes be identified with fair certainty. Evidence of drastic editing is readily apparent in the Gospel of John, where what was obviously meant as a conclusion to the whole work at the end of chapter 20 is immediately followed by an additional chapter, complete with its own separate conclusion. In other cases, however, the process of identifying stages of composition is subjective, tenuous, and controversial.

Theories about different editions may or may not have validity, but the casual reader is unlikely to realize just what a tiny proportion of any given "lost gospel" is likely to have such early origins. This can be illustrated from the accounts of various gospels which are given by recent critics, and the exaggerated claims made for these sources.

The Gospel of Peter

One text included in the *Complete Gospels* is the *Gospel of Peter*, which was popular in the early church. In the fragmentary form which we have it, the text mainly survives as an account of the passion and resurrection of Christ. Though the story is largely familiar from the standard New Testament, there are some unusual and vivid features. The cross itself is given a speaking role, and the report of the resurrection is impressive, reminding us of depictions in medieval art. As two angels lead Jesus from the tomb; "the heads of the two reached up to the sky, while the head of the third, whom they led by the hand, reached beyond the skies."[18]

For many years after it was rediscovered in the 1880s, most scholars were confident that *Peter* was derived from the canonical gospels, which were quoted extensively by a later author who had added his own narrative touches. This view, however, was fundamentally challenged by Crossan, who uses *Peter* as the basis for a revisionist account of how the gospels were composed. In his view, Jesus' followers knew nothing of the details of their master's death beyond the mere fact of the crucifixion, so that every single detail known to later ages (piercing of the side, dicing for his clothes) was invented as a kind of meditation on the Hebrew scriptures, to show how the death fulfilled countless ancient prophecies. For Crossan, *Peter* allows us to see the process of scripture-based reconstruction at work. He argues that *Peter*'s account is so distinctive from the canonical stories that it must have at its core an independent version of that first Passion story, what he calls the "Cross Gospel," which was also used in various ways by the four evangelists. Crossan argues that an original version of *Peter* is substantially independent of the synoptic gospels and even predates them, and this explains why in Table 4.1, the work is dated as "first edition, probably c. 50-100 C.E."[19] This apparently independent character explains why *Peter* is so often cited in Jesus Seminar works. In the Seminar's work on *The Acts of Jesus*, *Peter* is graced with a separate discussion of the sort otherwise accorded only to the four canonical gospels, plus Q.[20]

Crossan's view, though, is highly controversial, and reflects no scholarly consensus, even among radical New Testament critics. More conservative authors have been far more damning.[21] Ben Witherington notes that the evidence for this supposedly influential *Cross Gospel* is nonexistent, and the same applies for any early version of *Peter*. Neither is quoted in any of the indubitably early writings: "There is nothing in the *Didache*, nothing in *Hermas*, nothing in Ignatius, nothing in Justin Martyr, nothing in Clement, and the list could go on."[22] Again, one of Crossan's arguments for the independence of *Peter* is that the text uses traditions which are similar to those found in the four gospels, but not identical to the accounts of any one of them. This might mean that *Peter* is independent, but a more likely explanation is that the author was using a gospel harmony, of the kind that we know circulated in the mid-second century. And there are other difficulties. Closer analysis of the supposed *Cross Gospel* shows the presence of ideas which would more commonly be found well into the second century, far too late to have influenced any of the four evangelists. *Peter* first appears in history around 200, when a bishop initially permitted it to be read in a church, but was appalled at its heretical content, and ordered it suppressed. The specific heresies he found in it were characteristic of mid-second-century thought, indicating a composition date of around 150.

Crossan has also been criticized for his attempt to determine the ending of the *Cross Gospel*, and to situate the Resurrection appearances in this hypothetical text: Koester describes Crossan's opinions in this area as "seriously flawed."[23]

The point here is not to argue whether Crossan is right or wrong, and many scholars would sympathize with his general point about how descriptions of the crucifixion events were shaped by knowledge of Old Testament prophecies. What is striking is that the specific theory of the *Cross Gospel*, and thus the dating of *Peter*, represents the idiosyncratic work of one scholar, who has not been widely followed. Most scholars, and by no means just fundamentalists, would have severe doubts about any attempt to date *Peter* as anywhere near "probably c. 50-100 C.E.," and they would also see the work as wholly derivative. Nevertheless, *Peter* is given high honor in what is supposed to be the Jesus Seminar's objective new canon.

The Apocryphon of James

The argument that *Peter* sheds any light whatsoever on the earliest days of Christianity is extraordinarily weak, but a far stronger case can be made for this text than for most of the other noncanonical gospels. In fact, detailed study of the Christian materials found at Nag Hammadi finds that apart from possibly *Thomas*, there is no evidence that any of these texts uses materials older than the synoptic gospels, and when the synoptics were used, it was in the final versions that we have today.[24]

In several instances, even proposing that the noncanonical gospels might contain early materials is, to say the least, overambitious. One text in the *Complete Gospels* is the *Apocryphon of James*, which purports to be a letter in which James, the brother of Jesus, describes a series of revelations given by Christ to his apostles after the Resurrection. It is what is technically known as a discourse gospel, in that all the interest focuses on Jesus' speeches and dialogues, rather than his deeds or miracles. These words bear a general resemblance to what is found in the canonical gospels in terms of their message and structure, but the resemblances are to more than one of the four, and in a form quite different from that with which we are familiar. According to some scholars, this means that the *Apocryphon* is using oral traditions of the kind that went into the four gospels, but it is doing so independently.

There are a number of problems here. Supposed parallels between the *Apocryphon* and the New Testament passages are tenuous, and it really takes the eye of faith to see these resemblances: often, passages cited as parallels are describing broadly similar ideas which were commonplaces of early Christian thought and rhetoric.[25] Rather than believing that the "secret" text has access to some independent source, it is just as likely that the heretical authors are writing so late that they had become thoroughly acquainted with the canonical Christian texts, so that phrases and sayings have become jumbled together in their minds, just as later Christians would harmonize the distinct birth stories to form their familiar Christmas pageant. Instead of being independent witnesses of Jesus' teaching, the secret documents could equally be seen as historical fictions which use the canonical gospels as a springboard for their speculative tales and theological discourses. Other evidence, too, may point to reliance on canonical works. The choice of James as the recipient of this vision may have been inspired by Paul's reference in 1 Corinthians to the brother of Jesus having received a distinctive Resurrection appearance, though this encounter is never described in canonical sources. Curiosity about this event may well have inspired not just the *Apocryphon*, but also two separate *Apocalypses of James* likewise found at Nag Hammadi.

Even if the *Apocryphon of James* is using early sources, the actual date of the document is highly debatable. Crossan describes it as "late first century or early second century," which would make it contemporary with the synoptics.[26] In the *Complete Gospels*, however, it is described as likely stemming from "the first half of the second century," while the primary translator of the text comments that it "may have been written in Egypt in the third century C.E., though some would place it earlier."[27] That gives us estimates of, roughly, 100, 125, and about 225. Such a huge divergence illustrates the leeway that is possible on questions of dating, and how easy it is for critics to choose early or late dates, depending on how they intend to use the text in question. It is important, though, to decide what exactly is being dated. It is possible that Crossan is just claiming such a very early date for a supposed early core of the *Apocryphon*, though the remark as it appears seems to claim this status for the whole convoluted text. The only reason to push such texts into the early period, before 125 or so, is to suggest that these are just as ancient as the canonical gospels, and therefore possess equal authority.

The editors of the *Complete Gospels* consistently reinforce this inappropriately early dating by a subtle trick of organization, by dividing the various gospels into broad categories, including "Narrative Gospels" (the canonical four) and "Sayings Gospels," and the latter category includes Q, *Thomas*, the *Apocryphon of James*, the *Dialogue of the Savior*, and the *Gospel of Mary*.[28] Technically, this is defensible, as these five sayings sources are all composed of sayings and discourses attributed to Jesus, but bracketing these vastly different texts together looks like editorial sleight-of-hand intended to boost the significance of the apocryphal texts, at the expense of the canonical documents. An undeniably early text like Q is being placed aside much later Gnostic works, presumably to give the impression that these latter should in fact be regarded as equally primitive, and moreover that they represent an earlier evolutionary stage than the narrative texts. This is misleading. While Q and probably *Thomas* do indeed represent an early literary form, the *Apocryphon* and its like come from a quite different genre. Q excludes narrative because the stories in question were still in the process of development and consolidation; in contrast, the Gnostic texts omits narrative because that movement had no interest in the earthly career of Jesus, and dismissed as irrelevant events which occurred in the objective world of matter. The primitive style of the sayings source is thus confounded with the much later genre of the discourse gospel.

In other ways, too, the particular methods of the Jesus Seminar school tend to exaggerate the apparent similarities between the canonical gospels and later texts such as the *Apocryphon*. The Jesus of the four gospels is an unmistakably Jewish figure, who often has in his mouth the words of the Hebrew Bible, in stark contrast to the Hellenistic mystagogue found in most of the Nag Hammadi texts.[29] As we have seen, however, the critical scholars of the Jesus Seminar group go far toward removing Jesus from this Jewish environment. In assessing the veracity of the sayings attributed to Jesus, these researchers accept a working guideline that passages which include quotes from the Old Testament are unlikely to be authentic, and should be excluded from any account of the historical figure. The logic behind this decision is that such quotations derive not from Jesus himself, but rather represent meditations by early Christians, who were trying to understand his life as the fulfillment of Biblical prophecy; this process is said to be particularly evident in the account of the trial and crucifixion. The consequence, however, is that the Jesus presented as historical says little that indicates distinctively Jewish roots, but is rather a generic Mediterranean Wisdom teacher. This has the effect of making him sound much more like the redeemer beloved of the Gnostics, for whom the Old Testament tradition was anathema, literally diabolical.[30]

Other Texts

Similar problems occur when other extracanonical sources are discussed. In his influential biography of Jesus, Crossan summarizes the major sources for Jesus both inside and outside the canon, and in the process makes some remarkable statements about the dates of various alternative gospels. This systematic overclaiming is so important because Crossan's books have been such popular best-sellers, and have thus become the primary means by which many nonspecialists will acquire their information about the dating and historical value of the hidden gospels.[31] Of the *Gospel of the Hebrews*, for instance, he writes that it was "composed by the fifties CE in Egypt," which would be astonishingly early. He places this text at the very earliest stratum of the Jesus tradition, alongside the letters of Paul and the oldest contents of *Thomas*. Few other scholars, though, accept anything like such an early date. Robert J. Miller, another critical scholar active in the Jesus Seminar, notes that the *Gospel of the Hebrews* "must have been written in the early second century," partly because the work knows and uses our canonical gospels, and other scholars propose dates in the first half of that century.[32]

Nor is this the only example. Crossan again dates the *Gospel of the Egyptians* to "possibly by the sixties CE," while most other scholars suggest a second-century origin. The fact that this work is not included in the *Complete Gospels* suggests that the editors had qualms about Crossan's very early date. Once again, discussing an intriguing gospel fragment found at Oxyrhynchus, Crossan notes that "it could be as early as the 50s when Christians first began to create books about what Jesus had said and done."[33] Many things "could be" true in theory, but the problem is that this very brief fragment also includes a section of narrative describing how the Pharisees and priests criticized Jesus. According to most modern theories, narrative gospels were more likely to develop at the end of the first century, rather than the middle. This particular text need have been composed no earlier than the third century, when the actual manuscript was written.

Replying to criticisms that he consistently provides remarkably early datings for noncanonical texts, Crossan responds that he "date[s] them all just as everyone else does," but often, his estimates are not only far outside the scholarly consensus, but much earlier than those of even the most radical critics.[34] One egregious example concerns the *Sophia of Jesus Christ*, which Crossan cites as "latter half of the first century." The story here is even more complex than usual. The *Sophia* is one of two very closely related documents found at Nag Hammadi, and represents a later Christianized version of an earlier philosophical tract. According to its translator, the *original* document belongs "sometime in the first two centuries CE," and seems related to a system described by Irenaeus about 175. As a later version of the first document, the *Sophia* need not be earlier than the 170s, and might be much later, possibly around 200. Another analysis places it in "perhaps the second half of the second century, or at latest the third century."[35] Once again, Crossan's dating is around a hundred years earlier than the consensus.

When we hear that document X was composed at a particular date, we have to ask the grounds for this conclusion, especially if the date is buttressed by some qualifier like "arguably" or "some think." Caution is all the more necessary when some extracanonical source is described, because of the widespread tendency to be overoptimistic about their potential value. Just as higher criticism is consistently used to make the apocryphal texts look earlier, so it is employed systematically to downgrade the canonical texts. Looking at Table 4.1 again, we see the odd suggestion that the Gospel of Mark as we have it dates from 100, rather than from the 70s, as most scholars would suggest. The reason for this is curious, and involves a fragment of a so-called Secret Gospel of Mark: in this case, however, doubts about the value of the evidence do not depend just on rival interpretations of ancient texts, but on whether the material in question was bogus.

This is an unsettling story. According to Morton Smith, the reputed discoverer of Secret Mark, while at the monastery of Mar Saba in Palestine, he found an eighteenth-century transcript of what seemed to be a letter from the late second-century church father Clement of Alexandria, in which Clement denounced the heretical sect of the Carpocratians.[36] Supposedly, this group was using a fraudulent version of the gospel of Mark in which Jesus initiated a young man through secret and probably sexual nighttime rituals. Clement protests that the passage used was not found in Mark, either in the standard version or—and this was the surprising element—in the secret version of Mark approved for use by Christian initiates. To prove his contention, Clement then quotes the appropriate passage from Secret Mark. If authentic, this was an amazing find, indicating the possible existence of a whole clandestine version of Mark, and perhaps of other Christian gospels. The discovery might also suggest that Mark had gone through a complex series of stages and editions, reaching its present form much later than previously thought.

The problem is that there are serious and enduring doubts about the Clementine text involved, which has not been made available to scholars except in photographic form, and there are unresolved rumors of forgery.[37] The location of the find is fascinating, since this was the scene of the forgery described only a few years before in the then-popular novel *The Mystery of Mar Saba*. To appreciate the degree of coincidence involved, we might imagine the response if someone today announced an epoch-making paleontological find from the English site of Piltdown, which became notorious for the forgery of the Piltdown skull. The fact that Secret Mark came from Mar Saba is either strong proof of the text's authenticity, in that nobody would have dared invent such a thing in the 1950s, or else it is a tribute to the unabashed *chutzpah* of a forger. With so many doubts surrounding the document, it is surprising to see the evidence of Secret Mark included here as authoritative, and as proof of the late date of a canonical text.

With these caveats in mind, let us consider some of the works included in the *Complete Gospels* alongside the familiar texts. Though the book itself promises "all twenty" early Gospels, the only ones which predate the canonical Big Four are (obviously) Q, and, just conceivably, the "Signs Gospel" which, according to some theories, can be detected within our current text of John. Both are, however, hypothetical texts, the exact scope and limits of which are highly controversial. Of the other gospels included, *Thomas* may have first-century roots, but this text was substantially modified before reaching the form in which we have it, and it is difficult to speak with confidence of the tiny gospel fragments, like the Egerton Papyrus. With these possible exceptions, virtually all the texts included either are derivative from the canonical books or are much later Gnostic concoctions, such as the *Gospel of Mary*. Both the *Apocryphon of James* and the *Dialogue of the Savior* date from a period long after the last canonical gospel was completed. Disappointingly, perhaps, the *Complete Gospels* offers little to challenge the distinctly old-fashioned view that Matthew, Mark, Luke, and John are by far the best historical sources that we have for the life and times of Jesus, and that all the supposed rivals (*Thomas* perhaps excepted) are weak also-rans. Five gospels, perhaps; twenty, certainly not.

History and Legend

Not only are the canonical gospels earlier, but they are more likely to offer authentic history. This may seem a surprising statement, given that these documents are frankly theological writings, which do not pretend to historical objectivity in any modern sense. The Gospel of John states honestly enough that "these [things] are written so that you may come to believe that Jesus is the Messiah, the Son of God, and that through believing, you may have life in his name."[38] Throughout the gospels, canonical or otherwise, material is selected or excluded on the basis of how far it contributes to the author's theological goals.

Having said this, the canonical gospels enjoy one immense advantage over the Gnostic texts in that orthodox Christians at least believed that Jesus had lived and died in a real historical setting, and that it was possible to describe these events in objective terms. For Gnostics, by contrast, Christ was not so much a historical personage as a reality within the believer. Indeed, the Jesus of Gnosticism was much like the Buddha of Buddhism, in which the historical figure becomes only one manifestation of a universal and even pantheistic reality. Individuals, animals, and even plants have a buddha-nature which can be achieved and recognized, so there is nothing unique or even special about the specific historical individual who came to bear the title of Buddha. In fact, the term *buddha*, "awakened one," would fit well within the Gnostic mythological system, in which the soul is said to be sleeping in dead matter, and the lot of the average person is often presented through analogies of sleep and drunkenness. From earliest times, Buddhists felt free to attribute elaborate speeches and doctrines to the founder of the religion. In the Gnostic view, too, Jesus continued to speak through individuals in later ages, and it was appropriate to record these continuing teachings in new gospels.

Gnostics wanted a Jesus who said certain things, and they wrote documents asserting that he had done so.[39] Accordingly, the Gnostics neatly foreshadow postmodern attitudes toward subjectivity. Elaine Pagels describes the frustration of Irenaeus when he demanded the authority which Gnostics claimed for their doctrines: "Most offensive, from his point of view, is that they admit that nothing supports their writings except their own intuition. When challenged, 'they either mention mere human feelings, or else refer to the harmony that can be seen in creation.' . . . 'They are to be blamed for . . . ascribing the things that happen to human beings and whatever they recognize themselves as experiencing to the divine Word.'" As Irenaeus complained, "every one of them, just as it suits his own temperament, modifies the traditions he has received."[40]

Since the Gnostics had little regard for objective historical truth, their retellings of the story of Jesus claimed not a particle of historical authenticity. Founders of Gnostic schools happily composed their own gospels, and Irenaeus complained that Valentinus' followers "outstep all bounds of reverence in producing their own writings, and boast that they possess more gospels than there really are. Indeed, they have advanced to such a pitch of audacity that they give the title *Gospel of Truth* to a work composed by them not long ago."[41] Origen noted with distaste how "Basilides has presumed to write a 'Gospel According to Basilides.'" Other Gnostic leaders presented their opinions as writings credited to some apostle. Athanasius charged that heretics wrote their gospels "when it pleases them and generously assign to them an early date of composition in order that they may be able to draw upon them as supposedly ancient writings and have in them occasion to deceive the guiltless."[42] While the orthodox protested that this was outright forgery and deception, the Gnostics lacked any sense that the historical bona fides of a document mattered greatly. They would have been puzzled, and perhaps amused, if they had been asked whether the words attributed to Jesus in their particular gospels had any relationship to the sentiments of the historical figure of that name. Even raising the concept of the historical Jesus would have marked the questioner as hopelessly unspiritual, a slave to the material world, and one who failed to grasp even the most rudimentary stages of *gnosis*.

The historical value of the canonical gospels appears all the greater when contrasted with other texts which are included as *Complete Gospels*, such as the Infancy Gospels of Thomas and James. Both are charming fictions which no scholar would dream of taking seriously as historical sources.[43] The Infancy narrative of Thomas (not to be confused with the sayings gospel of that name) is a naive collection of miracles concerning what Jesus did as a toddler, how, for example, he made clay models of sparrows, which came to life at his command. The work named for James is a comparably mythical piece focusing on the early life of the Virgin Mary, and filling in the details in some stories in the New Testament. In both cases, of Jesus and Mary, the stories would long be influential, and found their way into popular stories and artistic representations.

The existence of such tales is not surprising, since people have always wanted to elaborate the lives of famous and admired people, who attract stories drawn from what seems to be a common worldwide fund of folklore. In these cases, the apocryphal stories were built around what were already the well-known infancy stories found in Matthew and Luke. But not even the most optimistic scholar or critic suggests that these so-called gospels draw on any early or independent tradition whatsoever, and it is amazing that such accounts have found their way into a would-be revised canon such as the *Complete Gospels*. Their inclusion could be justified only if they represented very early texts, and the editor of *Infancy Thomas* suggests, unconvincingly, that "its understanding of Christ is what one would expect to find in the popular traditions of the Christian movement in the late first or second century."[44] Though this implies that the text was written no later than the canonical gospels, other experts favor dates much later in the second century, probably at its end.

One suspects that the decision to include these late and fantastic stories in this collection is meant to imply that the narratives found in the canonical gospels should likewise be regarded as folklore and fairy tale, rather than representing any core of historical reality. This would be quite in keeping with the views of Robert Funk, who has argued that the Biblical canon should be radically reconsidered, as "a collection of scriptures without a fixed text and without either inside or outside limits, like the myth of King Arthur and the knights of the round table, or the myth of the American West."[45] From his point of view, though, the problem is that including blatantly fictitious concoctions like the infancy stories only serves to emphasize by contrast the high literary and historical qualities of the canonical texts.

Reviewing suggestions for a potentially revised New Testament canon, we are repeatedly struck by just how weak are the claims of most of the candidates. Furthermore, these weaknesses are scarcely a secret for the advocates of the alternative gospels, who must know that the early dates and independent authority which they are claiming for their pet documents are bitterly contested by other scholars of equal merit, and in no sense represent a consensus. The Jesus Seminar affects to believe that its efforts represent an impartial endeavor in social science, in which authentic Jesus sayings are collected in a "database," in a project which seeks an objective Scholars' Version of the early Christian scriptures. In practice, though, the group demonstrates a powerful bias, obsessively magnifying the noncanonical sources while denigrating the traditionally accepted scriptures. In the *Complete Gospels* project, particularly, this ideological agenda becomes quite blatant. Contrary to recent claims, the more access we have to ancient "alternative gospels," the more we must respect the choices made by the early church in forming its canon.[46]

Hiding Jesus: The Church and the Heretics

Where the bishop appears, there let the people be, just as where Jesus
Christ is, there is the catholic church.

IGNATIUS OF ANTIOCH, LETTER TO THE SMYRNAEANS

ASSERTING THE AUTHORITY of a hidden gospel has implications
far beyond the strictly defined agendas of textual scholarship, as
claims are also being made for the ideas contained in the documents. To argue that alternate gospels possess a value equivalent
to the canonical texts is also to declare that their messages, long
dismissed as heretical, are statements of Jesus' vision just as
authentic as what would become orthodoxy. In rediscovering Q
and *Thomas*, scholars also try to portray the "Q community" and
"Thomas Christianity" as varieties of heresy which actually predated orthodoxy. By rediscovering these heresies-that-were-not-
heresies, such as Gnosticism, modern scholars are validating other
visions of early Christianity, with countless implications for the
shape of Christianity today. Generally, too, these new visions follow the prescriptions of liberal and radical reformers within the
respective churches.

This liberal approach strikingly recalls much older ideas, as
reformers throughout history have commonly denied that they
were wantonly innovating, claiming instead that they were
restoring an idealized lost reality. A recurrent theme in Protestant
history has been the quest for the idealized pure church of the
primitive ages, which was distorted and eventually suppressed by
ecclesiastical power: the search for restoration meant stripping
away all the accretions of the centuries of Romanism and popery.
In some cases, too, it meant reexamining and romanticizing various past heresies as the repositories of Christian truth, the groups
that had kept the gospel alive through the grim millennium of

unchallenged papal power. In Protestant mythology, the long Catholic night was brightened by the existence of heresies such as the medieval Waldenses and Lollards, groups who insisted on reading the Bible in their native tongues. Ever since the Reformation, some Protestants have looked longingly at the Celtic churches of the British Isles as bastions of anti-Roman resistance. A few reformers even looked to the Cathars or Albigensians of the thirteenth century, whose starkly unorthodox theology posited an eternal battle between the forces of spirit and matter, light and darkness, and who can only by a generous stretch of language even be termed Christian. Nevertheless, these medieval Manichaeans were sometimes depicted, however optimistically, as proto-Protestants.[1]

Each age seeks to reconstruct early Christianity according to its own needs and ideals, and uses the proofs that carry the most conviction in that particular society. Whereas in earlier societies those proofs have generally depended on scriptural interpretation, a modern audience demands validation through what appears to be objective academic scholarship. As we have seen, the Jesus Seminar validates its revised New Testament as the Scholars' Version. But as the example of the Cathars indicates, the ex post facto vindication of past heresies is often misleading, and this is particularly apparent when we are dealing with the church's earliest centuries. Just as some gospels are more valuable, more authoritative, than others, so also it is difficult to accept the idea that orthodoxy was no more than one viewpoint among its many rivals. Though contemporary writers use the Gnostic gospels to portray alternative models of Christianity, we see that these rival movements were much later historically than their orthodox counterparts, and were actually formulated in reaction against a preexisting orthodoxy, so they cannot claim to represent equally valid or ancient views of Jesus. The more we explore primitive Christianity, the earlier we find some of the most "catholic" and orthodox practices.

The Two Ways

As much as the Gnostic texts themselves, the communities that used and wrote them have also been brought back into focus. In the process, scholars have been forced to confront some important questions about the definitions of a religion, and especially of its outer reaches: is there a point, for instance, at which a group that affirms itself to be Christian has strayed so far from the conventional description of that faith that it can legitimately be denied the Christian label? There are still today hard-line ultra-Protestants who would exclude Roman Catholics from the Christian family, while a great many Christians would deny such membership to, say, Mormons, Christian Scientists, Identity Christians, Unificationists (the so-called Moonies), or Unitarians. The underlying assumption in such exclusions is that there somewhere exists a minimum catalogue of essential doctrines, from which the suspect groups have strayed. Must a group accept both Old and New Testaments? Is it forbidden to give scriptural status to any non-Biblical materials? Must Jesus be seen as the unique redeemer? Can humans achieve godlike status?

If the process of definition is controversial today, it is so much more so with respect to the early centuries of the faith, when beliefs and ideological frontiers were far more fluid, and when all these controversial questions were so frequently raised. For the orthodox, groups such as the Gnostics, Marcionites, and Ebionites were so blatantly heretical, and so outrageously denied the basic tenets of faith, that they had only tenuous claims to the name of Christian, and some orthodox critics even denied them this title. As, however, we find more ancient evidence from the heretics themselves, modern scholars are reluctant to accept this easy categorization of Christian and non-Christian, orthodox and heretic, and they see such divisions as basically political in nature. For many scholars today, the heretics are long overdue for vindication.

In her widely read account of Christian origins, Elaine Pagels argues that Gnosticism was a potent voice of the early church, which for political and bureaucratic reasons came to be stigmatized as heretical. Pagels, like other recent authors, sees a revolutionary change in Christianity during the second century. In the first half of that century, an immense diversity of belief and practice was reflected in the coexistence of numerous different gospels, and there were effectively no central mechanisms to dictate uniformity. Even the followers of the Gnostic Valentinus are recognized by some orthodox writers not as a rival religion, but as a "school" (*didaskalia*) within the Christian movement. By 200, however, "Christianity had become an institution headed by a three-rank hierarchy of bishops, priests and deacons, who understood themselves to be the guardians of the only true faith."[2] In this newly polarized world, a whole segment of the Christian movement found itself labeled as deviant and aberrant. The Great

Church declared that its followers alone were orthodox, "literally, straight-thinking," and this church was catholic, or universal: outside it, there could be no salvation. Karen King suggests that this intolerance was entirely new to a movement which hitherto had debated rival interpretations without seeking to exclude them, and presumably the change reflected the recent growth of hierarchies and institutional structures.[3]

About 177, Irenaeus of Lyon popularized the words orthodoxy and heresy to designate the rival sides, and attacks on heretics became steadily more vituperative. A few years later, Tertullian denied the claim of heretics like Valentinus and Marcion even to be Christians: as such, "not being Christians, they have acquired no right to the Christian Scriptures." In a recent television program, Pagels comments that Irenaeus denounces his opponents as "heretics, which means people who make choices about what to think. Irenaeus didn't want people making choices. He wanted them thinking what the bishop told them to think."[4] In her view, the orthodox obediently followed irrational dogmas, while heretics continued to exercise their intellects freely. There were two rival streams within Christianity, and for Pagels, as for many other writers, the wrong side won.

A similarly loaded picture is presented by influential feminist theologian Rosemary Radford Ruether, who sees the hidden gospels as the fragmentary records of the alternative Christianities, which are falsely dubbed heresies: "We can only dimly glimpse a time when a great variety of Christianities, some experimenting boldly with the personal and social changes and theological interpretations of redemption, not only competed as equals with emerging clerical and patriarchal forms, but in many places were the predominant forms of Christianity. These, just as much as those who won as the 'orthodox,' saw themselves as building on ancient traditions going back to Jesus and the first generation of his followers." In the face of growing "clerical and patriarchal" orthodoxy, "Christians of other views are cut off from these Christian assemblies and forced to meet in separate gatherings that are increasingly marginalized as 'orthodoxy' wins social predominance." Gnosticism was one among several versions of a suppressed truth; for Ruether, "Valentinianism is another variant of radical egalitarian Christianity of the second century."[5]

Elaine Pagels concurs that political power was decisive in determining doctrinal boundaries—might not only made right, it made orthodox. A news story on her views remarked that the Nag Hammadi texts were "produced and collected by early Christians who lost a theological battle with what became the dominant faction of the church."[6] Pagels argues that doctrinal debates contributed directly to this political transition. Orthodox theology reinforced the power of the emerging church hierarchy, which used the canonical gospels as rhetorical clubs to suppress the dissidents. The orthodox were the Christians who believed in the literal, bodily resurrection of Jesus which occurred at a specific moment in historical time. Historicity is stressed in the creed which emerged from this era, which specifies that Jesus died "under Pontius Pilate," which is to say about the year 30, rather than in a spiritualized dreamtime. Similarly, all Resurrection appearances had occurred in a specific (and brief) historical period around this same time. Religious authority was in the hands of the spiritual descendants of those who had been chosen to receive Resurrection appearances at that time, in other words, the church that traced an organic descent from the apostles. Emphasizing the literal truth of the Passion and crucifixion of Jesus gave these churches a potent example to follow in accepting and even seeking martyrdom. As the heirs of successive new martyrs in each new generation, church authorities gained ever greater prestige: Tertullian boasted, "the blood of martyrs is the seed of the church." Finally, the orthodox emphasis on the unity of God and the denial that God had a spouse or a feminine component were used to justify the monarchical authority of the bishop, who represented God's power on earth: as above, so below.

At every point, the Gnostics denied or challenged those ideas that represented the foundations of the new institutional church. In consequence, while the orthodox church became rigidly formalized and bureaucratic, the Gnostics reputedly maintained the traditions of the earliest Jesus movement, which was democratic, antihierarchical, and anti-institutional. For Gnostics, moreover, the events of the Christian story were inward and subjective, symbolic and mythological. Contra the orthodox, the Passion and crucifixion were not historical facts but inner realities, which affected the individual psyche: Jesus himself never suffered such a death, having escaped by means of an illusion which deceived his persecutors. Without his example of voluntary suffering, why would rational believers put themselves in a position to accept martyrdom? As for the Resurrection, this could be seen and experienced by any individual believer at any time, in the third century or indeed the twenty-first, and no political authority was derived from a vision of Jesus' presence. In place of patriarchal monotheism, the Gnostics were happy to contemplate multiple divine beings, including female or androgynous ones; this made it easier to accept decentralized authority on earth, with women occupying prestigious positions.

According to modern revisionist scholars, the rise of orthodoxy was justified by the familiar totalitarian device of rewriting history, and it was in this process that the orthodox church decided what came to be the canon of the New Testament. To quote Ruether once more: "The 'myth of orthodoxy' begins to be shaped by leaders such as Tertullian and Irenaeus in the late second century as they identify this emerging patriarchal and clerical Christianity with the original 'apostolic' faith passed down from an established succession of leaders (bishops) from the apostles who possess the original faith. . . . A canonical New Testament begins to be shaped that privileges second century writings reflecting this view and that interprets earlier writings in its own terms and cuts off writings that reflect other perspectives." Robert Funk has similarly declared, "The New Testament is a highly uneven and biased record of orthodox attempts to invent Christianity."[7] The Gnostics, in contrast, refused to be constrained by the notion of a canon, and rejected the idea that the number of gospels could ever be fixed. Once again, the orthodox seem to stand for limits, for boundaries, for restrictions, the Gnostics for the unfettered exercise of creative imagination. This is a contrast in which a modern audience finds it difficult not to favor the defeated underdogs, as opposed to the fanatically superstitious victors, with their cult of blood and martyrdom. In a conflict between one movement labeled as clerical and patriarchal, and another radical and egalitarian, few modern readers find it difficult to choose sides.

The influence of the liberal historical view, and the Protestant mythology before that, is amply suggested by the popular treatment of early Christian history in recent media portrayals. Television documentaries are not the normal venue in which academics discuss cutting-edge ideas, but these presentations have a far greater impact on public discourse than any number of scholarly articles or conference presentations. In 1998, there were two television miniseries, both major productions featuring numerous leading experts and addressing quite technical issues in New Testament study. At Easter, PBS presented a four-hour series under the title of *From Jesus to Christ: The First Christians*, while some months later the Arts and Entertainment network offered *Chris-*

tianity: The First Thousand Years. Both represented strongly liberal perspectives on early Christian history.

The series *The First Thousand Years* studied several critical points of transition from the glories of early Christianity to the repressive horrors of later times, and in each instance, the change was symbolized by an individual: the mythology has its demonology as well as its hagiography. One crucial change occurred in the second century, when Saint Ignatius of Antioch attracted blame for what is cited as his megalomaniacal emphasis on the episcopate. In this view, the office of bishop introduced a kind of hierarchy which marked a radical departure from the proto-Christian system of autonomous house churches. But even this traitor to the authentic vision of Jesus pales besides later monsters such as the Emperor Constantine, who gave the church political power. In both crises, it is alleged, the Gnostics and other heretics represented the stubborn resisters against the power-grab by the over-ambitious episcopate, who suppressed the freedom and spontaneity of early Christianity.

According to *The First Thousand Years*, Christian doctrine and practice in the early second century were enormously diverse, and authority was very widely distributed among house churches, many of which were under the authority of women. However, extreme diversity was seen as a danger by a few leaders, especially Ignatius. Historically, Ignatius was the bishop of one of the greatest Christian communities. He was arrested around 110, and while being led to his trial and death, wrote several influential letters to the communities he passed through. For this program, however, Ignatius was an authoritarian revolutionary. According to Karen Jo Torjesen, "Ignatius, like Paul, is one of the key figures in early Christianity. He is working to centralize the authority over Christians in a town under a single person. There is a move to consolidate all of these little house churches into one larger organization. One of the moves in this direction is to bring a central authority to this collection of house churches in the form of a bishop." Ignatius's letters were the vehicles for his revolutionary manifesto, in which he "sets forth his design for centralized authority." Not only did Ignatius seek to stamp out local autonomy, but the new episcopal structure was modeled on that of the Roman empire, so that the primitive democracy of Christianity gave way to Roman, and ultimately Roman Catholic, authoritarianism.

In the second century, according to this picture, the episcopal heirs of Ignatius began the campaign to stigmatize and destroy rival doctrines under the damning label of heresy. They tried to prevent Christians from reading and writing gospels and other texts that did not have the church's official imprimatur. The program *From Jesus to Christ* presented a similar model. In Rome around 150 or so, we are told, there was indeed a bishop or Pope, but he coexisted with the schools of Justin Martyr (orthodox), Valentinus (Gnostic), and Marcion (dualist), and there was no reason why one rather than another should be seen as the voice of "real" Christianity.[8] Only gradually were the Gnostics and Marcionites ostracized and labeled as heretics and, eventually, as less than Christians.

For both these programs, the decisive fall of Christianity is associated with the Emperor Constantine, who granted toleration to the faith in 313, and who ruled for the next two decades as the effective head of both a Christian empire and its church. Constantine showered wealth and privileges upon the church and sponsored magnificent building programs, but one of his measures has become particularly controversial. This was his summoning of the Council of Nicaea in 325, the debate which led to the declaration of the orthodox position about the Trinity and the divinity of Jesus, and the restatement of those views in the so-called Nicene Creed. Historians have long regarded Constantine as a mixed blessing for the church: though he ended persecution, he also drew Christianity into an intimate relationship with political power. The Nicene settlement illustrates the heavily politicized nature of theological debates. Orthodoxy was determined not by the faithful but by "a convention of clerical bureaucrats" summoned by a brutal dictator. The new political status of the church was symbolized by the basilicas that became the pattern for most church building for centuries to come: these stately edifices were essentially throne rooms, to which one came to venerate the absolute ruler of heaven, whose earthly image was the emperor. The image of Jesus as Wisdom or *logos* gave way to that of Pantokrator, the absolute ruler of the Universe. Love yielded to power.[9]

Constantine, it is claimed, wanted a world in which there was one united empire, and accordingly there should be one church with one doctrine and one Bible, and these goals should be enforced if need be by political repression. In the PBS series *From Jesus to Christ*, the policy of "One empire, one church" is presented in the most sinister terms, with its connotations of Hitler's slogan *Ein Reich, ein Volk, ein Führer*. Constantine was supported by the great bishop Athanasius, the champion of Trinitarian orthodoxy, who also struggled to enforce a strict definition of the New Testament canon. Constantine's inexorable quest for religious uniformity resulted in a tragic contraction of Christianity's ideological frontiers. The Gnostics were forcibly suppressed by the legal weight of the Roman empire, their churches seized on behalf of the Catholic Church, and their scriptures consigned to oblivion. The televised presentations of Constantine's revolution-from-above suggest that his regime capriciously selected the Catholic tradition as the Christian mainstream, at the expense of others now labeled heretical. If political affairs had developed slightly differently, the world's religious history would have been changed beyond recognition. As William Dalrymple writes, semi-seriously, "in the uncertain world of early Christianity, it does not seem impossible that the Manichees or the Gnostics could have won the day. . . . Churches would be dedicated not to 'heretics' like St. John Chrysostom but rather to Manichaean godlings such as the Great *Nous* and the Primal Man; reincarnation would be accepted without a second thought, and Messalian mucus-exorcisms would take place every Sunday after Evensong."[10]

For the series *The First Thousand Years,* it was Constantine's policies that decisively drew the line between orthodoxy and heresy, and their respective scriptures: "Some of the third century's most devout followers of Jesus would not be recognized as Christians today. Many of the more mystical beliefs and factions within the church are today called Gnostics." In this perspective, mystical or radical Christians suddenly found themselves condemned as heretics, victims of Constantine's obsessive hatred of diversity. (Not until 380 did the emperor Theodosius formally outlaw branches of Christianity outside the Catholic norm, denying them even the right to call their meeting places "churches," but blaming everything on Constantine makes for a more convenient narrative.)[11] The remaining Christians, neither mystical nor radical, were the worldly, gullible sheep, who became ordinary believers: in short, mere Catholics. The growing physical magnificence of imperial churches contrasted tragically with the spiritual emptiness they concealed, and the intolerant and superstitious Middle Ages began shortly afterward.

Orthodoxy and Heresy

The problem with these reconstructions is the suggestion that both orthodoxy and Gnosticism are equally ancient and valid statements of the earliest Christianity, which they are not. What became the orthodox view has very clear roots in the first century, and indeed in the earliest discernible strands of the Jesus movement; in contrast, all the available sources for the Gnostic view are much later, and that movement emerges as a deliberate reaction to that orthodoxy. While the Gnostic texts certainly show that some early Christians developed mystical and spiritualizing ideas, the organized groups holding those views in their extreme form did not exist in the earliest stages of the movement, and cannot claim any direct linkage to the world of Jesus and the first apostles. It is not thus a case of two equal strands, but rather of one branch growing out of a well-established tree. Rather than speaking of orthodoxy and Gnosticism as two competing strands, one of which happened to gain the sympathetic ear of a friendly tyrant, it would be more accurate to speak of the orthodox position as the mainstream from the first century onward. By the third century, the orthodox or Catholic unquestionably represented the Great Church, and there was never any doubt that this was the group with which the empire would have to deal: long before Constantine, other groups like the Gnostics, Marcionites, and other miscellaneous sects were at best on the defensive.

As in the case of the "other gospels," assertions about the independent authority of the Gnostic tradition rely on misleading claims about the dates of the key documents. Basically, the orthodox position is thoroughly spelled out in texts from the first century onward, while the documents which Pagels, King, and others cite to illustrate rival Gnostic concepts are far later, and in many cases assume a knowledge of one or more of the four canonical gospels.

This point is illustrated by the debate over the key concept of the Resurrection, which is so fundamental to Pagels's argument. We recall that the orthodox regarded Jesus' resurrection as a specific event that occurred at a given moment in history, while Gnostics viewed it as a continuing and symbolic process. There is no doubt that the orthodox position reflected the ideas of the first century, as all the four canonical gospels had before 100 provided their famous accounts of resurrection and the various appearances to Jesus' followers. But when did the Gnostic interpretation emerge? Most of the evidence generally cited in support of such a view dates from well into the second century. In the (canonical) second epistle to Timothy, we hear of leaders who believed that a general resurrection had already occurred, which is close to the

Gnostic position, but the dating of this text is highly problematic: suggested dates of composition range all the way from 65 through 140. Pagels herself cites three sources to illustrate the Gnostic view, namely, the *Gospel of Mary*, the *Treatise on Resurrection* (or *Letter to Rheginos*), and the *Gospel of Philip*. As we will see, *Mary* was not written before 150, and perhaps a good deal later, and the standard translation of the Nag Hammadi texts attributes the *Treatise* to "a late second century Christian Gnostic."[12] It is not legitimate to use these much later works to claim that Gnostic ideas represent a rival current in the earliest phases of Christianity.

The case of *Philip* deserves closer examination, because Pagels uses the work so frequently to illuminate Gnostic positions on issues such as the feminine nature of the Holy Spirit, and the potential for the individual believer to "become Christ." *Philip* ridicules orthodox Christians who believe in a literal resurrection after death, as opposed to a symbolic awakening in the present life. If it were an early text, this would be a fascinating illustration of debates among the first Christians, and we might see this gospel as a remnant of the mystical, symbolic, anti-eschatological approach that has been proposed for *Thomas*. The problem is, though, that *Philip* is commonly agreed to be one of the latest items in the Nag Hammadi collection. The standard translation suggests that the work "was probably written in Syria in the second half of the third century C.E.," that is, between 250 and 300, and it is not even claimed as an early text in the various new canons proposed by the Jesus Seminar. Bentley Layton, one of the more cautious scholars working in this area, is prepared to remark only that the work must have been compiled before 350, which is the approximate date the actual manuscript was penned. The *Gospel of Philip* is as far removed from the time of Jesus or Peter as we are from, say, the French and Indian war, or the world of Voltaire, and there is no hint that this work contains any kind of independent historical tradition.[13] Just as late is the *Apocalypse of Peter*, which Pagels herself dates to the third century and describes as "probably one of the latest writings discovered at Nag Hammadi"; this does not prevent her quoting the text repeatedly to illustrate Gnostic contempt for the structures and hierarchy of the orthodox church.[14]

If these datings are correct, then the significance of the Gnostic gospels as historical sources is greatly diminished, and so is the importance of the ideas they describe. Throughout Christian history, various believers have accepted an enormous diversity of views, concerning, for example, the spiritual nature of the Resurrection, the feminine nature of God, the role of women in the church, or the direct inspiration which God provided to the individual believer. Radical ideas on these matters were widely known among heretical sects within the Roman empire, and they reappear with the medieval Brethren of the Free Spirit and with early modern movements such as the German Anabaptists and the English Quakers and Diggers. Finding what the Gnostics believed about Jesus might be intellectually interesting or spiritually rewarding, but it brings us no closer to the historical roots of Christianity than does exploring the religious beliefs of nineteenth-century Shakers or Mormons. The Gnostic texts no more than confirm what we already knew about the far fringes of early Christian belief.

The dating issue also helps us understand the growth of the church and its institutions. If the free-wheeling practices described by Gnostic gospels portrayed matters as they had existed in the first century, then we could imagine the growth of hierarchical institutions and dogma as a betrayal of pristine, democratic Christianity. In this scenario, the clergy gained an increasing stranglehold over ordinary believers, whose spiritual life turned outward from the personal, mystical quest to the more impersonal world of liturgies and official church ceremonies. Such a transition seems intuitively plausible, particularly for those familiar with standard sociological theories about how religious movements succumb to bureaucratization. The problem is that clergy, liturgy, and institutions all have an excellent claim to have been there first, or at least to have been in place long before anyone thought of writing texts such as the Gospels of *Philip* or *Mary*. Instead of representing the lost original truth of Christianity, the Gnostic world should rather be seen as the first of many popular reactions against the institutional structures of the existing church, of the sort that would be commonplace through the middle ages and beyond.

Early and Catholic

A great deal of early evidence reveals that something looking very like a hierarchical church existed at a remarkably early stage of the Christian story. Unpalatable as it may be to many, a great deal of what is supposed to be the ugly face of the later church, Catholic and "medieval," has clear origins before 125 at the latest. The reason this is not so widely known is that many seekers for

Jesus spend a great deal of time on the New Testament and related sources, but neglect the evidence from the Apostolic Fathers and the Patristic sources: perhaps we see a traditionally Protestant tendency at work here, a resolute commitment to *sola scriptura*. By the first quarter of the second century, we have clear evidence of a hierarchical church with a rich sacramental life, based on elaborate theological interpretations of Jesus' life and significance. We find bishops and clerical orders, who grounded their authority in the succession from the apostles, and we also observe structured liturgies, focused on the Eucharist. Already before 125, the church organized on these lines had a narrow tolerance on doctrinal matters, and a strong sense that the community needed to be vigilant in defense of orthodoxy.

To illustrate the institutional life of the early church, we are lucky to have a range of sources from outside the New Testament that can probably be dated to the years between about 90 and 120, and they might be even closer together in time than this. Respectively, these are the first letter of Clement, the letters of Ignatius, and a letter of the pagan writer Pliny. The *Didache*, the Teaching of the Twelve Apostles, may also be this early, though others would date it to the mid-second century.[15] The dates are important, as these texts all come from before the full flowering of Gnosticism, and almost certainly before the writing of any of the Gnostic gospels, including the extant versions of *Thomas*. At this early date, moreover, we never once hear of Christians organized on the lines of Greek or Asian philosophical schools, in which pupils mulled over Wisdom teachings attributed to Jesus. Nor do we hear of rambunctious Jesus-oriented Cynics wandering the streets and shocking the bourgeoisie with their antics. If in fact there ever was a Christianity of limitless diversity, free of church institutions, hierarchies, and dogmas, it must have ended very, very soon after the death of Jesus, if not before.

The "catholic" quality of early Christian life is illustrated by the letter of Clement of Rome written to the Corinthian community probably before 100, at a time when Corinthian Christians were undergoing bitter internal divisions. It is debatable whether Clement was regarded at the time as the bishop of Rome, and hence one of the succession of Popes, but he certainly had an exalted idea of the bishop's office: he came close to speaking in terms of a separate clerical order, founded upon apostolic succession. He writes that once the apostles had founded churches, "they appointed the first-fruits [of their labors] . . . to be bishops and deacons of those who should afterwards believe." He urged that the successors of those first appointees should be obeyed as the heirs of the apostles. The clergy, that is, bishops and presbyters, are then compared to the priests spoken of in the Hebrew Bible, with all their privileges and special status, and as in those earlier times, rebellion against that established hierarchy was seen as a grave sin against God. [16]

Similarly impressive ideas of clerical status are exemplified by the letters of Ignatius around the year 110. Among other things, he orders the churches with whom he is in contact to obey their bishops and clergy at all times: just as Jesus Christ represents the mind of God the Father, so "the bishops, though appointed throughout the vast, wide earth, represent for their part the mind of Jesus Christ." The Ephesian Christian community meets in communion with Jesus Christ, "to show obedience with undivided mind to the bishop and the presbytery, and to break the same Bread, which is the medicine of immortality, the antidote against death, and everlasting life in Jesus Christ."[17] Heretical enemies at Smyrna are rebuked because "from Eucharist and prayer they hold aloof, because they do not confess that the Eucharist is the flesh of our Savior Jesus Christ. . . . You must all follow the lead of the bishop, as Jesus Christ followed that of the Father; follow the presbytery as you would the Apostles; reverence the deacons as you would God's commandment. Let no one do anything touching the Church, apart from the bishop. Let that celebration of the Eucharist be considered valid which is held under the bishop or anyone to whom he has committed it. . . . It is not permitted without authorization from the bishop either to baptize or to hold an *agape* [love feast]; but whatever he approves is also pleasing to God."[18] The reference to the "catholic church" in Ignatius' Letter is the earliest usage of the phrase.

Cumulatively, this sounds not only catholic in a medieval sense, but rather like the highest Roman Catholicism of the Council of Trent. Not surprisingly, Ignatian quotes were popular with later Catholic writers who asserted ecclesiastical power and episcopal authority, while conversely, Protestant writers from the seventeenth century through the nineteenth waged war against the authenticity of some of the more extreme-sounding passages.[19] For over a hundred years, though, scholars have accepted that the letters attributed to Ignatius genuinely are early: they really do reflect the ideas of the very early second century, and probably of Ignatius himself.

We cannot conclude that the kind of monarchical bishops described by Ignatius existed everywhere throughout the Christian world, and there is a plausible argument that Rome itself was governed by more of a collegial system until well into the second century. On the other hand, there is no justification for the claim that Ignatius was setting forth a revolutionary manifesto, as opposed to describing the proper state of affairs as he and his particular community had long believed them to be. Even had Ignatius planned to revolutionize the office of bishop, as was suggested in the television documentary *The First Thousand Years*, it is extremely unlikely that the very diverse world of Christianity could have been transformed, and so rapidly, by the eccentric vision of one man, albeit an important martyr. It is vastly more likely that episcopal structures were already fundamental to the churches across the Mediterranean world, though the power and prestige of bishops certainly did grow as the second century progressed.

Already by 110, the bishops were regarded as the heirs of the apostles, and ultimately of Christ himself. Curious confirmation of the power of this doctrine comes from Ignatius' archenemies, the Gnostic thinkers themselves, who asserted that they too received their authority by apostolic succession. Basilides, the great Egyptian Gnostic of the mid-second century, claimed to trace his knowledge from two separate apostles, with an indirect chain from Peter himself, and a direct link from Matthias, who "recounted to them secret discourses which he had heard from the Savior in private teaching."[20] About the same time, Valentinus claimed an "apostolic succession" from a disciple of St. Paul named Theudas. The fact that such claims were made is far more important than their historical plausibility: apostolic succession already mattered.

From exactly the time of Ignatius, namely, in 112, we have other evidence which shows that Christian life was based on communal liturgical services rather than the kind of esoteric discussion and mystical speculation that we might imagine from the Gnostic gospels. In a famous letter, the Roman writer Pliny wrote to the emperor Trajan about his current investigations into the Christian problem in the province of Bithynia, in modern Turkey. Based on interrogations, he described how Christians "met regularly before dawn on a fixed day to chant verses alternately amongst themselves in honor of Christ as if to a God . . . after this ceremony, it had been their custom to disperse and reassemble

later to take food of an ordinary, harmless kind." Some testimony
was extracted under torture from two slave women who bore the
title of deaconesses.[21]

Possibly from these same years, we have the ancient liturgy
preserved in the *Didache*.[22] Though the document's original date is
uncertain, it is unlikely to stem from much later than 125, since it
portrays a primitive-sounding kind of church structure, in which
bishops coexisted alongside apostles and prophets. The *Didache*
might indeed represent very much the kind of service which the
Bithynian believers confessed to practicing. This text describes a
liturgical service in which a person blesses a cup and some broken
bread in words which recall Jesus' Last Supper, and we probably
also have the congregational responses. We cannot assume that
the service implied anything like later eucharistic theology, but
just as we find in the Bithynian evidence, we are clearly in the
world of a structured church. This is neither the Wisdom school
suggested by *Thomas* nor the allegorical thought-world of the
Gnostics:

> First, as regards the cup:
> We give Thee thanks, O our Father,
> for the holy vine of Thy son David,
> which Thou madest known unto us
> through Thy Son Jesus;
> Thine is the glory for ever and ever.
> Then as regarding the broken bread:
> We give Thee thanks, O our Father,
> for the life and knowledge
> which Thou didst make known unto us
> through Thy Son Jesus;
> Thine is the glory for ever and ever.
> As this broken bread was scattered upon the mountains
> and being gathered together became one,
> so may Thy Church be gathered together
> from the ends of the earth into Thy kingdom;
> for Thine is the glory and the power
> through Jesus Christ for ever and ever.[23]

The *Didache* shows that already there is great concern about
false doctrine being spread within the churches, indicating that
the community concerned had a definite concept of true and false
teaching, what later generations would call orthodoxy and heresy.

The congregation is instructed that "whosoever therefore shall come and teach you all these things that have been said before, receive him; but if the teacher himself be perverted and teach a different doctrine to the destruction thereof, hear him not; but if to the increase of righteousness and the knowledge of the Lord, receive him as the Lord."[24] Christian communities already believed that there was true doctrine, and there was false, and such a dichotomy is evident throughout the New Testament, in documents such as the Book of Revelation and the letters attributed to John. Neither these texts nor *Didache* itself actually use the word "heresy," but the concept is assuredly present, in the stark denunciations of "deceivers," "antichrists," and false prophets; in contrast, the word "heresy" seems relatively mild and nonjudgmental. For these early writers, it was quite conceivable for an intellectual current to place itself completely beyond the bounds of the Christian movement.

The evidence of these primitive texts makes it difficult to argue that the hierarchical church which later claimed the names of catholic and orthodox was a much later outgrowth or corruption of the primitive ideal, or at least, if there was a process of corruption, it happened at the absolute beginnings of the movement, in the 30s or 40s. As far back as the 1920s, G. K. Chesterton described the liberal commonplaces of his day about the regrettable rise of an "ecclesiastical, dogmatic and despotic Church utterly alien to the simple ideals of Jesus of Nazareth," but Chesterton rightly noted that "those who maintain that Christianity was not a church but a moral movement of idealists have been forced to push the period of its perversion or disappearance farther and farther back."[25] The more evidence we have acquired about the early church, with its institutions, liturgies, and creeds, the stronger Chesterton's argument appears. Conversely, there is no support for the high claims recently made about the Gnostics within the Christian tradition, which generally rely on texts and materials which are so late as to be worthless for the purposes they are used.

6

Daughters of Sophia

The Savior himself said, "I am come to undo the works of the female."
CLEMENT OF ALEXANDRIA, QUOTING *THE GOSPEL OF THE EGYPTIANS*

FEMINIST SCHOLARS AND THEOLOGIANS have been the most ambitious in using the newly found gospels to reconstruct the early churches in their own image. This is not surprising, given that gender issues have been so central in the study of religion over the last quarter-century, the period during which the Nag Hammadi texts have come into public view. As Elaine Pagels has written,"The Nag Hammadi source, discovered at a time of contemporary social crises concerning sexual roles, challenges us to reinterpret history—and to re-evaluate the present situation."[1] The new sources seem all the more valuable because they feature women so centrally as companions and apostles of Jesus, while women are known to have played an important role in the historical Gnostic movement. The hidden gospels might preserve memories of an age when women were far more important in the Jesus movement than later writings would indicate, when women were apostles and prophets, leaders and bishops. And if that was the case in the first century, how could a similar role be denied to any succeeding generation? Mary Magdalen is sometimes portrayed in modern writing as a founding mother of Christianity with a primacy equivalent to that held by Peter in Catholic sources. For a society engaged in endemic controversy over women's ordination and feminist revisions of liturgy and scriptural language, this is all highly relevant evidence.

Once again, though, a yawning chasm separates the findings that can legitimately be drawn from the texts, and the claims made for them. Partly, the claims reflect a misunderstanding of the impact of the Nag Hammadi documents: the discoveries of mid-century did not really burst upon a scholarly world unfamiliar with the feminist implications of the Gnostic tradition. In reality, these ideas had been very familiar since the end of the nineteenth century. More important, though, is the perennial issue of dating the texts themselves, particularly key documents such as the *Gospel of Mary*, which is so often quoted in feminist revisions of early Christianity. Contrary to recent accounts, *Mary* and related gospels are late documents that shed next to no light on the apostolic age, and their credentials as early evidence are embarrassingly weak. *Mary* has been so popular because it so exactly fits feminist perspectives of what an early gospel should have said about the events of the time. To paraphrase a famous saying, if a gospel like *Mary* had not existed, it would have had to have been invented, and in a sense, invented it was.

Early Feminists and the Bible

Ever since modern feminism originated in the late eighteenth century, activists for women's causes have had to confront what appear to be deeply misogynistic and repressive texts in the Christian Bible. Foes of feminism have regularly deployed texts about Eve and the Fall, as well as Pauline injunctions that wives should be submissive to their husbands and silent in church. Activist women needed a rhetorical counterattack, which they found, for instance, in Elizabeth Cady Stanton's *Woman's Bible*, published in 1895. While it did not seek to revise the scriptural text, the *Woman's Bible* offered a thoroughgoing feminist commentary that pointed out the inconsistencies in Scripture, and stressed the egalitarian nature of Jesus' teachings.[2]

Intense periods of feminist activism and consciousness have been reflected in attempts to reinterpret the position of women in Judaism and Christianity, and often this has led to an interest in alternative and heretical traditions, in the roads not taken. Late nineteenth-century activists saw Jesus and his first followers as protofeminists, whose radical ideas were swamped by a patriarchal orthodoxy. The idea that the Gnostics retained the core truths of a lost Christianity was commonplace among occult and esoteric writers, many of whom shared the contemporary excitement over women's suffrage and other progressive causes. Many of the leading occult thinkers were of course women, including Theosophists H. P. Blavatsky, Annie Besant, and Anna Kingsford.

Feminist and esoteric writers found abundant evidence that some forms of heretical Christianity held attitudes toward gender roles very different from those of the orthodox. Many patristic writings would have alerted them to the existence of early texts in which Jesus carried on dialogues with faithful followers such as Mary Magdalen and Salome, scenes which became a trademark of the Gnostic gospel tradition. The sheer volume of this literature was indicated by Hippolytus' remark about the Ophite sect, and "the very many discourses which they say James the brother of the Lord handed down to Mariamne" (presumably Mary Magdalen).[3] In the late second century, the pagan critic Celsus reports the existence of several fringe schools which claimed traditions from female apostles or leaders: "Celsus knows, moreover, certain Marcellians, so called from Marcellina, and Harpocratians from Salome, and others who derive their name from Mariamme, and others again from Martha." Though Celsus' enemy Origen denies that he has ever encountered such groups as independent sects, a sizable literature boasted a transmission of teachings from Jesus through female disciples.[4] Appropriately, when we do hear of Gnostic leaders and propagandists, they are often female: when bishop Epiphanius recalled the Gnostics who almost tempted him into the sect in the fourth century, the seducers were typically "deadly women."[5]

Feminists found additional ammunition in the lost texts which were even then coming to light in such abundance. When the *Pistis Sophia* became available in English in 1896, it revealed a tradition in which female disciples and supernatural figures played a vast role. Most of the text takes the form of a dialogue on spiritual mysteries between Jesus and his disciple Mary Magdalen, whom he addresses as "thou spiritual and light-pure Mary," "inheritress of the light," and who is depicted as his primary follower and disciple. Jesus addresses Mary, "thou blessed one, whom I will perfect in All mysteries of those of the height; discourse in openness, thou, whose heart is raised to the kingdom of heaven more than all thy brethren."[6] Of forty-six questions addressed to Jesus by the apostles, Mary poses thirty-nine. Other women are also prominent questioners, including Mary, Jesus' mother, and Salome. In one memorable scene, Peter is forced to interrupt on behalf of the excluded men: "My lord, let the women cease to question, in order that we may also question." Jesus is sympathetic, telling the women, "Give your male brethren the opportunity, that they too may ask."[7] This dialogue was well known to modern readers of the *Pistis Sophia*, and it is quoted, albeit as a humorous footnote, in King's Victorian edition of *The Gnostics and Their Remains*.

The *Pistis Sophia* also included some of the so-called *Odes of Solomon*, a very early Christian hymn-book, which is orthodox rather than Gnostic. In 1909 a complete text of these odes was published in English, and some presented a surprisingly female imagery of the divine. In Ode 19, for instance, we read that

> The Son is the cup
> and he who was milked is the Father,
> and the Holy Spirit milked him; because his breasts were full,
> and it was necessary for him that his milk should be suffi-
>   ciently released
> and the Holy Spirit opened his bosom
> and mingled the milk from the two breasts of the father
> and gave that mingling to the world, which was unknowing.

These Odes are cited appreciatively by modern feminist theologians such as Rosemary Radford Ruether, and are included in her collection of "readings towards a feminist theology," her alternative feminist canon.[8]

Also available at the beginning of the twentieth century were ancient liturgies that exalted the divine feminine. The most important, and powerful, are found in the apocryphal *Acts of Thomas*, which may reflect the practice of a Gnosticized Syrian church in the early third century. The work includes a Eucharistic invocation which proceeds:

> Come, O perfect compassion
> Come, O communion of the male
> Come, she that knoweth the mysteries of him that is
>   chosen . . .
> Come, she that manifesteth the hidden things and maketh
>   the unspeakable things plain . . .
> Come, the hidden mother . . .
> Come and communicate with us in this Eucharist, which we
>   celebrate in thy name and in the love-feast wherein we
>   are gathered together at thy calling.[9]

In addition, readers had easy access to early Christian tales which glorified female saints. One of the best known was Thecla, who enjoyed a considerable reputation in the middle ages. Her story is found in an apocryphal but largely orthodox text called the *Acts of Thecla*, probably written around 160, which describes how she abandons her fiancé to preach the gospel, and travels the world as a celibate companion and follower of Paul. The *Acts* basically constitute a novel with many obviously legendary elements, but nevertheless, it tells the story of the early church from the point of view of a heroic woman, whose bravery appeals to women followers and supporters, and who secures the conversion of noble women. Indeed, the book was apparently written by a presbyter in Asia Minor, partly "in support of women's freedom to teach and baptize."[10] The *Acts* were available in English translations from the 1870s.

With so much evidence readily accessible, the materials were present for a feminist revision of early Christian history. Just how thoroughgoing such an endeavor could be was indicated by Frances Swiney's important book *The Esoteric Teachings of the Gnostics* (1909), which is virtually forgotten today. Though she writes from an occult or theosophical perspective, Swiney has much in common with modern scholars such as Elaine Pagels or Elisabeth Schüssler Fiorenza, who attempt to restore the lost voices of the women of early Christianity. For Swiney, the Gnostics found their chief supporters among the emancipated women of the Roman empire, "early pioneers of the the liberation movement of their sex, dialectical daughters questioning the truth and authority of received opinions, earnest intellectual women."[11] She saw the Gnostics as the direct predecessors of the suffragette women of her own day.

Without the benefit of the Nag Hammadi texts, Swiney uses the *Pistis Sophia* to provide a strikingly full portrait of the Gnostic world-view. (She also seems to have known contemporary German writings, particularly on the concept of Gnosticism as a pre-Christian movement.) She saw the Gnostic faith as a far more spiritual and egalitarian doctrine than the crude beliefs of the orthodox church. Gnostics taught reincarnation; they believed "that the real human is male-female, devoid of differentiated sexuality; the duality of manifestation now existing being a transitory phase of existence"; while the notion of Christ's vicarious sacrifice for sins was a "monstrous doctrine" invented by the orthodox. "Though Gnosticism long predated Christianity, the Gnostics were the first Christians; they accepted Christ in the full realization of the word; his life, not his death, was the key-note of their doctrine and their practice." Their beliefs were expressed in gospels which, she believed, were accepted and regarded as canonical decades before a like veneration was extended to orthodox texts such as the letters of Paul. The surviving Gnostic fragments, "the few mutilated relics that remain of these writings, [are] the most valuable evidence of what primitive Christianity really was, and what was the contemporary opinion of Christ and his teaching."[12]

These noble Gnostic thinkers, "the guardians of the most sacred truths of existence," were subjected to orthodox persecutions which collectively represent "the bloodiest and the blackest records that history can show us"; these acts were inflicted by "the uninformed, narrow-minded fathers of the primitive church." Worse than merely obscurantist, the Christian reaction specifically represented male persecution of women: "The Gnostics kept true to the original pristine faith in the Femininity of the Holy Spirit. A truth universally suppressed in the fourth century A.D. by the male priesthood of the Christian Church." Male priests had systematically doctored the surviving texts: "It is very suggestive of a sinister motive that in most of the erasures and where pages are missing in these Gnostic writings, the subject treated is in the context of some hidden mystery, the interpretation of which was unacceptable to the masculine mind and to bigoted orthodoxy." The iniquitous exclusion of women from the faith and its scriptures was the direct cause of "the persecution, degradation and maltreatment of womanhood" through the succeeding centuries.[13]

The New Feminism

Though writers such as Swiney had developed an advanced feminist interpretation of Christian origins, such ideas became scarcer with the decline of the women's political movement from the 1920s onward. Matters did not change until the return of political feminism in the 1960s and 1970s, and the concurrent growth of feminist spirituality. Following the publication of Mary Daly's *The Church and the Second Sex* in 1968, feminist insights made massive progress in mainstream theology and particularly Biblical scholarship.[14]

A surging wave of books discussed female characters in the Bible, and explored instances in which either editors or later translators had suppressed feminine-oriented themes. Scholars such as Schüssler Fiorenza advocated a whole new range of approaches which should be applied in feminist research, including a "hermeneutics of suspicion," based on the presumption that patriarchal texts would exclude or demean women and the feminine. One landmark in the movement's development was the publication in 1979 of the collection of essays *WomanSpirit Rising*, which would have an enormous impact on the emerging academic field of feminist studies.[15] The book included studies from within the Judeo-Christian tradition by Ruether, Schüssler Fiorenza, and Phyllis Trible, while other writers spoke from a Wiccan or goddess-oriented position: the book reprinted an essay by Elaine Pagels entitled "What Became of God the Mother?" which naturally drew attention to Gnostic scriptures. The centenary of Elizabeth Cady Stanton's *Woman's Bible* was greeted by a substantial collection of feminist Bible interpretations called *Searching the Scriptures*, which showed how firmly women's perspectives had become established in the critical literature.[16]

Received views of the New Testament were substantially changed by pointing to aspects of the text that had long been neglected, which stressed feminine aspects of God or Christ. And such passages can indeed be found: in one Q instance, Jesus makes the strikingly feminine proclamation that he wished to have gathered the children of Jerusalem together as a hen gathers her brood under her wings.[17] Central to feminist readings of this and other passages was the concept of Wisdom or Sophia, the feminine manifestation of God, who had become prominent in texts of the intertestamental period. This distinctively female imagery might lie behind the oldest understandings of Jesus' divine role, the first Christologies. In the book of the Wisdom of Solomon (written around 50 B.C.?), Sophia is "a breath of the power of God and a pure emanation of the glory of the Almighty . . . she is a reflection of eternal light, a spotless mirror of the working of God, and an image of his goodness." The figure of Wisdom boasts that she was with the Father from the beginning of time, and she is credited with the deeds attributed to God in the Hebrew Bible: it is Wisdom who protects Adam, saves Noah, delivers Moses from Egypt, and so on.[18]

This Hebrew image may have contributed to the understanding of Jesus who, in several instances in the Gospels, seems to be identified with Wisdom rather than with more familiar images such as Messiah or Son of God. As we have seen, scholars of Q and *Thomas* have stressed the central importance of this concept in those texts, and Stevan Davies has described *Thomas* as "a document of sophiological Christianity."[19] Wisdom ideas have many parallels with the exalted notions of Christ found in New Testament epistles such Colossians and Philippians, and the role of Wisdom is much like that of the *logos* in the Gospel of John, "the

Word" who was with God in the beginning, and who was God.[20] This kinship of ideas may explain why some early Christian communities actually included the book of Wisdom in their New Testament.[21] It may also support arguments that the Gnostics, who were so fascinated with the mythical figure of Sophia, might have retained theological ideas from the very earliest days of the Jesus movement, which were suppressed by a steadily more patriarchal orthodox church.

Intimately linked to the interpretation of scriptural texts was the role of women within historical religious communities. We have already seen how contemporary scholars have developed a mythology about the fall of the Jesus movement, of how the democratic spirituality of Jesus became the legalistic authoritarianism of the Catholic Church.[22] Feminist scholars have their own particular version of this story, stressing how this historical transition was uniquely grim news for Christian women. A substantial literature now argues that women played a critical role among the earliest followers of Jesus, and maintained their high position in the church's first century or so, until they were excluded by the growth of Catholic orthodoxy. Obviously, these arguments have an importance far beyond the purely academic, as the existence of female prophets, presbyters, bishops, or apostles in the first centuries would destroy the ideological arguments advanced today to prevent women from being ordained in the Roman Catholic Church and the other hold-out denominations. In 1993, Karen Jo Torjesen published a book entitled *When Women Were Priests*, with the polemical subtitle, "Women's leadership in the early church and the scandal of their subordination in the rise of Christianity."[23]

Feminist scholars have some grounds for arguing that women occupied high social roles in the earliest church, and enjoyed real power. Documented cases in the New Testament include Lydia, whose household was the mother church of the city of Philippi. Paul addresses a certain Junia as "prominent among the apostles," and he not only respected but accepted the teaching of another woman named Priscilla. A hundred years ago, Adolf von Harnack suggested that Priscilla might be the author of a New Testament book, namely the Epistle to the Hebrews. Another of Paul's correspondents named Phoebe seems to have enjoyed a supervisory role in her church at Cenchreae, perhaps close to what would later be called a bishop.[24] Phoebe and others were duly noted, and their role stressed, by Cady Stanton's *Woman's Bible*.

By the late second century, though, the high status of women seems to have all but vanished in the orthodox church. The orthodox venerated letters attributed to Paul, who ostensibly wrote, "I permit no woman to teach or to have authority over a man; she is to keep silent . . . yet she will be saved through child-bearing." This decline of status is reflected in the later treatment of Paul's women associates. Medieval manuscripts assume that any-one so distinguished and apostolic as Junia must have been male, and therefore convert the name to Junias, while the manuscript history of the New Testament shows a subtle but systematic effort to reduce Priscilla's role in comparison with that of her husband, Aquila.[25] In contrast, the heretical sects still gave women a high role: this meant the Gnostics, of course, but also the Montanists, who followed the teachings of inspired women prophets, as well as the Marcionites. Irenaeus offers a horrified case study of the followers of a Gnostic called Marcus, whose group offered women the chance to participate in eucharistic services as both priests and prophets, worshipping a maternal deity. His disciples, likewise, "have deceived many silly women, and defiled them." Elaine Pagels offers a nice paraphrase of one orthodox polemic against such a woman heretic: "We know that Tertullian, one of the lead-ers of the church in Africa, spoke about a woman he called simply, 'that viper,' because she was baptizing people. And he said, 'These heretical woman, how audacious they are. I mean they, they teach, they baptize, they preach, they do all kinds of things they shouldn't do. It's horrible, in short.'"[26]

This kind of evidence indicates that some long-range transfor-mation was occurring as the church grew, though the change, the "fall into patriarchy," was neither as sudden nor as revolutionary as has been argued. There would always be very powerful women within the church, in the late ancient world and throughout the middle ages, both lay women and religious. Nor is it clear that the earliest church was as woman-friendly as is sometimes claimed. This point is well made by Pagels: "I don't see a picture of a golden age of egalitarianism back there. I see a new, unformed, diverse, and threatened movement which allowed a lot more fluidity for women in certain roles for a while, in some places and not in others."[27]

But such subtleties are rarely discussed in the recent accounts of women in early Christianity, in which an idealized early church is seen as falling prey to hierarchy and misogyny sometime in the early second century. In the television series *Christianity: The First*

Thousand Years, it was noted that the Christianity of the first century was a movement based in the homes of more substantial believers, and according to the narration, "often early Christian churches were led by women." Torjesen stated that "house churches were presided over by the householder, which could be the father of the household or the mother of the household. The household really was considered women's domain, so the house churches were in a space that recognizes and is comfortable with women's authority." Once again, Ignatius of Antioch becomes the chief demon figure. In the early second century, it is claimed, Ignatius was instrumental in centralizing these churches under a monarchical bishop, who ruled according to the patterns of Roman tradition, in which female authority was not welcomed. In consequence, Christianity followed Roman ways, "and demotes women accordingly": "women now lose the power they had achieved in the early church." This last sentence was spoken not by one of the program's experts but by the narrator, suggesting that the view is indisputable fact.

A similar story pervades contemporary feminist writing on the early church, and is represented, for instance, in the materials presented by the reformist Catholic organization FutureChurch. According to the historical sketch they offer, "female leaders flourished alongside male leaders in the egalitarian and orthodox [sic] Valentinian and Montanist churches of Asia Minor until the fourth century when they were suppressed. By this time, Constantine had succeeded in using Christianity to unify the crumbling Roman empire. The inclusive, charismatic discipleship of equals which enhanced Christianity's rapid early growth, had been domesticated."[28] Miriam Winter's fictional *Gospel of Mary* tells how new and more authoritarian structures emerged during times of persecution and doctrinal controversies: "There was even talk of a canon, of making certain traditions authoritative for all. Women everywhere were disheartened. Their leadership was no longer recognized. Their experience was being misinterpreted. Their teaching, preaching and prophesying had been disqualified on theoretical grounds. . . . Was it the end of the age of freedom? Would wisdom disappear in the heat of theological definition? Soon no one would remember how it had once been." [29]

Mary Magdalen and the Hidden Gospels

But if there was a lost "age of freedom," an era of female autonomy, might that have left its traces in scriptures, if not those within the traditional canon, then in the excluded texts? Torjesen argues that women's perspectives were systematically excluded during the process of creating the New Testament canon: "Books celebrating women's apostolic activity (*Acts of Thecla*), containing women's words (collections of oracles of women prophets), and transmitting women's teachings (*Gospel of Mary*) which had nurtured the religious life of many churches, were not included in the canon, which was defined in terms of male leadership." Using the hermeneutics of suspicion, feminist scholars avidly sought what might be the suppressed words of the women of the early Jesus movement, evidence of feminine images of the divine, as well as women in leadership roles, and they found rich materials in the Nag Hammadi texts.[30] The major collection of feminist essays entitled *Searching the Scriptures* included forty essays on various documents from the early Christian period, from many of the leading contemporary scholars. Most concerned New Testament books, but all five of the opening essays concerned noncanonical or marginal texts, including the *Wisdom of Solomon, Odes of Solomon, The Thunder, Perfect Mind*, the *Trimorphic Protennoia*, and the *Book of Noreal Hypostasis of the Archons*. The last three of these came from Nag Hammadi. The whole volume containing these essays is structured around the theme of *Sophia*, with sections covering "Manifestations of Sophia," "Submerged Traditions of Sophia" (the New Testament epistles), and "Envoys of Sophia."

Central to the rediscovery of women's Christianity is the figure of Mary Magdalen, who is portrayed as a principal apostle of Jesus in several Gnostic texts. She is a key figure in the *Gospel of Philip, Pistis Sophia*, the *Sophia of Jesus Christ*, and *the Dialogue of the Savior*, and her role in the church is discussed in the conclusion of the *Gospel of Thomas*.[31] Conventionally, Biblical scholars assume that scriptural accounts of apostles such as Peter or John or Thomas were written in order to make statements and claims about the later communities who looked back on those individuals as their founders and patrons. Should we similarly believe that scenes involving Mary Magdalen reflect a real historical phenomenon, in that a primitive woman-oriented church was treasuring recollections of its supposed foundress? Do these documents retain recollections of women's authority in the earliest times, accounts that were suppressed in the mainstream (what Schüssler Fiorenza calls the "malestream") ? Feminist scholar Jane Schaberg argues that the role of Mary Magdalen in the noncanonical sources "shows the importance of breaking out of the canon."[32]

Long before the Gnostic gospels became easily available, the theory of a historical suppression of Mary's role in Christian origins could have been developed independently by anyone who read the canonical New Testament critically. In all of the canonical gospels, Mary Magdalen and at least one other female disciple are the first to witness Jesus' empty tomb, and are thus the first witnesses of the fact of Resurrection, although only in John does Mary Magdalen receive a special Resurrection appearance in her own right. In Paul's writings, however, there is no mention of Mary or the other women disciples, and the list of Resurrection appearances reported in 1 Corinthians includes no reference to the women, unless they are counted generally in the "five hundred" to whom Jesus appeared on one occasion. There are several possible explanations for this absence. We might argue that the first disciples knew only of a Resurrection appearance in Galilee, and only years later did early Christians develop the story of the empty tomb, as the notion of Jesus' literal physical revival from the dead gathered strength. In this case, the story of the women at the tomb would represent a later narrative addition, which was not known to Paul. Many writers, however, have suggested that Paul and other early Christians deliberately omitted Mary Magdalen as a witness, chiefly because she was a woman, whose testimony counted little in Jewish law. Raising doubts about this view, though, we have seen that Paul was quite comfortable in acknowledging the prestige and apostolic authority of women leaders. A later tradition suggested that Jesus "had cast out seven demons" from this Mary, indicating that she was mentally unstable, and therefore doubly unreliable.[33]

Other evidence that Mary might have been deliberately excluded from the Christian tradition comes from the image of her that develops in the later church, where she is portrayed as a reformed prostitute. This image arises from the merger of several female figures in the New Testament, including the penitent woman who wipes Jesus' feet with her hair, and even the woman taken in adultery whom Jesus saves from stoning. Historically, though, there is no suggestion in the New Testament that Mary was originally portrayed in either role. Nevertheless, the word Magdalen came to be a euphemism for prostitution up to modern times, and Magdalen Homes were refuges for prostitutes or unmarried young mothers. In Western art, paintings of the penitent Magdalen were often soft-core images of seminude women. Feminist writers see the denigration of this woman apostle as not merely historical accident, but a deliberate attempt by orthodox church leaders to discredit her reputation. As has often occurred with powerful women throughout history, a smear involves allegations of sexual excesses. Pagels has said that she suspects that "there were Christians who were trying to challenge her status among certain groups who saw her as a great one of the disciples."[34]

The question then arises which of Mary's words or activities might have been omitted from a rigidly patriarchal tradition, and it was in this context that the hidden gospels seemed to offer the greatest promise. The work most often cited as a fresh resource is the *Gospel of Mary*. This Gnostic text was known long before the Nag Hammadi discovery, but it was not published in a scholarly edition until 1955, and remained untranslated for years afterward. Not until the revival of feminist Biblical scholarship in the 1970s did academics begin to emphasize its possible significance. The gospel takes the form of a special revelation delivered by the risen Jesus to Mary Magdalen, whose authority is hotly debated by the male apostles. "When Mary had said this, she was silent, since the Savior had spoken thus far with her. But Andrew answered and said to the brethren, 'Say what you think concerning what she said. For I do not believe that the Savior said this. For certainly these teachings are of other ideas.' Peter also opposed her in regard to these matters and asked them about the Savior. 'Did he then speak secretly with a woman, in preference to us, and not openly? Are we to turn back and all listen to her? Did he prefer her to us?'" Mary protests, and is supported by Levi, who denounces Peter for hot-headedness, and declares that "if the Savior made her worthy, who are you to reject her? Surely the Savior knew her very well. For this reason he loved her more than us."[35]

This passage has proved irresistible to feminist writers, who find asserted here not only the apostolic status of Mary Magdalen, but her preeminence among the followers of Jesus. In the television series *From Jesus to Christ*, Pagels remarks that "the *Gospel of Mary Magdalen*, for example, shows us a Christian community in which Mary Magdalen is regarded as a disciple, as a leader, as one of the major teachers in the group, and one who claims that women should be allowed to teach." Moreover, the male apostles are depicted as obtuse and unwilling to hear the spiritual claims of women, in a way that foreshadows the later misogyny of the church. Karen King writes that by the end of the Gospel, "Peter, Andrew and the others have not understood the Savior's teaching. The reader must wonder what kind of good news such proud and ignorant men will announce."[36] Modern writers have seen the exchanges between the Magdalen and the apostles in *Mary* as literary evidence of an authentic movement by male clergy to suppress the role of women in the church. To quote King again: "This Gospel lets us hear an alternative voice to the one dominant in canonized works like I Timothy, which tried to silence women, and insists that their salvation lies in bearing children. We can now hear the other side of the controversy over women's leadership, and see what arguments were given in favor of it."[37] Ruether's *Womanguides* includes the *Gospel of Mary* as "this affirmation of the church as an egalitarian spiritual community over against that patriarchal church which identified its episcopal hierarchy with an apostolic descent from the prince of the apostles, Peter."[38]

In this reading, Mary symbolizes the nameless women who stood against the rising authoritarianism and centralization of the new male hierarchy, symbolized by the jealous male apostles. Such a conflict is also implied in other hidden gospels, including *Thomas*, in which Simon Peter asks Jesus to "make Mary leave us, for women do not deserve life."[39] One striking story of this kind occurs in the *Gospel of Philip*, where we read in a mutilated passage that "[Jesus] loved [Mary Magdalen] more than all the disciples, and used to kiss her often on her mouth. The rest of the disciples [were offended]. They said to him 'Why do you love her more than all of us?'" Mary is Jesus' "consort" or "companion," using a Greek word that indicates a sexual relationship. Jesus is actually described having sexual intercourse in another still lost work, the *Great Questions of Mary*, a text described with horror by the fourth-century writer Epiphanius: in this instance, the woman involved is not exactly Mary but a figure created from her body.[40] If stories of Jesus' sexual activity were to be accepted as true, not only would arguments against the ordination of women crumble, but so equally would the idea of priestly celibacy: if Jesus had a sexual relationship with the Magdalen, how could modern priests justify their own rejection of sex?

The exchanges in *Mary* and other texts might be a symbolic representation of faction struggles in the church, but some have gone further in accepting their historical credentials, to read them as accounts of Mary herself. A few scholars regard these stories as recording actual debates between historical individuals, which occurred at a time when Mary herself occupied a critical leadership role in the early church, perhaps as a rival to Peter. The most enthusiastic advocate of *Mary* is Karen King, a core member of the Jesus Seminar, who argues that "discoveries of new texts from the dry sands of Egypt, along with sharpened critical insight, have now proven that [the traditional] portrait of Mary is entirely inaccurate. She was indeed an influential figure, but as a prominent disciple and leader of one wing of the early Christian movement that promoted women's leadership. . . . historically, Mary was a prophetic visionary and leader within one sector of the early Christian movement after the death of Jesus."[41]

The *Gospel of Mary* is priceless evidence for scholars and activists campaigning against contemporary restrictions on women, and largely because of its obvious political usefulness, *Mary* has had an impact second only to *Thomas* among the Nag Hammadi writings. It is one of the twenty *Complete Gospels* published by the Jesus Seminar, and *Mary* is prominently advertised on the book's cover because it "suggests that women held prominent roles in the early church."[42] *Mary* also reached a mass audience through the recent television documentaries that have done so much to popularize the new gospels, and the revisionist account of Christian origins they are used to support.

Confronting the Myth

But as we have already seen, we have to be very careful before accepting the evidence of the hidden gospels for conditions in the earliest church, and this is particularly true when evaluating claims about Mary Magdalen, and pivotal texts such as the *Gospel of Mary*. As always, so much depends on the date at which this was written. In the *Complete Gospels*, King suggests that the *Gospel of Mary* "may arguably have been written sometime in the late first or early second centuries," though elsewhere, she states that "a date in the first half of the second century may be appropriate." As evidence for these early dates, King argues that "the *Gospel of Mary*'s setting, its characters and many of the Savior's teachings invoke first century gospel traditions." She further believes that the visionary revelations in *Mary* belong to the tradition of Christian prophecy, which was a well-recorded phenomenon in the New Testament and other first-century documents.[43] King's estimate would put the text around the same time as the four canonical gospels, which would be an explosive finding for interpreters of early Christianity, since the work is so extraordinarily different from anything we would expect from that era.

King's dating for *Mary* is, however, unusually early. As so often with these noncanonical works, we have no certain clues about dates, as the work is not quoted by external authorities, and all that can be said with absolute certainty is that it must be placed somewhere between, say, 50 and 350. Any closer estimate has to rely on internal evidence, basically comparing the ideas and language contained in *Mary* with other early texts, and deducing the period in which a work like this is most likely to have been composed. On these largely subjective grounds, most scholars would place the work at the end of the second century, if not later. Torjesen places it somewhere in the second century, Ruether in the early third. Interestingly, some radical scholars of the Jesus Seminar group seem less than enthralled by claims for *Mary*'s early status. Crossan, who often tends to claim extremely early dates for uncanonical sources, does not include *Mary* among the sources he lists as having been written before 150, and Funk writes coolly that "it is still unclear what we will learn from the study of the *Gospel of Mary*," presumably indicating that he too does not see it as a primitive source.[44] A consensus of recent scholarship would place the writing of *Mary* not much before 180 or 200, about a hundred years later than King's figure, but there is no intrinsic reason why it should not be later still. The oldest fragments of the text date from the third century.

One reason for suggesting a late date for *Mary* is that the work contains a kind of Gnostic mythologizing which is characteristic of the later second or early third century, and suggests the influence of Valentinus. The Gnostic elements are apparent from a brief summary of the work, contradicting King's assertion that "the internal evidence of the *Gospel of Mary* itself provides no support for assuming the existence of a fully developed Gnostic myth behind the text." Mary Magdalen describes a vision in which she observes the ascent of the soul through the heavens, in which it meets, and is interrogated by, successive powers like Wrath and Ignorance. At each level, the soul learns the codewords that will ease passage to the higher sphere: "They ask the soul, 'Whence do you come, slayer of men, or where are you going, conqueror of space?' The soul answered and said, 'What binds me has been slain and what turns me about has been overcome, and my desire has been ended and ignorance has died. . . . From this time on will I attain to the rest of the time of the season, of the aeon, in silence.'" Not only is this obviously Gnostic, it is far removed from the prophetic or visionary genre in which King seeks to place it.

These passages are nothing like the kind of oracular pronounce-
ment we usually find in prophetic utterances, and the whole
work should rather be regarded as a theological discourse which
happens to be described in the form of a vision. [45]

For these reasons, a late second-century date for *Mary* is quite
probable. Indeed, it is curious that any commentator has suggested an earlier period, even qualified by the word "arguably."
However, the idea of an early Gospel in which a woman emerged
as head of the apostles was so clearly tempting on ideological
grounds that the desire to buttress its authority is understandable.
Nor can we put a significantly earlier date on other major documents that mention Mary, such as the *Sophia of Jesus Christ* or the
Dialogue of the Savior, while the *Gospel of Philip* comes from well
into the third century.

Quite as remarkable as the claims about the very early date is
the notion that Mary herself seems to emerge as "a prophetic
visionary and leader . . . of the early Christian movement." This
statement deserves comment as an example of what I have
called inverted fundamentalism. Traditionally, fundamentalist
approaches to the Bible exaggerated the importance of sources
within the New Testament, always seeking opportunities to establish their value as literal historical sources. Contemporary academics treat such claims coldly, emphasizing that the authors of
the New Testament books were not writing objective history in
anything like a modern sense, and that the gospels had an overwhelming theological and rhetorical agenda. Liberal scholars generally assume that scriptural works reflect the interests and controversies of the communities that created them, long after the
events described; these texts were simply not eyewitness testimony. From this perspective, few modern scholars would treat
the accounts of the apostles given in the canonical New Testament
as literally historical descriptions of their careers or attitudes, but
this is exactly how King is treating the Mary portrayed in the
gospel which bears her name. The criteria applied to noncanonical
sources are very different form those used for their canonical
counterparts.

But why does it matter so much that the key texts about Mary
Magdalen come from the period between 150 and 200, rather
than from fifty or a hundred years earlier? Everything depends on
the information that we hope to find in these texts. They certainly
can be used to illustrate the ideas and rhetoric of some strands of

heterodox Christianity in the late second century, but we cannot find here any significant evidence about the earliest church or, specifically, about the time of Mary Magdalen herself. *Mary* and comparable works completely lack any factual material about the Magdalen or her life, beyond what could be found in the canonical gospels. Nor do they necessarily make any statements about the status of women as such.

However evocative, these texts do not originate in a time of conflict when women's authority was in the process of being suppressed; if such an event ever occurred, it was long past before *Mary* was composed. These uncanonical texts were written at a time when the episcopal hierarchy was already well established, when the early house churches were a distant memory, and when the canonical gospels were already widely known as the principal authorities for the life of Jesus. *Mary* and its like come from a time when the church had already fixed its gospel canon at four. Despite claims that *Mary* was excluded or omitted from that canon, presumably because of its subversive feminism, the work was much too late a candidate even to be considered. Though Torjesen suggests that texts such as Mary had "nurtured the religious life of many churches," the gospel originated at a time when the Gnostic movement was already quite distinct from any kind of mainstream church life.[46]

Once we understand the historical setting of the Gnostic gospels, it becomes questionable whether the portrait of Mary Magdalen as chief apostle reflects any kind of gender conflict within the church, still less an authentic historical tradition about her career. Gospels like *Mary* arose from the controversies of the late second and early third centuries, an era of intense literary warfare between orthodoxy and heresy. This chronology helps us to understand the demeaning portraits of Peter and the apostles in these documents, written so long after their deaths. The authors were less interested in attacking the actual historical figures of Peter, Andrew, and their like than in challenging what they viewed as the arrogant pretensions of the orthodox churches, who claimed descent from Jesus' chosen followers. The message of *Mary* and the rest is that orthodox congregations and their leaders are just as worldly, simplistic, and naively literal-minded as their vaunted apostolic founders, and thus too spiritually blind to understand the great truths passed on by Jesus. By attacking the apostles, one was undermining the bishops; this is incidentally powerful testimony that the ideology of apostolic succession was already a potent weapon in the arsenal of orthodoxy, which the heretics were forced to confront.

The Gnostic attack on the apostles necessitated an outside figure who could serve as a counterpoint, someone who recognized Jesus' mystical message, and was thus wiser and more spiritual than the established leaders. Mary had many qualifications for this subversive role, and her elevation as rival apostle and patron saint of Gnosticism may have arisen from a close reading of the canonical gospels. Like any modern reader, Gnostics could easily see that although Mary was intriguingly close to Jesus, she was not counted among the Twelve, and her importance was quite obvious from the canonical accounts of the Resurrection. Gnostic readers presumably noticed the paradox that Mary was identified as the first witness of this event, and yet was not cited in this role by either Paul or by later church tradition; if Peter had falsely claimed that he was the first to see Jesus, then his primacy crumbled, and so did the claims of his episcopal successors. Apostolic prestige was also questioned by the canonical accounts which presented the women followers as truer disciples than their male counterparts. In Luke, the women proclaim the Resurrection to the apostles, only to be met with incredulity, thus indicating that the women possessed greater faith and sensitivity; "but these words seemed to them an idle tale, and they did not believe them." As Elizabeth Cady Stanton noted, "The men who visited the tomb saw no visions, but all the women saw Jesus and the angels, though the men, who went to the tomb twice, saw nothing."[47]

Even if women had not played such a strong part in the Gnostic churches, it is likely that the movement's texts would for doctrinal reasons alone have made Jesus' special companion a woman. The Gnostic world-view demanded that spiritual beings exist in male and female pairs, forming a common whole, a syzygy; how could Jesus exist without his counterpart, with whom he merged in spiritual—and perhaps sexual—union? We may also find here the common mystical idea in which the individual soul is seen as female, awaiting a spiritualized sexual union with the divine. These symbolic ideas probably lie behind the curious text in *Philip* which portrays Mary as Jesus' "consort." A close relationship between the two was also suggested by the Gospel of John, which by all accounts was the canonical text most favored by the heterodox.

Perhaps, too, suggestions of a sexual relationship between Jesus and Mary were inspired by the practices of the Gnostic groups themselves. Hostile writers like Epiphanius explicitly stated that some Gnostic groups did practice forms of ritual sex, in which, for example, a couple would offer semen or menstrual blood in a kind of eucharistic rite. Practices of this sort have existed in esoteric groups through history, and the tale is not inherently impossible, but we can scarcely use the orthodox critics as reliable witnesses on Gnostic practices. Epiphanius and other writers also add far more outré charges, including ritual cannibalism, which are probably drawn from the common fund of horror stories directed against fringe religious groups over the centuries, including, on occasion, Jews and Christians themselves.[48] If, however, we do accept that sex had acquired a ritual significance in some Gnostic groups during the third or fourth centuries, then erotic passages such as that in *Philip* should be seen as attempts to justify later practices by back-projecting them to the time of Jesus himself. These texts say nothing of historical value about matters in the first century.

The Gnostic image of Mary Magdalen as Queen of the Apostles is purely a literary construction and contains not a shred of historical memory, and much of what appears to be primitive in these texts is rather a deliberate literary device of much later writers. If *Mary* and comparable texts are the best evidence that can be mounted for a supposed gender conflict within early Christianity, then the case for that controversy is extraordinarily weak. Contrary to the common feminist assertion, the evidence for a general suppression of women's spiritual authority within Christianity is slim. This should be recalled when reading Elaine Pagels's statement that "from the year 200, we have no evidence for women taking prophetic, priestly and episcopal roles among orthodox churches."[49] This remark invites the obvious question as to just how extensive the evidence for such a role was before the year 200. It was in fact scanty.

Reconstructing the Women's Church

Besides *Mary*, other texts demonstrate a tendency by feminist scholars to inflate claims about the value of lost gospels and scriptures as evidence for the early church. It has, for example, been argued not just that women were pivotal to the earliest church, but that we can observe a whole alternative feminist theology in early Christianity. Once again, though, the documents used to substantiate this idea are open to different interpretations, and the case made is far from convincing.

Some Gnostic texts differ substantially from their orthodox rivals by speaking of the divine in explicitly feminine terms. One striking example from Nag Hammadi is a mysterious text called *Thunder, Perfect Mind*, a poem spoken in the voice of a divine female figure. It is a matter of debate who this person is imagined to be, though the beginning of the text has links both to Jewish views of Wisdom and to Gnostic mythology. She declares:

> I was sent forth from the power,
> and I have come to those who reflect upon me,
> and I have been found among those who seek after me. . . .

Karen King describes the document as part of a "remarkable collection of oracles from another unnamed woman prophet," who is assumed to be part of a Christian group; *Thunder* also has parallels to the text of a lost Gnostic *Gospel of Eve*.[50] And there are other similar texts. In the *Apocryphon of John*, we find a hymn about the descent of (female) divine Wisdom, the *Pronoia* of God.[51] Yet another text of this sort is the so-called *Hypostasis of the Archons*, in which the ignorant and inferior creator-God of Genesis tries unsuccessfully to thwart the higher, female, spiritual forces.[52]

Many Gnostic scriptures also present a notion of divine androgyny. Ruether's *Womanguides* illustrates the Christian mystical ideal of achieving androgyny from Nag Hammadi texts such as the Gospels of *Philip* and *Thomas*, as well as the *Gospel of the Egyptians*. As Jesus tells Salome, it is possible to enter the kingdom "when you make the male with the female into a single one so that the male will not be male and the female not be female."[53] As interpreted by contemporary feminist writers, this theme is important because it attempts to overcome strictly defined gender boundaries, to enter into a more fluid and liberating concept of gender roles.

The importance of such texts, it is claimed, lies not in any one passage, but in the cumulative evidence that can be drawn from so many examples. King argues that "by placing the teaching of the *Gospel of Mary* side-by-side with the theology of the Corinthian women prophets, the Montanist women's oracles, *Thunder, Perfect Mind*, and Perpetua's prison diary, it is possible to discern shared views about teaching and practice that may exemplify some of the contents of women's theology."[54] But has this "women's theology" been correctly identified? Or to be more precise, in what sense are the ideas presented part of any notionally Christian tradition? One difficulty with using Nag Hammadi texts is that by no means all of these have any Christian character whatever, a point established by the presence of part of Plato's *Republic*. Other texts arise from a Gnosticism which used no words or names associated even loosely with Christianity; these works might have arisen from a highly deviant Judaism, or even from purely pagan roots. One example of this syncretism is the *Paraphrase of Shem*, "a non-Christian Gnostic work which uses and radically transforms Old Testament materials, especially from Genesis."[55] The *Apocalypse of Adam* also reflects Jewish Gnostic ideas, stemming from older Jewish apocalyptic traditions.[56] Some other works that do occasionally mention Jesus or Christ use the names in an intellectual framework that draws variously on Jewish, Manichaean, and Hellenistic pagan thought. The Nag Hammadi texts were, after all, found in Egypt, and many of them show strong signs of composition within that ancient mystical culture. They particularly suggest the sort of synthesis we might expect in a syncretistic, cosmopolitan community such as Alexandria.[57]

We cannot assume that the group that produced or used any particular text found at Nag Hammadi had any Christian credentials whatsoever, and that certainly applies to the texts that appear to present a divine feminine. It has long been well known that the Gnostics used female images of the divine, and that their *pleroma* contained many feminine images, but it is uncertain whether these notions arose from developments within the Christian tradition or reflected contacts with other intellectual traditions. While both Jews and Christians of Jesus' time knew of feminine faces of God, especially in the form of Wisdom, texts such as *Thunder* draw more heavily on pagan sources. Despite claims for its Christian status, most of *Thunder* would fit better into the voice of the great goddess Isis, or any of her ancient counterparts from across the Near Eastern world, such as Inanna and Astarte.[58] The unnamed speaker declares:

I am the mother of my father
and the sister of my husband
and he is my offspring.

Like *Thunder*, the *Apocryphon of John* as we have it is only tenuously connected with any Christian tradition whatsoever: Susanne Heine calls it "a very popular second century writing . . . which has undergone a Christian revision." These texts are not remnants of a protofeminist theology from within Christianity, but should rather be seen as additional testimonies of the power of goddess images throughout the world of the pagan Mediterranean. It is scarcely fair to reconstruct alternative Christian theologies on the strength of documents that are not even Christian.[59]

Equally inappropriate is the feminist use of the figure of Thecla, the heroine of the *Acts*. Scholars have long since concluded that this work is obviously a romance, and draws much from the most fantastic aspects of the Hellenistic novel. A series of miracles saves Thecla from the beasts of the arena, including a moment when a lioness demonstrates sisterly solidarity by defending her against male animals. The late and legendary qualities of these *Acts* have not prevented modern writers from treating Thecla as a real figure, a founder and paladin of women's Christianity. King writes, "One of the most famous woman apostles was Thecla, a virgin-martyr converted by Paul."[60] Though King describes Thecla's story as "somewhat fabulous," she does not indicate that the tale is all-but-unanimously regarded as pure fiction from start to finish (once again, contemporary scholars who seek to rehabilitate Thecla's historicity are reviving speculations of the late nineteenth century). Yet even if acknowledged as fiction, the existence of the Thecla story is assumed to represent what Ruether calls an "alternative Christianity . . . its primary promulgators were probably communities of celibate women teachers who prepared other women for baptism."[61] The existence of such an alternative Christianity is as speculative and ill-documented as the story of Thecla herself or, indeed, of her lion.

Feminist interpretations of the hidden gospels represent a triumph of hope over judgment. If a source dating from perhaps 180 or 200 purported to describe the events of the apostolic age, it is very unlikely that reputable scholars would assume that this text was historically authoritative, unless there were clear signs that it contained some kind of independent tradition. The chance that the work would produce any useful information about the earliest Jesus followers would be all the slimmer if it obviously stemmed from a Gnostic source, because the mythological character of that movement's writings is so well known. In cases such as the *Gospel of Mary*, though, neither the late date nor the character of the source has prevented the text from being seized upon as a lost pearl. The expectation was that a treasure trove of lost gospels should produce testimony to a feminist golden age, and, however improbably, *Mary* proved the best candidate. In the same way, works such as *Thunder, Perfect Mind* are taken to support ideas of a primitive feminist theology, no matter how tangential that text is to any school of Christianity whatsoever. The willingness to claim such texts as part of a lost women's canon is troubling testimony to the ideological character of some modern interpretations of the hidden gospels.

7

Into the Mainstream

Seek for the pleasure of seeking, and not for the pleasure of finding.

JORGE LUIS BORGES

IN AN EMOTIONALLY CHARGED FIELD such as Biblical study, there is nothing novel about the assertion that scholarship is ideologically motivated, and the critical study of the Bible has long been driven by the desire to establish particular positions, conservative or radical, Catholic or Protestant. Often, too, the political concerns of a given period determine the texts and passages that will become the main intellectual battlefronts in that era. Some contemporary theorists would deny that truly objective or value-free scholarship is even a possibility. What has changed fundamentally in recent years is the nature of the prevailing ideology, which asks quite novel questions about, for instance, gender and sexuality, canon and authority. The liberal and feminist tone of contemporary writing on the lost gospels is what we might expect from the academic and religious culture of the late twentieth-century West.

Scholars write books making sweeping claims for the hidden gospels, and a substantial public is buying and reading these works. New Testament scholarship has long attracted a lay audience, and the idea of finding an authentic fifth gospel has been a popular dream since at least the 1890s. In the late twentieth century, however, the expansion and democratization of the mass media have carried the new approaches to early Christianity to readers who might not be expected to take an interest in religious scholarship. Ideas and theories that seem quite arcane in their appeal—the nature of Q, the existence of gospels of *Thomas* or *Mary*—have become the subjects of best-selling books and widely watched television documentaries. Not only have ordinary readers and consumers followed the new discoveries with avid attention, but they have been willing to accept quite radical scholarly interpretations arising from these finds. Incongruous as it may appear, the Gnostics have finally reached the mass market they never found, or sought, in their own day.

The modern-day popularity of the writings owes less to their value as startling new historical sources than to their ideological usefulness in current social and ecclesiastical debates. The degree of enthusiasm suggests that the hidden gospels had the appeal they did because they filled a preexisting need. Indeed, these texts have gone far toward providing scriptural warrant for a major social movement that has had far-reaching effects on American religion. To speak of a social movement, we do not need to find that large numbers of individuals subscribe to a single party or umbrella organization, and formal institutions might be disparate and loosely structured. What is required is that substantial numbers of people share broadly similar views in support of a common set of social goals, and that their interest and activism be sustained over a period of time. By this definition, we can readily speak of a substantial social movement favoring a radical reconstruction of contemporary religious belief and practice.

Several different constituencies can be identified within the larger audience. One may be found in institutions of higher learning. The new market for noncanonical materials and suppressed traditions here can be explained in terms of the changing nature of the academic world and the widespread sympathy for postmodern approaches. Intimately linked to this trend is the changing position of women, who have come to play an ever-growing role in the universities, at a time when a thoroughgoing restructuring of women's expectations has transformed most aspects of Western society and politics. Women have long been recognized by the mass media as a crucial component of the reading and viewing audience, and it is natural that writers and publishers should devote so much effort to recapturing what appears to be the lost history of women's role in Christianity.

Quite as important is women's rapidly growing role within the churches, less in terms of their actual numbers in congregations than in their representation among clergy and seminarians, and in the small groups that have become so vital a part of American religion.[1] Together, lay and clergy women provide a major new element of the potential audience for claims about the true origins of the Jesus movement and the historical roots of gender issues within religious communities. Also within the churches, and on their fringes, radical reinterpretations of Christianity find an audience among so-called seekers, those interested in spirituality but alienated by formal religious structures. At least as they have been presented, the hidden gospels have become so popular because they appear to speak to so many contemporary concerns, religious and secular.

Institutions

Much recent writing assumes that newly discovered sources such as *Thomas* have fundamentally changed our knowledge of Christian origins, but as we have noted, this is not the case, since most of the materials required for a radical revision of the apostolic age have been available for a century or so. Around 1910, scholars already knew a good deal about Q, *Thomas*, and assorted Gnostic sources; they were at least familiar with the idea that heretics might have preserved authentic relics of the earliest Christian belief, whether or not they accepted this perspective. To take just one example, the venerated and widely read scholar Adolf von Harnack was already asking many of the critical questions.

Yet with all these building blocks at hand, most of the truly subversive approaches to early Christianity had nothing like the impact that they would in later years, at least among respectable scholars and church leaders. Ideas that were known, but not fully explored, involved issues such as the absence of key doctrines in Q, the idea that Jesus might have been valued for his sayings and teachings rather than his supernatural status, the evidence for women's leadership in the early church, and in summary, the sense that Gnostic texts might be portraying early Christianity just as accurately as the canonical gospels. Though all these approaches were known to some extent at the start of the twentieth century, they were more commonly found on the esoteric fringe, at least in the English-speaking world. The ideas lacked the institutional bases which they would acquire at the end of the century, when they would be freely discussed in major universities and presented by solid journals and respectable presses.

The process of institutionalization is complex. Ideas can exist in isolation, held by a few individuals, but they can make a significant social impact only when they achieve wide distribution through books and news media, whatever the media technologies are in a given period. This is most likely to occur when the ideas in question acquire institutional roots, when they are appropriated by particular interest groups or movements. Once ideas have found a home, so to speak, they will be discussed and developed; when publishers know that there is a guaranteed market for related works, these will be widely presented, so that ideas become self-perpetuating and self-sustaining. We can see this process in action in the nineteenth century, with the massive development of critical Biblical studies: though individual scholars had held such radical views before that point, the amazing upsurge of work from the 1820s onward became possible only when new types of research acquired an institutional home in German universities such as Tübingen and Jena. Likewise, it was in the second half of the twentieth century that the study of alternative Christianities in North America progressed from being the preserve of quirky occultists to providing a principal focus for academic research, and became thoroughly mainstreamed. The crank views of one generation can become the commonplaces of the next, and vice versa; or as Presbyterian feminist Mary Ann Lundy has aptly observed, in a religious context, "yesterday's heresies are becoming tomorrow's Book of Order."[2]

Professors

Changing attitudes about the history of Christian origins partly reflect developments in higher education, as the study of the New Testament became at once more widespread and more secular in tone. In contrast to the contemporary situation, the academic world was considerably smaller a century ago, and serious study of the Bible was generally confined to quite conservative departments in universities and seminaries. Historically, much of the academic work on religion and religious texts shared common origins and assumptions with the well-established fields of Classics and what used to be called Orientalism, before that term fell into disgrace. Scholarship involved the intricate study of the documents and scriptures of particular religions, paying scrupulous attention to philological detail. As academics were reluctant to make overambitious claims about the significance of their materials, the professional ethos was hostile to popularization for a general public. Some important scholars did indeed write for general magazines, including potent names such as J. Rendel Harris and Edgar Goodspeed, but they were in a minority. Most attempts at popular writing tended to be done outside academe, and if there was an institutional framework for radical Jesus research, it was chiefly found in occult bodies such as the Theosophical Society and its offshoots. It would have been professional suicide for an academic scholar to venture too far into this mystical underworld, although the occultists may have been more correct in their conclusions than many could have suspected at the time.

What changed in the mid-twentieth century was not that new ideas became possible, but that they acquired a quite different institutional basis, chiefly in the secular universities. Prior to the 1960s, critical Bible scholarship in the United States was dominated by a few major universities and seminaries, such as Harvard, Chicago, Yale, Princeton, and Union Theological Seminary; Biblical matters were also taught in many smaller and less prestigious institutions, but scholars here made nothing like a comparable mark on the field. Over the next two decades, the broad field of religious studies expanded dramatically, particularly in state schools, and largely as a response to the growing interest in spirituality and comparative religion. The change is reflected in the development of the National Association of Biblical Instructors, which historically represented the teachers in smaller schools. In 1964, a new professional self-confidence encouraged this organization to reorganize as the American Academy of Religion (AAR).[3]

Religious Studies has since become a thriving branch of the academic profession. Today, over half of all colleges and universities that offer a B.A. degree or higher have some program in religious or theological studies: such programs exist in over 1200 institutions, some of which have very large operations, and that is in addition to over 270 seminaries. Over a third of all public colleges and universities have a program in religion or theology, as do 60 percent of all private colleges offering a B.A. or higher.[4] The same years witnessed a rapid growth in the number of doctorates in religious studies and Biblical scholarship. Today, some 7000 or 8000 participants attend the annual "religion meetings," the joint convention of the AAR and the Society of Biblical Literature. Put simply, there are vastly more scholars undertaking research and writing, and publishing ever more books and articles in response to the professional demands set forward by their institutions. More scholars need more topics to work on, and they are apparently finding them with little difficulty. The swelling number of graduate and undergraduate students provides a whole new market for scholarly work in religion.

As well as expanding, the religious studies field has developed emphases beyond those of the older, strictly textual-based scholarship. Contemporary radicals such as Robert Funk suggest that a major paradigm shift occurred as Biblical research moved from denominational-run institutions—the "God schools"—into secular universities, with the implication that only now were scholars able to liberate themselves from the shackles of ecclesiastical control. Funk offers a somewhat distorted history of American Biblical scholarship, a tradition which, according to him, "retreated into the closet" following controversies such as the Scopes trial and the associated debate over evolution: "The fundamentalist mentality generated a climate of inquisition that made honest scholarly judgments dangerous. Numerous biblical scholars were subjected to heresy trials and suffered the loss of academic posts. They learned it was safer to keep their critical judgments private." "It was not until the middle of the twentieth century that biblical scholars began to exit ecclesiastical precincts—church colleges and seminaries—in large numbers and to stake out homes in secular institutions."[5] Only then, for the first time in two millennia, could scholars pursue their research free of religious constraints.

This statement represents a caricature, which takes no account of the long tradition of incisive and independent-minded Bible research in both Europe and North America. Read in the context of a history of nineteenth- and twentieth-century Biblical scholarship, such as the celebrated work of Bishop Stephen Neill, these comments appear farcically inaccurate.[6] Still, it is true that the study of the Bible was changed substantially by the shift to the state universities. As a humanities discipline, religious studies came to be closely involved with the concerns of other academics in fields such as literature and history. Among other things, this meant a growing interest in the characteristic approaches of postmodern thought, including an interest in rhetoric and narrative, of questions of authorship and authority. It also implied grave skepticism about canons and orthodoxies, religious or secular. A commitment to interdisciplinary approaches is suggested by the extensive borrowings from anthropological theory in recent research on Jesus and his age, such as Crossan's influential interpretation of Jesus as a member of a Mediterranean peasant society.[7]

Current religious studies scholarship devotes much attention to the role of women, a trend that clearly reflects the growing role of women in the academic profession. With a few important exceptions, before the mid-twentieth century, it was not academics but activists who stressed women's role in early Christianity, and this is not difficult to comprehend given the thorough exclusion of women from academic positions in those years. Even in socially advanced Germany, no woman received a doctorate in theology or Biblical studies until 1906. Given the late acceptance of women in university departments, and the opposition they often encountered, it is only natural that when a wave of women scholars did arrive, they should have been particularly drawn to the study of struggling and excluded women in history, and the noncanonical aspects of religion. Germany's first female doctor of theology was Carola Barth, who chose as her dissertation topic the appropriately fringe subject of Valentinian Gnosticism.[8]

In the 1960s there was a massive expansion of women's representation in universities through Europe and North America, as both students and professors, and this had a dramatic effect on the topics and methods of academic study. Though this has been a general trend in the humanities disciplines overall, it was particularly marked in the religious studies field. Nationally, women today make up over a third of doctoral candidates pursuing degrees in religion and theological studies. By the mid-1990s, women represented 40 percent of new academic hires in these fields, if we combine figures from universities, colleges, and seminaries. Of the individuals elected annually as president of the AAR, only three of the twenty-six incumbents chosen between 1964 and 1989 were women, a tiny proportion; but women served in six of the ten years from 1990 through 1999. The change is particularly marked at some of the leading seminaries. At Union Theological Seminary, the current faculty includes a female majority, fourteen out of twenty-seven professors; at the Episcopal Divinity School in Cambridge, the figure is nine out of sixteen; at Harvard Divinity School, women comprise a third of the faculty, thirteen out of thirty-nine. Women's impact across the board is immediately apparent from the course schedules and the specialties of the individual professors. At the Episcopal Divinity School, Gale Yee is listed as "Interim Director of Studies in Feminist Liberation Theologies; Visiting Associate Professor of Hebrew Bible and Women's Studies." Another faculty member here, Carter Heyward, uses her web page to describe her core assumptions, which she describes as "feminist liberation theology, and it is also Anglicanism at its best."[9]

By no means all female academics in such units work on topics directly related to women's relationship to religion and spirituality, but many do. As a result, any sect or movement in which women have played a significant role is likely to be the subject of numerous books, articles, and dissertations, most of which have appeared just in the last fifteen or twenty years. Courses in "women and religion" flourish both in religious studies departments and in the women's studies programs which often grew up alongside them. In 1984, Immaculate Heart College Center in Los Angeles inaugurated an influential master's program in feminist spirituality, the first of its kind in the United States, and a model for other ventures. One side-effect of all this is to create a large textbook market for solid academic studies that address women's issues in religion, generally from a committed feminist standpoint.[10] Obviously, not all religious studies academics are postmodern firebrands, and a sizable number pursue research that is very conservative, in terms of both intellectual methodology and the individual's personal attitude to religion. Also, many of the most radical scholars in the field are male; for example, women make up only a tiny fraction of the Jesus Seminar. Nevertheless, disciplinary changes have created a sizable profession, substantial sections of which have a powerful interest in any religious tradition which can be seen as countercultural, noncanonical, and subversive, above all when women occupied a prominent role in its development.

Most academics welcome the expansion of perspectives in recent years, but in some ways greater breadth has been accompanied by less depth, by a diminishing sense of the contributions made by scholars of the past, and this change helps explain the misleading emphases in the current study of the hidden gospels. Traditionally, Bible scholars were acutely aware of working in a tradition that has developed organically over several centuries, and they felt an obligation to show how an argument relates to the countless thousands of books and articles which have appeared over the years: a work has merit insofar as it works within that great tradition, and yet builds something new upon it. For multiple reasons, however, contemporary scholars tend to be less deferential to the insights of the past. Many see their work as belonging to the realm of social science, in which little useful is to be found in works published more than a few years ago. At the same time, radical and feminist academics often presume that older generations of scholars were so hidebound in their patriarchal and clerical prejudices that little of value is to be found in such works, which in practice means most scholarship from before the 1960s. The less older works are cited, the more the assumption that they have nothing to say is confirmed, and the less need there is to consult them. As we have witnessed, the overall result is the tendency to believe that all the worthwhile research on heresies and alternative Christianities has been done within the last thirty years or so, and that only very recently have we been freed from the intellectual shackles of past generations.

The changing nature of the academic profession makes it clear why the Nag Hammadi texts and related materials should have inspired so much interest among professors and doctoral students, who approach these works with questions and concerns quite different from those of an earlier generation. It is equally apparent why those academics should so enthusiastically proclaim the importance of those texts, and become so committed to their supposed revelations. According to the traditions of the field, people work in extreme detail on a narrow body of material, which requires a long-term, if not lifelong, commitment: it would be quite possible to devote decades of one's life to elucidating just one of the Nag Hammadi texts.[11] This commitment might extend over generations, in that a successful and active scholar attracts graduate students to work with him or her, on topics growing directly out of that person's areas of interest. Particularly in Biblical studies, a field that strongly recalls its Continental European roots, there is a powerful tradition of the "doctor-father," the mentor who not only teaches graduate students but also exercises a benevolent guidance over their subsequent careers. In consequence, a fascination with a particular type of text or methodology is inherited by intellectual successors, who carry this interest with them to other institutions, where they influence their own students in turn. The concept of apostolic succession is not confined to ecclesiastical circles alone.

No scholar will undertake such a lengthy project on a particular book or document without a powerful idea that the text is of considerable importance, that it is eminently worth studying, and one is therefore likely to make the most ambitious claims possible about the document's importance. It is unthinkable that someone who has spent twenty years studying, say, *Thomas* would write that the work is basically irrelevant to our understanding of early Christianity or ancient religion, and that it should interest nobody other than specialists. There is a natural tendency to advocate one's own particular text as being extremely early, independent, and significant, though the high critical standards of the field provide some limitations on the assertions that can be made. The tendency of individual scholars to focus so intensely on a particular type of literature also means that virtually all the scholarship on those particular texts is undertaken by people who have a vested interest in making them appear as important as possible. To take the literature on *Thomas*, none of the recent wave of books has been written by a scholar who believes that the document is late or derivative, because such skeptics, who abound, probably would not be bothering to specialize in that field. To use an analogy from another and far less reputable field of religious study, people do not generally become experts on the Shroud of Turin without a solid presumption that this supposed relic is genuine; it is scarcely worthwhile becoming an expert on something one believes to be insignificant.

Highly critical, skeptical traditions are particularly marked in some of the more prestigious schools, which have become the centers for the Jesus Quest, and for advocacy of the hidden gospels. The localized quality of such work is evident by observing the Jesus Seminar, which the media all too often present as the organized voice of cutting-edge New Testament scholarship. In fact, this portrayal is misleading, since the group never claims to have involved more than 200 scholars, and the number of active participants is usually far less, around twenty or thirty. This is minuscule compared with the several thousand members of the mainstream Society of Biblical Literature, or the more internationally oriented Society for New Testament Studies. Moreover, the Seminar's core group is strongly identified with a handful of institutions, to the total exclusion of many other major universities and seminaries in which important (though less instantly newsworthy) work is being done.[12]

Of the seventy-six scholars listed as active in the Jesus Seminar in 1993, about a third had some affiliation with just two units, namely, Harvard Divinity School, and the religion department at Claremont Graduate School.[13] Claremont alone accounted for fourteen of the doctorates of the Seminar's fellows, including several names that we have already encountered here, such as Marvin W. Meyer, Robert J. Miller, and Stephen Patterson. Karen Jo Torjesen serves as that department's cochair, and Burton Mack taught here. Claremont provides a useful example of how traditions become established in a particular university. The key founder of this unit was James M. Robinson, who from the 1950s onward was a critical figure in bringing to North America the latest Continental thought about the quest for the historical Jesus. He has been described as "the pivotal figure of avant-garde German New Testament studies in America." An article which he published in 1964 remains central to subsequent efforts to reinterpret Q as a collection of Wisdom sayings, and in 1981, he founded the International Q Project. Robinson was also the senior editor for the project that from 1966 undertook the translation of the whole Nag Hammadi library into English. Naturally enough, the Nag Hammadi enterprise attracted a distinguished corps of graduate students, who in turn reinforced and developed the interest in the noncanonical texts. Claremont also became a center of feminist thought in religion. Torjesen began a master's program in women's studies in religion in 1990, and a doctoral program was added in 1998. [14]

A similar story emerges at Harvard Divinity School. The Harvard faculty is both diverse and distinguished, but within this group too we find several exponents of the more radical theories of Jesus research and the development of the gospels, including Helmut Koester, Elisabeth Schüssler Fiorenza, and Karen King. Koester is one of the leading advocates of the independence and authoritative status of the Gospel of *Thomas*, and, like Robinson, he took the important step of urging his pupils to learn Coptic in order to study texts like those from Nag Hammadi. In 1971, Robinson and Koester cowrote the very influential book *Trajectories through Early Christianity*, which had a profound influence on a generation of New Testament scholarship.[15] Both men did much to popularize in North America the ideas of Walter Bauer, whose classic statement about the relationship between early Christian orthodoxy and heresy had appeared in the 1930s. Koester's many doctoral students include Elaine Pagels.

The Churches

Much like the universities, the mainstream churches have become another institutional base for current theorizing about Christian origins, as well as a market for books and media presentations. Two trends are at work here. One is a massively greater openness by the mainline organizations to liberal and skeptical theology; the other is the quite revolutionary impact of women within the churches.

Skepticism as such is by no means new to church life; there never was a golden age of faith when all believers monolithically accepted the creeds and canons. At least since the eighteenth century, liberals in mainline Protestant churches have been restive about historic doctrines like the Trinity, the infallibility of scripture, the incarnation of Christ, and the Resurrection, and in each case, debates revolved around the authority of the scriptures.[16] For some, the pressures grew too great to remain within church orthodoxy, while others adapted to a situation in which they assented to the creeds with inward reservations. New scientific insights also made their impact, raising doubts about even more aspects of "Bible truth," and new psychological approaches made suspect the whole theological world-view based on sin, guilt, grace, and vicarious sacrifice. For feminist theologians, the notion of the father demanding the blood sacrifice of his son for the sins of the world was an apotheosis of child abuse.

By the late twentieth century, skeptical views were all the more commonplace among clergy and seminarians themselves, as the church organizations usually had neither the will nor the legal ability to penalize unorthodoxy. Though he is an extreme example, Episcopal bishop John Spong has published a series of best-selling books which basically deny every supernatural aspect of the Christian world-view, including the incarnation, the virgin birth, and the Resurrection, and challenge large sections of Christian moral teaching about sexuality. He also proposes that such doctrinal revision should provide the basis for a new reformation: to quote one of his titles, he argues "why Christianity must change or die." Not surprisingly, he is a lauded speaker at events organized by the Westar Institute, the parent organization of the Jesus Seminar.[17] If a bishop could say so many outrageous things with impunity, there seemed to be no remaining frontier, whether legal, moral, or intellectual, to mark where the faithful should not stray.

An atmosphere of thoroughgoing laissez-faire was reflected in the activities of the many small groups that exist within churches for prayer, scripture reading, and discussion. Though such groups have existed for decades, they have gained importance in recent years because of the increasing self-confidence of the laity in major denominations. Researchers such as Robert Wuthnow argue that small groups should properly be seen as the organizational core of religious activity in many churches. From the 1980s onward, such groups were often discussing quite radical ideas about theology and Christology, and providing a flourishing market for books on these subjects. Based on the impressionistic evidence of conversations with those attending conferences and events organized by the Jesus Seminar, a large part of the lay audience seems to be composed of members of liberal mainline churches, particularly Methodist, Presbyterian, United Church of Christ, and Unitarian Universalist, whose interests in new scholarly insights grow directly out of long-standing involvement in the activities of church discussion groups.[18]

Small group discussions have also been fostered by new media technologies, which transmit lectures or conferences into a church or discussion room, where they can then be debated for several successive meetings. In 1994, for example, New York's Trinity Church sponsored a conference, "The Jesus Summit: The Historical Jesus and Contemporary Faith," which was broadcast via the Episcopal Cathedral Teleconferencing Network (ECTN), and the program was subsequently distributed in video form. The summit took place at San Francisco's Grace Cathedral, with Karen King as moderator, and a panel made up of Borg, Crossan, and Mack. Clearly, non-traditional approaches to Bible scholarship were very well represented. An even more widely distributed example of this phenomenon was the 1996 conference sponsored by the Trinity Institute on "Jesus at 2000": the event was held in Corvallis, Oregon, and made available through satellite downlink via ECTN, which broadcast live to over 300 sites nationwide. Presenters included Borg, Crossan, and Torjesen.[19] More recently, ECTN organizes webcasts through the Internet, making critical scholarly views more generally available than ever before.

Issues of canon and Biblical authority are weighty enough in their own right, but they also have critical implications for doctrinal and moral debates. Since the 1980s, all the mainline Protestant churches have been riven by controversies involving homosexuality, whether homosexual individuals could be ordained to the ministry or priesthood, or whether the churches could bless same-sex unions. On both matters, strong liberal constituencies exist in most major churches, and are very well represented in seminaries and the academic world. Bishop Spong, for example, is a vociferous campaigner for gay ordination.[20] One reason this whole area is so contentious is that the Bible contains a number of passages that appear to condemn homosexual conduct in the strongest possible terms; since such passages are found in the Pauline letters, it is not possible to argue simply that they represent older Jewish principles that had been superseded under the Christian dispensation. Granting any degree of approval to homosexuality thus involves a direct contradiction of the scriptural text, or at least an assertion that Biblical injunctions were valid only for the particular society in which they were proclaimed. The battle-fields of ecclesiastical controversy have shifted to matters in which it is increasingly difficult to reconcile a liberal stance with any dependence on Biblical authority, where it contradicts the assumptions of contemporary culture. This trend inevitably creates sympathy for critical studies of the New Testament that challenge older assumptions about the authority of that text, and even seek to restructure the canon.

Seekers

The collapse of doctrinal boundaries was one component of still more far-reaching religious trends. Though most mainline churches reported dramatic declines in their membership from the 1960s onward, popular interest in religion continued unchecked. This enthusiasm was reflected in the growth of evangelical churches, but there also developed a large population of "seekers," people interested in religious matters, but reluctant to commit to formal church organizations. (This category is distinct from the liberals within the mainline churches, usually a much older population.) The interests and enthusiasms of the seeker group go far toward explaining the marketing of materials about the hidden gospels.[21]

Seekers are at best cool toward clerical structures and creeds and toward denominational labels. They practice a cafeteria approach, which appropriates beliefs and symbols with little regard to the traditions from which they originate, provided that they seem suitable for the individual doing the selection, and are useful in the continuing struggles of daily life. This is the eclectic approach that has been termed "flexodoxy." The new spirituality is heavily influenced by psychology and therapy movements as well as by many of the New Age ideas that surfaced, or rather resurfaced, in the 1960s. In turn, recovery movements increasingly acquire many of the features which would once have denoted a religious sect, so that the boundaries between religion and therapy become ever more porous. Usually, eclectic individuals draw a sharp distinction between spirituality (good) and religion (outdated and repressive). Focus group studies indicate that people in their twenties and thirties associate religion with negative terms such as exclusive, doctrinal, judgmental, and confining, while spirituality conjures up far more positive associations, such as "inclusive," "creative," "engaging." This religious/spiritual division is reflected in a popular interest in Jesus as spiritual teacher, though not in any of the institutional forms of the Christian religion. Crossan summarizes this facet of American thought neatly when he writes, "There is out there, for twentieth century Christianity, those I call the Jesus-likers—a phenomenon akin to that of the God-fearers for first-century Judaism."[22] By the 1990s, the seeking population was swelling as the baby-boom generation approached middle age, and asked ever more questions about ultimate meaning.

The seeker phenomenon, which crosses faith boundaries, is reflected in the outpouring of books on religious themes, both scholarly and inspirational. Some of the most popular depict a middle-aged individual rediscovering faith after many years of thoroughly secular life, and usually in a tone of amazement that someone of this generation could possibly find his or her way back to organized religion. This was the theme of works such as Nora Gallagher's *Things Seen and Unseen*, Winifred Gallagher's *Working on God*, Gary Dorsey's *Congregation*, and the works of Frederica Mathewes-Green on Eastern Orthodoxy. Appealing to a similar general market were the very popular works of Kathleen Norris, like *The Cloister Walk* and *Amazing Grace*, which presented the Christian monastic tradition in a fresh and sympathetic manner. Similar interests are reflected by the popular success of television presentations which deal with serious scholarly matters in accessible form: apart from the PBS series *From Jesus to Christ*, the same network also produced Bill Moyers's widely seen series on Genesis. In music, the striking success of albums of Benedictine chant was commonly reported in the media as a manifestation of a new interest in spirituality; also popular were the lyrics and settings taken from the medieval mystic Hildegard of Bingen.[23]

Much of the seeking activity occurred beyond the margins of the churches and, as at the beginning of the twentieth century, involved esoteric and New Age groups who are deeply interested in the figure of Jesus, though conceived in Gnostic mode. Now as then, the Jesus of this movement was seen in syncretistic terms, someone who could equally well speak for Buddhism or Hinduism as for any form of Christianity. Largely ignored by most writers on Christian trends, the New Age Jesus continues to flourish, and to stimulate countless books from presses both major and marginal. One of the best-known of such efforts was Jacob Needleman's study, which bore the evocative title *Lost Christianity*. Esoteric adherents have access to their own distinctive verse-by-verse New Age commentary on *Thomas*, complete with appropriate mystical "affirmations" and mediations throughout, while the implications of the Gnostic discoveries were discussed at length in New Age periodicals. Also immensely popular has been the book *A Course in Miracles*, and the vast literature it has spawned since its first appearance in 1975. The *Course* claims to be a series of revelations dictated by Jesus himself through a channeling process. The book shares the fundamental Gnostic principle that the material world is the product of false perception, of error and delusion, from which one can be saved through a relationship with Jesus as "elder brother," rather than unique redeemer. Also Gnostic is the rejection of the value of the crucifixion, and the absolute emphasis upon the Resurrection. Many of the familiar narrative elements we have noted earlier also occur in the New Age tract known as the *Celestine Prophecy*, although this does not adopt the "hidden gospel" format. Nevertheless, this is supposedly an ancient Peruvian tract written in Jesus' own language of Aramaic, and again, the document has been brought to light despite the plots and machinations of the Roman Catholic Church.[24]

One aspect of the quest for an acceptable Jesus involved a rediscovery of Celtic Christianity, which has provided the theme for hundreds of books in the last ten or twenty years: Celtic texts, saints' lives, prayers, and blessings are all widely available. According to the common perception, the church which flourished in the Celtic areas of the British Isles between about 400 and 1100 was crucially different from the religious bodies that dominated contemporary Europe, because the Celts somehow retained ideas and practices inherited from earliest Christianity. In popular accounts, the Celtic church exemplified all the most attractive features of the Gnostics, from whom they might have received a spiritual inheritance; other enthusiasts traced Celtic roots to Druids and, of course, Essenes. (A good case can be made that the medieval Irish church knew and used a large number of noncanonical Bible texts, though nothing as early or wildly unorthodox as the sort of gospels which would emerge from Nag Hammadi.)[25]

According to their admirers, the Celts practiced a pure, non-Roman Christianity. They venerated nature; they taught a religion based on love and free inquiry rather than fear and judgment; they practiced varieties of pantheistic mysticism, and perhaps taught reincarnation and shamanism; and their church gave a high role to women. The Celtic church reputedly had many points of contact with Eastern religions such as Buddhism, and its mystical tradition perhaps contributed to the linked mythologies of King Arthur and the Holy Grail, which have so long fascinated esoteric believers. To use the loaded title of one book, this is a story of *The Celtic Alternative: The Christianity We Lost*. It is a sign of how favorably the tradition is viewed that it is commonly termed "Celtic spirituality" rather than using the embarrassing words "Christianity" or "church." As in the case of the Gnostics, this is a highly romanticized account, which vastly exaggerates the differences between the ideas and beliefs of Celtic and Roman Christians.[26] Nevertheless, the Celtic fad, which reached new heights in the 1990s, further popularized the idea that a true alternative Christianity with strong New Age components was out there waiting to be discovered, and that this idealized faith might possess some kind of apostolic succession from the Gnostics.

Spiritual seeking is reflected, and further stimulated, by the abundance of religious-related materials on the Internet, which encourages a privatization of intellectual life. Both *Thomas* and the Nag Hammadi texts have a substantial presence on the Net, and Stevan Davies runs a "Gospel of Thomas Homepage" with an impressive array of scholarly and devotional materials. A catena of sites forms the Gnostic Ring, which refers the surfer to various discussion circles, magazines, and independent churches. A typical site is Nazarene Nirvana, which "explores the links between pre-Nicene Christianity and eastern spiritual traditions." (Even neo-Catharism has its own website.) The entire texts of the Nag Hammadi collection are available through the "Gnostic Society Library." Needless to say, advocates of ancient Celtic spirituality are also thoroughly at home with this modern technology. There are "virtual sanctuaries" and sites dedicated to Celtic prayer, not to mention whole Celtic church denominations that exist entirely on line.[27]

Unlike the early twentieth century, there is no hard and fast boundary between what was once dismissively called the "Jesus of the cults" and the figure imagined by many within the mainline churches. Though New Age movements attract only a tiny number of formal members, their general ideas have gained a wide influence, including many both within the churches and in the larger penumbra of the seeker population. Among ordinary believers, surveys repeatedly find that startlingly high proportions of Christians accept New Age ideas. According to Wendy Kaminer, anywhere between a quarter and a half of self-described Protestants and Catholics believe in extrasensory perception, psychic healing, UFOs, and astrology, while smaller numbers are sympathetic to ideas of reincarnation and channeling. The influence of New Age ideas is shown by the wide readership attracted by the writings of Matthew Fox, whose ideas on creation spirituality developed during his career as a Roman Catholic monk, and were subsequently continued within the framework of the Episcopal Church. Fox draws heavily on the medieval Catholic mystics, including Hildegard, but also shares a great deal with feminist spirituality and radical ecology. His "Cosmic Christ" represents a mystical and pantheistic concept instantly intelligible to New Age believers: in 1994, he celebrated his Planetary Mass at San Francisco's Grace Cathedral, an event pervaded by New Age and Buddhist concepts.[28]

The shifting boundaries between fringe and mainstream can be observed in the physical setting of a progressive church such as Grace Cathedral or the Cathedral of St. John the Divine in New York, both of which explicitly invite seekers. Visitors to Grace are told that the cathedral is for "pilgrims of the spirit . . . people who are willing to allow their drifting to be transformed into pilgrimage." On entering the church, the eye is immediately caught by the great labyrinth spread out on the floor, which visitors are encouraged to walk as a spiritual exercise: informational materials nearby explain the origins of the labyrinth, which are traced back through ancient Crete, traditional Celtic society, and Qabalistic Judaism. In the cathedral's brochure, Grace's bishop promises that, "in this space, you can walk the labyrinth of life to the tune of the Spirit which you uniquely hear. Immunity from religious control is granted you upon entry." While it would be easy to dismiss a phenomenon of this sort as a fluke, a manifestation of an unusually avant-garde church in a city noted for its experimental outlook, the labyrinth has in recent years become a popular form of spirituality nationwide. Indeed, Grace Cathedral's website permits the curious to locate other labyrinths in their own neighborhoods. Soon after Grace laid out its own labyrinth in 1991, another was established at Trinity Cathedral in Sacramento: this example features interfaith symbols, including a Celtic cross, a (Hindu) Om symbol, a Buddha, and a Chinese Kwan Yin. Labyrinth programs are held in churches and retreat centers of many denominations. These events commonly feature meditation programs and activities described as dream-quests, based on texts drawn from mystical writers such as Hildegard. Such programs commonly employ Hildegard's concept of *veriditas*, or "green-ness," the springlike spirit of divine life pervading the creation.[29]

Seekers and the Hidden Gospels

In such an intellectual environment, new discoveries about extra-canonical gospels seem liberating, as many seekers find their guid-ing texts in the purportedly scholarly reconstructions of a gender-neutral New Age–oriented early Church. The hidden gospels sug-gested how very early communities could have regarded them-selves as faithful followers of Jesus without the need to accept the complex and sometimes troubling theological doctrines that received dogmatic form in the Nicene Creed. The Q gospel appeared to bring to light a period in which Jesus was venerated for his teachings rather than his divine nature. Those reluctant to believe that Jesus experienced a literal bodily resurrection can take great comfort in the apparent fact that many early Christians likewise saw the resurrection event in symbolic and spiritual terms, and laid no emphasis on the atonement. Seeing Q rather than Mark as the primary gospel also avoids other problems: "the passion story is too bloody for late twentieth-century sensibilities, and it also raises issues of anti-Semitism."[30]

Rediscovering the Gnostics focused attention on a movement that viewed Christ as a complex psychological reality, rather than a supernatural Savior. This made eminent sense in a culture influ-enced by Jungian thought, and dubious about attempts to seek objective certainty. For Pagels, the salvation that is the Gnostic's ultimate goal can be expressed in terms such as self-knowledge, balance, inner reconciliation: the "kingdom" is not a supernatural realm but a state of transformed consciousness. Writing of the Valentinians, Rosemary Radford Ruether comments that "the lan-guage of these other texts is more mythical, that is, closer to con-crete human experiences of relationality, as opposed to the severely abstracted style of the orthodox creed."[31] Gnostic Chris-tianity seemed to preach to the right brain. In the Gnostics, like the Celts, modern-day seekers saw their reflection, or at least the more hopeful believed that they did.

Recent books on the Jesus Quest have been directly aimed at the potential audience of Jesus-likers, seekers who are interested in religious matters, and specifically in Christianity, but who are repelled by anything seen as dogma. Bishop Spong enthused that Funk's highly skeptical *Honest to Jesus* would "excite, encourage and give hope to countless millions who are drawn to Jesus but who are repelled by the theological structures of the past which have captured Jesus"; in contrast, "traditional, uncritical believers" will feel threatened. Marcus Borg argues that scholarship aimed at discovering the historical Jesus "contributes to a vision of the Christian life that is more persuasive and compelling than the vision of Christian with which they grew up." His work seeks to move "beyond dogmatic religion to a more authentic contemporary faith."[32]

Other scholars are much more confrontational in extracting antisupernatural and antireligious meanings from the hidden gospels, or at least using them for a frontal attack upon "religion." Based on his Q research, Burton Mack offers a total repudiation of traditional Christianity: "It's over. We've had enough apocalypses. We've had enough martyrs. Christianity has had a two-thousand-year run, and it's over." Equally militant is Robert Funk, who has issued his "21 Theses for a New Reformation," deliberately modeled on the ninety-five historic statements that Martin Luther supposedly nailed to a church door. Funk's version declares that "there is not a personal god out there external to human beings and the material world. . . . It is no longer credible to think of Jesus as divine. . . . The doctrine of the atonement . . . is subrational and sub-ethical. . . . Jesus did not rise from the dead, except perhaps in some metaphorical sense."[33]

Without dogmas, rituals, traditional prayer, or anything resembling the supernatural, Christianity must be reconstructed for a new age. On occasion, Funk's own Jesus Seminar itself attempts to provide the institutional nucleus for such an alternative ultraliberal Christianity, as it tries to attract a mass lay public beyond the closed group of scholars. Faithful followers ("associates") enthusiastically attend frequent national gatherings in addition to local road shows, in which selected experts make presentations in cities across the nation. The passionate commitment apparent in such events has much in common with traditional religious services, though the greatest enthusiasm is aroused by the denunciations of traditional pieties, rather than by their faithful reaffirmation. Attacks on "supernaturalists" receive particularly heartfelt applause, as do scornful references to right-wing religious figures such as Pat Robertson or the Pope. Recently, the group has even developed its own semiserious rituals, as members and associates are initiated into an "Order of David Friedrich Strauss": this is named for the famous nineteenth-century pioneer of radical Jesus scholarship, who wrote the critical *Life* of Jesus, and whose intellectual quest ultimately led him to an absolute rejection of Christian belief.

In understanding such dedicated attacks on traditional Christianity, it is difficult to avoid observing that the scholars in question are often struggling (and perhaps overreacting) against their own fundamentalist backgrounds, and thus have a natural sympathy for the most liberal perspectives. Among the more radical New Testament critics, we often find similar stories: Mack was a minister in the conservative Church of the Nazarene; Spong often writes about his strictly fundamentalist upbringing in the North Carolina of the 1940s and 1950s; Robinson's own background was conservative and evangelical; Crossan is a former Catholic priest. Funk himself had been not only a fundamentalist, but a preacher who led revivals in rural Texas. These personal histories may explain the group's natural preference for a religious style based on seeking, rather than dogmatic authority, and their rejection of a narrowly defined canon of inspired scriptures. This interpretation adds a pointed irony to the Jesus Seminar's warning to scholars, "Beware of finding a Jesus entirely congenial to you," since that is conspicuously what Funk, Mack, Crossan, and the others have been doing.[34]

Memories of fundamentalist backgrounds may also account for the acute sensitivity to claims that the core of Jesus' message was represented by apocalyptic ideas, rather than ethical or mystical teachings. As we have seen, denunciations of the Doomsday Jesus are central to the writings of the Jesus Seminar, and their usefulness in this regard goes far toward explaining the group's powerful predilection for the hidden gospels. Funk argues simply that "All apocalyptic elements should be expunged from the Christian agenda." The reason for this hostility is not hard to find. Doomsday preaching has traditionally been associated with the most conservative evangelical tradition, to the extent that contemporary liberals regard it as embarrassing at best, and perilous at worst, when it justifies the extreme right-wing radicalism of militias and antigovernment groups. Charlotte Allen writes that "The non-eschatological Jesus of the American New Quest is a congenial figure for many American academics who associate eschatology with snakehandling and polyester blends, or who fear that putting apocalyptic sayings into Jesus' mouth supports the political goals of the Christian Coalition."[35] The most strident critics of Christianity blame the apocalyptic tradition for much of the wars and violence carried out in the name of religion through the centuries, the massacres of Jews and political enemies. Such memories and prejudices well equipped iconoclastic New Testament critics to present their views in a way that would appeal to noncommitted seekers and Jesus-likers.

Women and the Churches

Another massive change within the churches over the last quarter-century involves the importance of women within ecclesiastical structures, as gender issues have come to the foreground of debate in most mainline denominations. From the late 1960s, the issue of women's ordination made the churches the setting for intense debate over women's proper role. The debate focused on the nature of Biblical authority, given the explicit prohibitions on women's ministry in some of the Pauline texts. These controversies also raised the historical issue of the nature of ministry, and asked whether the early church had intended the all-male apostolate to represent the gender composition of the clergy for all subsequent ages.

Usually, the more exalted the concept which a denomination held of the office of the priest or minister, the slower it was to ordain women, and the more fiercely debate raged. Conflict was particularly acute in the Lutheran and Episcopal churches, both of which treated the priestly office as particularly sacred. The ordination of women in the Lutheran denominations in 1969 and 1970 set off a firestorm of protest from more conservative groups. In the Episcopal Church, the decisive move came in Philadelphia in 1974, when eleven women were ordained in an irregular proceeding that was technically illegal. But their position was regularized when in 1976 the church made the official decision to ordain: the church acquired its first female bishop, Barbara Harris, in 1989. By the end of the 1970s, women clergy were active in all the major Protestant denominations.[36] The main exception among the Western Christian churches is the Roman Catholic communion, in which a powerful movement for women's ordination has repeatedly met defeat since the 1970s.[37]

The speed with which women clergy have established themselves in the respective denominations is startling, and underlines the revolutionary nature of the change which has occurred in American religious life. Between 1983 and 1996, the number of women who described themselves as "clergy" in the United States increased from 16,000 to 44,000. By the end of the decade, almost 50,000 women were serving as ministers and rabbis in

America, and the proportion of women clergy in particular Protestant denominations varied from 10 to 20 percent of the whole. Women make up one-seventh of Episcopal clergy and one-sixth of the ministers in the Evangelical Lutheran Church of America, while the figure among Unitarian Universalists stands at around one-third. The change has been obvious in the seminaries, which were so long a male preserve. Women today make up about a third of the students nationwide, and constitute an absolute majority in some of the largest and most prestigious institutions. So large a presence has naturally had its impact on the cultural and political tone of the institutions in question, where feminism of all different shades has become an unchallengeable orthodoxy.[38]

The numbers of women clergy have been rising quickly, as ever more women graduate from the seminaries and take positions vacated by an aging generation of male priests and ministers. In 1972, about a thousand women all told were studying for the Master of Divinity degree, which normally leads to ordination; this figure has now grown to around nine thousand, and woman make up 30 percent of prospective holders of the M. Div. degree. Gender parity should be achieved within the present decade. The increase is just as marked in Jewish institutions, as women rabbis have become an ever-more familiar part of the cultural scene. Even in the Roman Catholic Church, women continued to make significant advances, though outside the priesthood. According to a committee established by the U.S. Catholic bishops, women by the late 1990s held almost half of the professional staff positions at diocesan level.[39]

With such a professional transformation under way, it is not surprising that so many writers have drawn supportive images and role models from the gospel texts which have been newly found or publicized, particularly those involving Mary Magdalen. Scholars writing in the field have made no secret of their strong partisan commitment to an expanded role for women's ministry: they avowedly see themselves as activists within a movement, rather than objective commentators. Deirdre Good states that "contemporary readers, lulled by religious authorities into dismissing texts like *Pistis Sophia* as unworthy of attention, can find in the Mary of ancient and venerable texts a female model of spiritual authority and religious power." Susan Haskins, biographer of Mary Magdalen, remarks that her subject "was the first witness to the Resurrection—what's more important than that, in Christianity? She was apostle to the apostles, told by Christ to go tell them he had risen. There should be a role for women to preach and teach today—a role too often denied." Torjesen cites the literary evidence of the *Gospel of Mary* to support her view that women served as bishops and presbyters in the early church, and should hold similar roles in the modern world. Karen King agrees that "the *Gospel of Mary* . . . argued that leadership should be based on spiritual maturity, regardless of whether one is male or female."[40]

Based on such testimonials, Mary Magdalen has become a virtual patron saint of Christian feminism, but a Mary viewed largely through the hidden gospels. To cite the example of San Francisco's Grace Cathedral once more, a chapel contains Robert Lentz's striking icon of Mary Magdalen bearing the inscription "apostle to the apostles, the great apostle, the apostle of the resurrection, and equal to the apostles": the words are written in the ancient language of Syriac, suggesting that the image is intended to restore the truths of the most ancient church. The icon was unveiled on July 22, 1990, the historic feast of St. Mary Magdalen, with the aim of celebrating Barbara Harris's consecration the previous year as the first woman bishop in the Episcopal Church. In 1998, the Catholic pressure group FutureChurch began to make this feast day a national observance in support of advancing women's role within the churches. Activists at parish level were encouraged to "start an annual liturgical celebration of the feast of Mary Magdalen on July 22. Invite a local religious educator to present recent Biblical scholarship about Magdalen (i.e. she wasn't a prostitute, was a preeminent apostolic leader in the infant church etc.)." Within a year, about a hundred lay groups nationwide were involved in this grassroots Magdalen Project.[41]

As women's voices have increasingly been heard within the churches, so sensitivity to women's concerns has grown, and this has been particularly evident in matters of language. In changes that are likely to have enduring effects on all churches, there has been a widespread tendency to adopt gender-neutral language in liturgy and scripture translation, for instance, to replace references to the father, son, and holy spirit with the "Creator, Redeemer, and Sanctifier." Though the impulse driving this reform has nothing to do with ancient heresy, the Gnostics of old would be amused to see their doctrine of divine androgyny finally vindicated by the catholic and orthodox. Feminine-oriented christologies have also revived, often by reviving the tradition of Sophia. In 1984, the Cathedral of St. John the Divine in New York displayed a statue of the crucifixion featuring a female "Christa." When the *National Catholic Reporter* held a competition for an artistic image to represent "Jesus 2000," the winning entry used as its model the face of an African-American woman. Such manifestations naturally stir controversy, which in turn encourages progressives to seek for supportive scriptures and role models. In the Presbyterian Church, for instance, issues such as gender, homosexuality, inclusive language, and the uniqueness of Christian revelation have provoked ongoing guerrilla warfare between conservatives who find their voice in the newspaper *Presbyterian Layman*, and various progressive and feminist groups like the National Network of Presbyterian College Women.[42]

The radical change in the composition of the clergy naturally has an impact on the dissemination of ideas. At the most basic level, women clergy and seminarians are likely to buy books relevant to their concerns, as is anyone, male or female, interested in the quiet revolution in progress within the denominations. In response, mainline publishers not only sell books which employ strongly feminist approaches to religion, but use radical rhetoric in advertising them. In 1991, for instance, Penguin USA published a paperback version of Uta Ranke-Heinemann's *Eunuchs for the Kingdom of Heaven*, an intemperate manifesto which denounced Catholic misogyny. The blurb announced "Exposed! The Centuries-Old Oppression of Women by the Catholic Church," and by way of recommendation, boasted that the book had been condemned by New York's Cardinal O'Connor: the work was touted as "horrifying in its revelations."[43] In addition, publishing houses affiliated to the mainstream churches offer books with a strongly feminist emphasis. One example is the Minneapolis-based firm of Fortress, the official publishing house of the Evangelical Lutheran Church of America, and a prominent name in religious publishing. Among Fortress's titles are works by feminist scholars such as Rosemary Radford Ruether, Luise Schottroff, Carter Heyward, and Karen King.[44] As all are well-respected names, there is nothing surprising about their inclusion on Fortress's list, but it does confirm just how commonplace feminist thought has become within the churches. This is what congregations are now reading. Presumably, a book arguing the long-orthodox view that the ministry should be an all-male preserve would have a very difficult time getting published by such a mainstream house.

New ideas soon find their way to parish level, especially in the small groups noted above, which tend to be disproportionately

female in composition. Particularly in the mainline churches—
Methodist, Episcopalian, Lutheran, and so on—books such as
Pagels's *Gnostic Gospels* or Torjesen's *When Women Were Priests* have
long been mainstays. In addition to regular small group activity,
members of mainline churches are involved in retreats and conferences, which cover the full spectrum of ecclesiastical attitudes
and styles, and many draw on ideas which suggest New Age origins. By such means, feminist religious thought gains influence at
parish level, and so does the willingness to consider innovative or
heterodox approaches to the canon and to noncanonical texts.

These trends are suggested by the monthly calendar published
in the newspaper *Episcopal Life*, a principal organ of the Episcopal
Church, which claims to be read in some 230,000 households.
Each issue offers a dozen or so such events, most of which are
fairly mainstream, including monastic retreats, prayer workshops,
and short courses on liturgy and ministry; virtually all these
events also attract members of other mainline Protestant
churches, as well as Roman Catholics. Some groups focus on Bible
study, but with a strong emphasis on critical scholarship; for
example, in 1999, the Kirkridge Retreat Center in Pennsylvania
played host to a program led by Crossan on "The Birth of Christianity."[45] Usually, a few advertisements each month have what
we might call a radical or New Age approach, of a sort that would
have been very unlikely to appear in the pages of a mainline
church newspaper a generation ago. In a typical entry, a retreat
house in Brewster, New York, offers "Spirit Quest: a spirit-filled
weekend retreat dedicated to a holistic relationship with God,
Mother Earth, self, and one another." During 1999 and 2000, the
Kirkridge Center offered a series of programs, which included
"Celtic Spirituality and the Book of Creation," "Entering the
World of the Heart" (presented by writer on Buddhism, Joanna
Macy), and "The Labyrinth: Traversing a Sacred Path." The North
Carolina–based Stillpoint Ministries also presents programs on
subjects like Celtic spirituality. One 1999 retreat here concerned
"The Women Around Jesus" and addressed "the radicalism of
Jesus in relation to women in a restrictive, patriarchal society."
Another Stillpoint event advertised in *Episcopal Life* and other
mainline papers sounded purely feminist, if not neopagan: this
was "Maiden, Mother, Crone: Three Gates of the Feminine Soul . . .
group sharing, reflection, mask-making, dance meditation, culminating ritual."[46]

Many such events draw heavily on feminist perspectives, and

some are geared entirely to women. An ecumenical retreat for women clergy organized by the New England Women Ministers Association promised that "women will create a labyrinth, learn how to walk the sacred path, and create healing symbols and rituals." The Center for Progressive Christianity organized a forum at St. Mark's Episcopal Cathedral in Seattle, with topics including "liturgical dance, the environment . . . the Chartres labyrinth, alternative spiritualities, mental illness, full inclusion of lesbians and gays." In the Roman Catholic Church, too, such retreats can offer remarkably progressive approaches: in 2000, the diocese of Arlington, Virginia, ordered the suppression of a series on women's spirituality, organized by the radical pressure group the Women's Alliance for Theology, Ethics and Ritual (WATER).[47]

Re-Imaginings

Not only have feminist religious ideas acquired institutional foundations within the churches, but so have quite extreme aspects of women's spirituality. Religious feminism is a very broad category, with many degrees of commitment and radicalism, and some clergy women hold conservative attitudes on issues of liturgy and social policy. As some of the programs mentioned here suggest, however, the more experimental and innovative segments of the feminist spirituality movement seek to expand the boundaries of Christian doctrine very considerably. The activities of some of the most enthusiastic believers demonstrate the interaction of Christian thought with ideas that would once have been considered utterly marginal, and which overlap with neopaganism or the New Age. In the last decade, the acute controversies provoked by these trends confirm how institutionalized radical theological ideas have become—and often, how far activists have ventured into Gnostic thought and language. Once again, the literature on the hidden gospels and the Jesus Quest speaks very directly to contemporary concerns.

Some of the more radical aspects of women's spirituality grew out of the feminist campaigns within the Catholic Church, but also attracted interest from liberal Protestant groups. There were several interlinked pressure groups that originally focused on women's ordination as Catholic priests, but when this was denied, the movement shifted in a more extreme direction: as the Woman Church movement developed in the mid-1980s, it distanced itself increasingly from traditionally Christian concepts. There followed a series of conferences, retreats, and consciousness-raising events held across the country, often under the auspices of Catholic colleges and religious institutions. In 1985, Ruether's book *Women Church* proposed a wholesale reorganization of the institutional church on the model of the base communities pioneered by Latin American liberation theologians. In ideological terms, Christian feminists borrowed freely from neopagan traditions, the Goddess revival movement, and the Gnosticism of the hidden gospels.[48]

The single event that most sharply focused conservative concerns about religious feminism was the Re-Imagining controversy of 1993.[49] Re-Imagining was the title of a conference held in Minneapolis, and sponsored in part by the Presbyterian and Methodist churches. Some 2000 women attended, and scandalized the traditional-minded faithful when they tried to integrate new women-oriented rituals and symbols into the event. The gathering included a feminist Eucharist involving milk and honey, and prayers were offered to Sophia, the patron of the movement: in an invitation to "the banquet table of Creation," the invocation proceeded, "Sophia, we celebrate the nourishment of your milk and honey." Another ceremony declared, "Our maker Sophia, we are women in your image." Though the event was dismissed as pagan Goddess worship, its advocates plausibly claimed roots in current Biblical scholarship. As we have seen, some well-regarded theologians hold that Jesus should be seen rather as "Sophia's child" than Son of God.

The Re-Imagining conference became the basis for a whole movement manifested in several successive gatherings: the movement also sought to perpetuate itself through formal organizations with titles such as Voices of Sophia. At St. Paul, Minnesota, in 1998, the Re-Imagining Revival was "a four-day extravaganza of feminist theology and worship that the organizers called Christian but that most Christians would call horrifying. . . . of course much of traditional Christianity is demeaned. A reference to the Nicene Creed at the conference was met with hoots of derisive laughter. The conference ended with participants biting into large red apples to express their solidarity with Eve. . . . 'To bite the apple is to recommit ourselves to resisting all those forces who oppress us.'" The gesture of the apple has an impeccably Gnostic pedigree: the ancient Ophites took their name from the serpent which had instigated the revolt in Eden.[50]

Such events may seem far beyond the pale of normal activism within even the most liberal churches, but they featured participation by some of the best-respected names in feminist theology, some of whom hold distinguished positions within the major seminaries. These leaders are highly regarded not just on the furthest frontiers of feminist spirituality, but within the liberal mainstream of their respective churches. One Re-Imagining speaker was Mary Ann Lundy, who in consequence of the 1993 event lost her senior administrative position within the Presbyterian Church (USA), but who then became Deputy Director of the World Council of Churches. Other activists in Re-Imagining included Carter Heyward, who teaches at the Episcopal Divinity School, as well as Beverly Harrison and Delores Williams, both Presbyterians, who hold positions at Union Theological Seminary. It was Delores Williams who declared, famously, at the first Re-Imagining, "I don't think we need a theory of the atonement. . . . I don't think we need folks hanging on crosses and blood dripping and weird stuff." In the 1998 event, Carter Heyward announced "While nobody, even Jesus, is divine in and of him or herself, everybody, like Jesus, is able to god, and I use this 'god' as a verb. . . . That is what we are to do . . . to god, and that is what the Jesus story is all about."[51] Like Williams's rejection of the atonement, Heyward's statement immediately indicates why modern liberals would find such a resonance in the works of the ancient Gnostics.

The movement has also had some impact within lay organizations. In 1998, the ecumenical group Church Women United honored five women theologians as "prophetic voices": four of the five spoke at the first Re-Imagining conference.[52] In addition to sensational events such as the original Re-Imagining, the same activists present their messages at ongoing conferences, seminars, and teaching programs. In 1999, the Kanuga conference center in North Carolina organized the program "Jesus—A Feminist/Womanist Perspective," led by Carter Heyward and Delores Williams. The chaplain of the event was Bishop Barbara Harris, and the event was advertised in mainline newspapers including *Episcopal Life*. So was the program which Heyward and Williams organized in 2000 at the Kirkridge Center, on the theme of "Jesus, Power and Sexuality."

Since the first Re-Imagining event in 1993, conservatives have launched fierce criticisms of what they see as the subversion of Christianity by forms of paganism or even witchcraft. While it is misleading to taint all forms of feminist religious thought by the indiscretions of a small wing of the movement, the conservatives are correct in observing that in contemporary liberal Christianity, the boundaries between regular practice and heterodoxy are very porous. In such a climate, the label of heresy not only fails to carry a stigma, it suggests a laudable open-mindedness. It is not difficult to see why so many contemporary religious believers should have such a favorable attitude toward the heresies of old, and a curiosity about their suppressed truths.

8

The Gospels in the Media

Scientists unearth lost scrolls written by Christ!
THE SUN, AUGUST 10, 1999

NEW FINDINGS IN JESUS SCHOLARSHIP have been made widely available through the mass media, which clearly recognize the existence of a profitable general market. The media try to fill the needs of this market by offering ample coverage, which in turn sustains popular interest in what can be quite arcane historical and textual arguments. As a result, the once-hidden gospels have very much been brought into the light of day.

For almost half a century, the media have demonstrated a powerful if undiscriminating hunger for the latest critical claims and theories about the real Jesus and the hidden gospels. They generally accept radical interpretations of Christian origins as the most influential, and indeed as irrefutably correct. In addition to the news media, major publishers demonstrate a consistent taste for controversial and would-be subversive materials, such as those emanating from the Jesus Seminar. A still more extreme taste for the sensational is indicated by the media fascination with books that postulate outrageous conspiracy theories: as we will see, the Dead Sea Scrolls have proved uniquely attractive for such bizarre efforts. The interested lay person is placed in a difficult position, in that even wide and critical reading of books from major presses, and the supposedly responsible news media, can give the impression that quirky academic ideas represent serious trends in scholarship.

The dominance of these eccentric views is quite overwhelming, and it is not surprising that some conservatives posit a deliberate bias against mainstream Christianity, or even against Christianity as such. There is no evidence to support such a claim. If the media err, they do so through misunderstanding rather than malice, and a genuine failure to understand the nature of the scholarly profession: the media have an understandable preference for ideas that appear daring and newsworthy. The consequence, though, is that major publishers and news organizations have become an integral part of a social movement, rather than merely commentators on it. Believers in what I have called the new mythology of Christian origins therefore constantly receive fresh reinforcement for their views.

Jesus in the News

Public interest in the sensational possibilities of archaeological discovery dates back at least to the mid-nineteenth century finds in the Middle East, and enthusiasm reached a new plateau when the Sayings of Jesus were found at Oxyrhynchus in the 1890s. The modern obsession with how this kind of material might affect Christianity dates from the 1950s, when a combination of several distinct stories created widespread expectations about potentially revolutionary new finds. Moreover, these discoveries occurred at a seminal time in the media's coverage of religious issues, when public interest was excited by the churches' role in the American civil rights struggles, as well as the Catholic reform movement symbolized by the second Vatican Council. In response, many news outlets began to hire specialized religion correspondents, and vastly increased the space devoted to religion-related issues.[1]

The best-known archaeological story of the mid-century involved the Dead Sea Scrolls. The Scrolls have made a major contribution to scholarship on Judaism of the Second Temple era, and to the study of the Bible text, but since the earliest days, much of the interest surrounding them focused on the quite different matter of Jesus and his movement. If these texts did indeed date from the first centuries before and after Christ, according to conventional dating, surely they would at least make some mention of these great events? Accordingly, the media in the 1950s and 1960s leaped on every suggestion of a possible linkage to Jesus or to his contemporaries such as John the Baptist. Much of the interest focused on the parallels between the views of the Qumran sect associated with the Scrolls and early Christianity, particularly in their respective concepts of the Messiah. The Scrolls describe their coming Messiah in terms very much like those that Christians would apply to their own Jesus, and in a famous article published in 1955, Edmund Wilson suggested that

Qumran rather than Nazareth should be seen as "the cradle of Christianity." His piece appeared not in a scholarly journal, but in the popular *New Yorker* magazine. The Scrolls were a mainstay in publications such as *Time* and *Newsweek* through the 1950s and early 1960s, and indeed in much of the popular press.[2]

Still more sensational claims stemmed from a member of the scholarly team deputed to reconstruct and translate the Scrolls, namely, the curious figure of John M. Allegro, who was among the first to publish popular accounts of the Scrolls and their implications. Allegro can charitably be described as an eccentric scholar, who from the late 1950s made a series of presentations claiming that the Teacher of Righteousness who founded the Qumran community had been crucified and that his followers awaited his Resurrection, and his second coming in messianic glory (in most cases, the texts cited by Allegro did not exist, at least not in the form he claimed). Statements of this kind had an enormous impact, particularly in Europe, and by 1964, Bishop Stephen Neill commented on a "rather widespread idea that the Scrolls have somehow 'disproved Christianity.'" Suggestions of explosive secrets still to be revealed about Christian origins culminated in 1970 when Allegro published his book, *The Sacred Mushroom and the Cross*, possibly the single most ludicrous book on Jesus scholarship by a qualified academic. The book argues that the New Testament is a coded record of a clandestine cult that used hallucinogenic mushrooms to produce mystical visions: "Jesus" was a cult codeword for "Semen which saves," "Peter" meant "mushroom."[3] Allegro's baneful influence apart, both scholars and the media were bound to explore the Scrolls' implications for both Jewish and Christian origins.

By the end of the 1950s, the public was sensitized to the possibility that exciting or disturbing new finds might appear at any day, which helps explain the intense interest over the translation of the *Gospel of Thomas* in 1959. A popular edition of *Thomas*, presented as *The Secret Sayings of Jesus*, rapidly sold 40,000 copies in the United Kingdom. Other scholarly and popular books rapidly followed. The media treated *Thomas* as a major story, and usually presented the new gospel as just that, a genuine addition to the words of Jesus, a fifth gospel. The liberal *Christian Century* announced the finding of Thomas with the dramatic headline, "New Words of Jesus Found in Egypt," and *Time* reported the "New Sayings of Jesus." Some writers seriously discussed the prospect of including *Thomas* in a revised canon.[4] Also around this time, the media were reporting Morton Smith's remarkable discovery of what was claimed as a hitherto lost fragment of Secret Mark, a finding with remarkable implications for the construction of the gospels. Despite doubts about its authenticity, early reports of the secret gospel created widespread media interest, and Smith reported his find in a conference presentation in late 1960. The news was duly trumpeted by major newspapers and magazines.[5]

Between about 1955 and 1970, the news media were regularly offering headlines about secret gospels, hidden gospels, fifth gospels, new psalms, and so on. This media interest has never entirely died away, though the focus of concern has shifted somewhat over the years. The Scrolls remained good copy through the 1960s and 1970s, and every new theory was dutifully reported in national newspapers and magazines. The usual themes were neatly combined in 1972 when it was claimed that a fragment of the Gospel of Mark had been found among the Scroll collection, indicating yet again a link between the Qumran community, Jesus, and a hidden gospel.[6] Through the 1960s and 1970s, too, few years passed without some media furor about a new find or interpretation about Jesus and his times. Some stories ran sporadically over several years, such as the idea that Jesus might have been married, or otherwise sexually active. The tag here was the work of William E. Phipps, whose book *Was Jesus Married?* appeared in 1971. Also of recurrent interest were theories that Jesus might have been a militant political revolutionary or Zealot, a story that seemed all the more newsworthy during the radical years of the late 1960s and the interest in liberation theology.[7] This series of miscellaneous speculations, each usually based on the writings of only a handful of scholars, demonstrates the enduring perception that the reading public was always hungry for some new tidbit of information about Jesus and his times, especially something sensational—Jesus as husband, guerrilla leader, or sorcerer.

From the late 1970s, the publication of the Nag Hammadi texts shifted attention once more to the revelations these documents might contain about the early church, and especially the pivotal role of *Thomas* as a possible new source. The breakthrough in creating public awareness of the hidden gospels was the publication of Elaine Pagels's *Gnostic Gospels* in 1979. The book attracted respectful attention in all the major news media, but also had a great impact on more popular outlets. Typical of the latter coverage was an enthusiastically uncritical story in *People* magazine, under the dramatic title, " 'Jesus Kissed Mary Magdalen on the Mouth': The Gnostic Gospels Could Rewrite Religious History." Just how explosive such a headline could be is suggested by the international furor detonated some years afterward by the film *The Last Temptation of Christ*, in which it was precisely the suggestions of Christ's sexual relationship with the Magdalen that detonated widespread public protests and even violence. The *People* article was expansive in its claims about the authority of the new documents: "Some scholars believe the [Nag Hammadi] manuscripts included lost gospels of the New Testament. They may have originated in oral form as early as A.D. 50." The documents promised a "demystification of Christ's life," suggested by his sexual relationship with Mary. They were regarded as heretical, but only by "church bureaucrats" such as Irenaeus (in contemporary parlance, "bureaucrat" is a word at least as unattractive as "orthodox").[8]

As in earlier years, interest in the Jesus quest was reflected in popular culture treatments, and particularly novels, all of which ultimately harked back to *When It Was Dark*. Later novels in this tradition include James Hall Roberts's *The Q Document* (1964), which portrays a Nazi forgery conspiracy, while Irving Wallace's spectacularly successful *The Word* (1972) describes a fake gospel concocted by an embittered ex-convict. As interest in *Thomas* burgeoned in the 1980s, so did the fictional genre revolving around rediscovered gospels, genuine or false, and the perplexing world of subterfuge, conspiracy, and assassination in which New Testament scholars appeared to operate. These themes appeared in novels including Larry Witham's *The Negev Project*, Paul Maier's *A Skeleton in God's Closet*, Alan Gold's *The Lost Testament*, and other works imagining the quest for surviving lost gospels. A gospel of Matthias, the thirteenth apostle, features in Wilton Barnhardt's novel *Gospel*, while J. G. Sandom's *Gospel Truths* describes the hunt for a lost text of *Thomas* hidden in Chartres cathedral.[9]

The quest theme reached a mass market with the overheated 1999 movie *Stigmata*, in which a girl who develops the bloody wounds of Christ also scrawls words that prove to be the Aramaic text of "the Jesus Gospel." This fictional gospel reports Jesus' words to his disciples at the Last Supper, and these same words were supposedly contained in a scroll found near the caves of the Dead Sea Scrolls. Though this work is cited as the one authentic gospel, and thus "the most significant Christian relic ever found," all the words quoted are from the familiar *Thomas*. The plot revolves around the efforts of the Roman Catholic hierarchy to suppress this gospel, through murder if necessary, in order to prevent the destruction of the church. An epilogue explains that the real *Gospel of Thomas* was discovered in 1945, but notes that the document was still rejected by the Vatican, even though scholars around the world acknowledge it as the "closest record we have of the words of the historical Jesus."

During the 1980s, publicity about Nag Hammadi merged into renewed coverage of the quest for the historical Jesus, which from 1985 onward found expression in the Jesus Seminar. The Jesus Quest established itself firmly in the media mainstream, and since the late 1980s, most popular magazines have published major features on the supposedly revolutionary implications of the new scholarship for Christian orthodoxies. Remarkably technical articles on the subject have appeared in mainstream periodicals such as *GQ* and the *Atlantic*, apart from the whole spectrum of religious and denominational publications. *Time*, *Newsweek*, and *U.S. News and World Report* have all devoted several major special issues to the New Quest.[10]

Though news coverage has been wide-ranging, it has not been nonpartisan, in that certain critical scholars and their views have been adopted as almost the official position on New Testament issues, although these opinions do not represent the scholarly mainstream. By far the greatest beneficiary of media favor has been the Jesus Seminar group, which has played the public relations game quite wonderfully, marketing its particular interpretations as if they represent a new scholarly orthodoxy, compared with which all more traditional interpretations are dismissed as hidebound or cowardly.[11] Since the mid-1980s, the doings of this group have made regular national news, as the seminar's Fellows met to carry out their celebrated voting procedure to determine the actual words of Jesus. The fact that all but a tiny core of the Lord's Prayer was eliminated as inauthentic was regarded as a sensational story in 1988, and set the stage for other reports in later years. The Seminar's activities were ideally suited for the news media because their meetings occurred on a predictable annual schedule, so that after the first couple of years, the media knew infallibly that it was worth their while to have correspondents in place to observe the proceedings.[12] The controversies engendered by the seminar's claims were at least as valuable for the media in offering interesting stories as the original statements. In effect, the reports of claims and counterclaims constituted a wonderful prepublication campaign for the seminar's edition of *The Five Gospels*, which appeared in 1993, and for their subsequent volumes *The Complete Gospels* (1994) and *The Acts of Jesus* (1998).[13]

The ideological slant of media coverage is suggested by the special coverage which many news outlets regard as a necessity for their Easter and Christmas issues, when it is customary to explore what scholars currently think about some aspect of Christian belief, for example, the reality of the star of Bethlehem. At Easter 1996, the magazine *U.S. News and World Report* published a major feature entitled "In Search of Jesus," which presented contemporary positions on Jesus by means of detailed case studies by several scholars, namely, Robert Funk, Marcus Borg, John Dominic Crossan, John P. Meier, and Luke Timothy Johnson.[14] The first three all belong to the Jesus Seminar; Johnson is a major critic of that group; while Meier's is another conservative voice: he is particularly skeptical about the reliability and usefulness of the non-canonical gospels, including *Thomas*. The article was scrupulously fair to the extent that arguments were summarized accurately, and both sides, radical and conservative, were permitted to present their views in a balanced way. The problem, though, which would not be apparent to the vast majority of readers, is that the choice of experts grossly misstates the state of the field of New Testament scholarship, namely, the ratio of three radicals to two conservatives. The views of Borg, Crossan, and Funk simply do not represent the opinions of 60 percent of academics studying the New Testament, either in the United States or globally; 6 percent might be a better estimate. The same impression emerges when Johnson's conservative but strictly mainstream views are summarized as the voice of "the counter-offensive," suggesting an embattled or minority stance.

The same week, *Time* presented a still lengthier report, 5000 words to *U.S. News*'s 3000. This similarly described the competing views in the form of a balanced debate, between Funk and Crossan, on the one hand, against more conservative critics such as Johnson, N. T. Wright, and Craig Blomberg, on the other. Though the numerical balance of forces was somewhat different, the agenda was still effectively set by the Jesus Seminar, whose workings and conclusions were intricately described. Visually, too, the article conveyed a provocative message through the captions attached to lavish reproductions of Christian art. Under a representation of the crucifixion, we read, " 'Father, into your hands I entrust my spirit' is a revision of a Psalm verse, which the Seminar says shows how freely the Evangelists attributed words from other sources to Jesus"; for a picture of the Last Supper, "The Seminar says Luke's verses are so laden with Christianizing propaganda as to be beyond recovery." The captions are accurate to the extent that the views of the Seminar are accurately reported, but all but the most careful readers are left with the impression that they are reading the considered views of the academic profession. And on the central event of Christian faith, the Resurrection, "Jesus rising from the dead was blackballed by the Seminar, an unsurprising move since liberal scholars have always given that seminal miracle little credence." (This is incorrect: though liberal scholars have often seen the Resurrection in symbolic or spiritual terms, that is quite different from denying it.) The further impression is that there is a crude dichotomy between scholars, who are by definition radical skeptics, and believers, who are naive fundamentalists.[15]

Equally representative of the media's sympathy for the more radical Jesus scholarship was the ambitious series *From Jesus to Christ—The First Christians*, broadcast on American public television in 1998. This was a high-profile series aimed at a general audience, and the show was heralded by coverage and interviews in many popular publications, such as *Salon* magazine. While it included a diversity of expert speakers, the series was heavily weighted toward the interpretations of the Jesus Seminar group: Crossan was among the most visible speakers, partly because he is such an articulate and telegenic personality. Equally telling was the overall structure of the series, which presented the Jesus narrative in the stages in which, according to radical scholars, it is assumed to have developed. The first of four programs, about the life and times of Jesus, said little about his career or teachings except that he was baptized by John, and executed. The second described the career of Paul and the growth of Christian belief, while only in the third program was there significant discussion of the canonical gospels and their account of the teachings of Jesus. This particular unit, moreover, began with the Jewish War, the Fall of Jerusalem, and the siege of Masada, implying that since the gospels postdated these events (roughly, around the year 70) they could serve only as a reliable historical source for the events of the late first century; the texts revealed little about the actual times of Jesus. The very title of the series indicates how "Christ" was a distorted later concept imposed upon a pristine and nonsupernatural original Jesus—roughly, the simple sage we encounter in Q and *Thomas*.

At every point, this series offered an interpretation which subtly reflected the particular historical slant of the Jesus Seminar scholars. In the first program, for example, on Jesus himself, a viewer might have been surprised at the emphasis placed on the archaeological importance of the Hellenistic Galilean city of Sepphoris, which stood near Nazareth, but which is not once mentioned in the New Testament. The significance of Sepphoris, for the uninitiated, is that the presence of such a major Greek city makes it easier to place Jesus in a Greco-Roman context, and ideally to portray him as a sage or Cynic rather than a rabbi, a Wisdom teacher instead of an apocalyptic prophet. Sepphoris is the sort of culture in which Jesus followers might conceivably have produced Wisdom-oriented proto-gospels such as *Thomas*, or the core Q gospel imagined by some critics. The Resurrection was featured not in the program on Jesus, but in the subsequent unit on Paul, on the grounds that such doctrines were evolved by the church, and could have no historical validity. When challenged about the lack of emphasis on a historical Resurrection, the series' chief academic adviser replied that Jesus "arose, and *only generations later* do we start to get that empty tomb scene built. That would be historically inappropriate, in my view, to foist back on the days of Paul, or on the days of Jesus."[16] The word "generations" would suggest a gap of at least sixty years before the evolution of the empty tomb idea, which is at the upper end of what even radical scholars would suggest.

And the pattern continues. Another recent media venture into popularizing Jesus research was *The Search for Jesus*, a prime-time ABC documentary hosted by Peter Jennings in 2000. This inevitably featured "usual suspects" like Borg, Crossan, Funk, and Marvin Meyer. Extreme skeptics did not monopolize the program, as N. T. Wright represented more conservative opinion, but Jesus Seminar scholars predominated throughout. As so often in such efforts, Crossan emerged as the most visible expert, and any casual viewer would likely have concluded that he was in fact the voice of academic orthodoxy, speaking ex cathedra.

Publishers

A similar ideological slant is obvious from the "Jesus books" that achieve the widest distribution and publicity. The huge scale of the Jesus publishing industry today will be apparent to anyone who looks at the packed shelves of the religion section in any major bookstore. Between 1993 and 1998 alone, American sales of books about religion rose by 16 percent, roughly double the overall growth for trade books in the same period. This abundance is scarcely a new phenomenon, as there has probably not been a year in American history in which books on Christianity did not make up the largest portion of the overall output of the nation's publishers, but there are peculiarities about the sort of books that get published today. The most important commercial publishers, who have by far the most extensive distribution networks, have a powerful predilection for the more radical kinds of Jesus research. Many of the best-advertised titles represent the views of a fringe of the academic profession, while the more restrained serious scholarship appears from specialist religious-oriented presses, which make far less impact in the chain bookstores. Evangelical bookstores largely carry evangelical works, Catholic stores sell Catholic books, but secular commercial stores seem dominated by quite radical critical traditions. Responsible mainstream scholarship has no such natural constituency, outside the specialized bookstores of universities and seminaries.

These publishing patterns are exemplified by the publishing firm of Harper San Francisco, which in the late 1970s became one of the first companies to market religion and spirituality titles for a general readership. Harper has also been the major outlet for the Jesus Seminar's products. Harper copublished *The Acts of Jesus* and *The Complete Gospels* with the Seminar's own Polebridge Press. Other Jesus Seminar members regularly published by Harper San Francisco include Crossan (*The Historical Jesus* and *The Birth of Christianity*); Funk (*Honest to Jesus*), Borg (*The God We Never Knew*), and Meyer (*The Gospel of Thomas*). Harper also published all the Biblical works of Bishop Spong, as well as Karen Jo Torjesen's *When Women Were Priests*, books by Burton Mack (*The Lost Gospel* and *Who Wrote the New Testament?*), and *The Fifth Gospel*, Robert Winterhalter's New Age commentary on *Thomas*. At the 1999 convention of the American Academy of Religion–Society of Biblical Literature, Harper had the largest display of any publisher present, and of the titles highlighted on the New Testament and early Christianity, a substantial majority reflected radical or ultra-critical perspectives. Other works illustrated equally unconventional approaches to Judaism and the Old Testament, with feminist writing such as Judith Plaskow's *Standing Again at Sinai* and Ellen Frankel's *Five Books of Miriam*, and Michael Wise's *First Messiah*, on messianic images in the Dead Sea Scrolls.[17] The firm also does a lively trade in works on New Age and Celtic spirituality, including several titles by Matthew Fox, and it is particularly strong in feminist approaches to religion.[18] Of course, Harper publishes a diverse range of religious works, including Luke Johnson's potent attack on the Jesus Seminar in *The Real Jesus*, but the proliferation of ultracritical books gives the impression that true scholarship is more or less confined to this part of the spectrum. The same small group of names occur again and again as the recognized authorities, who repeatedly write forewords and blurbs for each other's books.

The sheer number of published works in this radical tradition is overwhelming. In addition to scholarly historical works, similar views are reflected in theological and philosophical books, and in devotional publications. Just as the first Protestants hoped to give ordinary believers access to the Bible in handy pocket editions, so modern believers can now turn to translations of both Q and Thomas, these supposed witnesses to the earliest Christianity, in which the words of Jesus stand in traditional red-letter print.[19] The existence of such an extensive literature on *Thomas* inevitably conveys a message about the crucial significance supposedly attached to this text. Surely so many professors would not be writing about it if it were not a fifth gospel? As a result, an average nonspecialist reader browsing bookstore shelves is all too likely to confirm an impression derived from the news media that the Jesus Seminar represents the core of contemporary New Testament scholarship. The historical truth of early Christianity appears to rest in lost gospels such as *Thomas* or *Mary*, while nobody, apart from a hardcore Bible Belt fundamentalist, accepts the canonical gospels as anything other than late, theologically motivated fictions.

Most of the books just mentioned represent solid if partisan scholarship, and they are reviewed respectfully, even enthusiastically, in professional journals. However, other works that achieve wide distribution are far more dubious. A media preference for the heretical is indicated by the serious treatment granted in recent years to a series of fringe or questionable ideas, far more outrageous than anything produced by the scholars of the Jesus Seminar; publishers demonstrate a striking indifference to the scholarly consensus. The sympathy shown by both commercial presses and media outlets to the far fringe indicates that the standards prevailing in religious publishing are quite peculiar when compared with other areas of the trade, and with other academic fields.

Major presses regularly publish quite eccentric works, which most scholars would dismiss out of hand, in a way that could not happen in, say, American history. In history, another vast market in its own right, powerful filtering mechanisms prevent major presses from venturing too far into fringe scholarship. It is unthinkable that a major commercial publisher, a Doubleday or a Harper, would publish a volume arguing that, say, Franklin Roosevelt was a career Soviet agent, or Harry Truman a secret transvestite, though such a book might sell well if only on the strength of the resulting notoriety. The manuscript would never pass the review of respectable scholars, and even if it did, the press would likely conclude that including a title like this would discredit it with authors and reviewers, to an extent that simply would not be worth any short-term profit. The hypothetical book would have to move further down the hierarchy of potential presses until ending up with some marginal enterprise, from which it would achieve strictly limited distribution.

In Biblical studies, however, and particularly works on the New Testament, truly eccentric works appear with some regularity, despite the derision of mainstream scholars. Allegro's phantasmagoric work on the Jesus movement, *The Sacred Mushroom and the Cross*, appeared from the major publishing house of Doubleday. One of the religious best-sellers of the 1990s was Michael Drosnin's outrageous *The Bible Code*, which argued that the Hebrew Bible text contained deep-coded references to future events in Jewish history, including the 1995 assassination of Israeli Prime Minister Yitzhak Rabin. In other words, the Torah contained a kind of exceedingly well-hidden gospel. Apart from its intrinsic implausibility, Drosnin's argument depends on the established Biblical text never having changed by so much as a single letter since its first composition, a view which is held only by the most extreme fundamentalists (and which is starkly contradicted by the textual evidence of the Dead Sea Scrolls). Despite its obvious problems, Drosnin's work achieved enormous visibility, and was published by Simon and Schuster. (*The Bible Code* has in addition spawned a subgenre of books explaining or building upon the original thesis, and even inspired the popular apocalyptic movie *The Omega Code*.)[20]

Fringe ideas and books receive media coverage far more extensive than that accorded to more respectable works. The response to Jesus-related stories is illustrated by the controversy over the work of German papyrologist Carsten Peter Thiede, who in 1994 argued that a small manuscript fragment of St. Matthew's Gospel was written far earlier than was previously supposed, namely, around 60 or 70, rather than about 200. The implications were stunning, since a Matthew written so early might plausibly have been written by firsthand observers of the events described, even by an apostle. The existence of the text would further indicate that situations and doctrines commonly believed to have developed at the end of the first century really dated from the most primitive stages of the religion. The problem was that Thiede's very early dating was immediately rejected by most of the scholarly community, as experts with at least equally solid credentials examined and overwhelmingly rejected his argument. Though Thiede himself is well regarded as a technical expert, his book received negative comments throughout the Biblical studies profession. Most scholars simply would not cite the book as a reliable source on the dating of Matthew, and its arguments are discounted.[21]

Despite the professional hostility, Thiede's claim swiftly made international news, after it first appeared in the London *Times* as a Christmas news item in 1994. By 1996, a book exploring the implications of the supposed discovery was published by some of the most powerful publishers in both England and the United States. The British firm of Weidenfeld published it as *The Jesus Papyrus*, while in the United States, Doubleday sold it as *Eyewitness to Jesus*. Doubleday promoted the work with brochures implying an Indiana Jones discovery. The new finds were allegedly "as important as the Dead Sea Scrolls . . . A gripping human story," involving "a mysterious 2,000 year-old journey of papyrus" and "startling discoveries." This is a story of an "inquisitive Victorian missionary," an "earthquake of biblical proportions," a "persistent German scientist," an "award-winning British journalist." Taking up this feed, newspapers around the country made it a significant news item that Easter, with headlines suggesting an epoch-making breakthrough in Biblical studies. The *Times-Picayune* headlined "Scholar Argues Age of Gospel—Could Have Been Work of Witness," and the *Dallas Morning News* reported, "Matthew Put Much Closer to Jesus' Time." The actual stories were not uncritical, since they included skeptical comments by other Biblical experts, but the prominence given to accounts of the supposed discovery could not fail to give the impression that this was a major event. *Time* magazine presented a substantial (900-word) discussion of the *Eyewitness* argument as its major Easter story: Thiede was left the last word, and the article concluded, "Apparently the age-old battle over the truth of Scripture, far from being over, has just begun." Meanwhile, *U.S. News and World Report* cited the book prominently in its review of current Jesus research, remarkably enough portraying it as a conservative counter to the Jesus Seminar.[22]

The Media and the Scrolls

The media's sympathy for the further reaches of scholarship is suggested by the long-running coverage of the Dead Sea Scrolls, which have proved particularly fertile ground for the most torrid fantasies. Speculations about the Scrolls were encouraged by the very long process of bringing them before the public gaze. A prestigious committee of scholars had been working since the 1950s on the arduous task of reassembling and editing the fragments, and enormous progress was made within the first decade, but thereafter, the process seemed to slow to a crawl, and even highly qualified scholars were excluded from access to the full range of materials.

The apparent efforts to withhold or even suppress the evidence of the Scrolls have made this material the focus for grotesque sensationalism. One recurrent rumor held that the Scrolls might contain some uniquely explosive secret, perhaps about the origins of Christianity, that they might in fact represent hidden gospels. In 1987, the *Jerusalem Post* reported John Allegro's contention "that the delay in publishing the findings of Cave Four is the result of a conspiracy by the Christian church," because the finds showed "how the Essenes' ideas and practices were adopted by precursors of the first real Christians two centuries before Christ." Even more outrageous stories were carried in quite reputable sources. The Associated Press carried a story claiming that the Scroll collection included a letter from Samson to Delilah, and the *Washington Post* reported that some prophecies from Qumran had been found in Chinese characters. Supermarket tabloids hold no monopoly on nonsense.[23] Given the florid speculations, it was not surprising that such enormous excitement should have erupted in 1991 when a dissident group of scholars broke the monopoly of the official Scroll committee and secured the release of the complete texts. Respected writer James Charlesworth recalled how at this time, "Virtually every major U.S. newspaper has set reporters hot on the trail of the newest developments in the story, and they in turn have set upon biblical scholars such as myself."[24] Interviews followed on popular television programs such as *Good Morning America*, and on CNN specials.

Despite the fevered expectations, the Scrolls contain little detrimental to Christian claims, and may even support Christian beliefs to an extent that would have seemed shocking some years ago. Assuming the Scrolls do not contain a direct reference to Jesus or the early Christian movement—and most scholars agree they do not—then the main concern involved parallels between the Scroll community, the *Yahad*, and the first followers of the Jesus Way. We now know that the Dead Sea community apparently practiced rituals and held doctrines hitherto believed to be distinctive to Christianity, including regular ritual meals: in addition, the community's description of a banquet ushering in the messianic age seems to throw light on the origins of Christian ritual eating, and perhaps the eucharistic meal itself.[25] Even so, the importance of these parallels is open to debate. A critic of Christianity might argue that the early Christians took ideas from that older *Yahad*, proving that there was nothing special or innovative about their beliefs, and that Jesus was firmly entrenched in first-century Jewish teachings. This view can be seen as subverting Christian claims, but in contrast, conservatives have used the very same parallels and linkages to argue for the plausibility of the New Testament accounts of Jesus. If both the Jesus movement and the Dead Sea community held the same views, then this shows that the ideas in question must be ancient, and must therefore have originated in an early Jewish context.

Again and again, the Scrolls show that much of the ideas and language which the early Christians were thought to have borrowed from the Greco-Roman world did in fact have deep roots in Jewish culture, making it more likely that the gospels were accurately reflecting the thought-world of Jesus and his apostles. The more Jesus is placed in an authentic Jewish context, the less plausible it is to attribute the exalted ideas and titles applied to him in the New Testament to an increasingly Hellenized Gentile church: these ideas were well established in Palestine decades before Jesus' time. "Early Christianity, we learn, was not a hybrid of Judaism and Hellenism—it was rooted in the native soil of Palestine." So much for the insights of a century and a half of the most radical Biblical criticism.[26]

This perspective can be used to validate some of the most hotly contested claims about the authenticity of New Testament statements about Jesus. Scroll evidence now strengthens the likelihood that Jesus really did make claims about his messianic status, and did everything short of making an explicit statement that he was indeed the Christ (and not, for example, Wisdom incarnate).[27] Another beneficiary of the Scroll material was the Gospel of John, which critical scholars had long dismissed as the most Hellenistic of the four canonical gospels, and the least historically reliable. Nineteenth-century scholars doubted whether it could have been written much before 150 or so, and the Jesus Seminar does not grant its certificate of authenticity to any of the words attributed to Jesus in this text. In contrast, evidence from the Scrolls places John ever more firmly in a religious context that is strictly Jewish, and far earlier than many would once have believed. John's dualistic ideas of the conflict between Light and Darkness would have found a receptive home among the authors of the Scrolls, showing that this theme reflected early Jewish ideas, rather than the Gnostic language of a century or two later. Overall, the Scrolls were good news for conservative and evangelical scholars, who could use this undoubtedly early Jewish source as a potent weapon against the much later Nag Hammadi texts invoked by the Jesus Seminar: my scrolls can beat your codex.[28]

But a minority of researchers found very different implications in the Scrolls, which were presented as new hidden gospels, vital records of the earliest Christians themselves.[29] It was these arguments that made the most public impact in terms of newspaper headlines and books from major commercial presses, while the conservative interpretations were little publicized outside the scholarly journals. The media response to the Scrolls demonstrates acutely the problems of media coverage of matters Biblical.

Some particularly speculative claims derived from Robert Eisenman, who claimed on the strength of a controversial and confused fragment that the Scrolls spoke of "the execution of a Messiah-like leader." Others built this claim into the story that the mysterious leader had been crucified, and this account was reported as a major story in the *New York Times* in 1991. The suggestion was that early Christians might have rewritten the story of Jesus to include such a messianic ending to his career, though it is now commonly agreed that the passage in question does not in fact include such a phrase, and there is no evidence that the *Yahad* had any concept of a pierced or crucified messiah.[30] This story is of a piece with other such sensational claims that have circulated for years before being demolished, such as the notion that the Messiah described in the Scrolls was known as "son of God . . . and son of the Most High," and thus prefigures Jesus. Subsequent scholarship shows that this language was in fact applied not to the Messiah but to an enemy of God, an Antichrist figure.[31] Time and again, the media trumpet claims about such alleged discoveries which promise to "rock the foundations of Christianity," while rarely even noting when such claims are disproved or withdrawn.

Eisenman also wrote a massive book entitled *James the Brother of Jesus*, in which he integrated the story of early Christianity into the world of the Qumran sect. Despite its highly controversial ideas, the book was published by the major firm of Viking Penguin, and received respectful treatment in the mass media. According to most interpretations, the Scrolls are the records of a sectarian movement that looked to a persecuted founder known as the Teacher of Righteousness, who was persecuted by a so-called Wicked Priest: both men lived and died sometime in the second century B.C. For Eisenman, however, the Scrolls describe much later events, involving known historical persons. The Righteous Teacher was James the Just, who headed the movement after his brother Jesus was executed as a Zealot, a political revolutionary: James himself was executed around 62. In this view, one of James' acts as leader was to order the expulsion of Paul, who is described in the Scrolls as the Man of Lies, for his blasphemous teachings. The New Testament thus becomes "one of the most successful historical rewrites ever accomplished."[32] Eisenman's interpretations, and particularly his dating of events, are starkly at variance with those of virtually all other scholars in the field. Crucially for his argument, too, his datings for key manuscripts have been systematically contradicted by carbon-14 tests, which more or less kill the book's central thesis and confirm that the Scrolls concern matters long before Jesus' time. Almost certainly by coincidence, Eisenman's ideas recall George Moore's *Brook Kerith*, published as far back as 1916, and the fictional Jesus tradition harking back to Venturini before that.

Still stranger was the sequence of books produced by Michael Baigent and Richard Leigh, which argued among other things that Jesus survived the crucifixion, married Mary Magdalen, and retired to France, where his offspring became the medieval French dynasty of the Merovingians. Paul, in this account, was a Roman agent. In common with many other esoteric writers over the centuries, the authors' scenario also invoked the medieval Cathars and Knights Templar as guardians of the great secret.[33] In the *Dead Sea Scrolls Deception*, published under the mainstream label of Touchstone, Baigent and Leigh further argue that the great truths in the Scrolls have been systematically concealed by a Roman Catholic conspiracy: inevitably, John Allegro was a major source for their ideas. In understanding the long delay in releasing the full body of Scrolls, they argue that "some other vested interest may be at stake, a vested interest larger than the reputations of individual scholars—the vested interest of Christianity as a whole, for example, and of Christian doctrine." The church lived in dread of what might be found from "these texts, issuing from so close to 'the source,' and, unlike the New Testament, never having been edited or tampered with."[34] Note the suggestion that the church had already doctored the New Testament beyond any hope of recovering its authentic message, though the true hidden gospel might still be recovered from the Qumran treasures. As in so many comparable speculations, both the Ebionites and the Celtic church were believed to have retained the essence of the original teaching.

Just as odd was Barbara Thiering's incredible *Jesus and the Riddle of the Dead Sea Scrolls*, although this too appeared from a first-class publisher, namely, Harper. Thiering argues that the gospel story of the life of Jesus is actually a coded account of ritualized performances within the community at Qumran: John the Baptist was the Teacher of Righteousness, and Jesus was the Wicked Priest denounced in the Scrolls. Jesus survived his crucifixion and settled down to marry Mary Magdalen, who bore him children (the couple ultimately divorced, leaving Jesus to enter a lonely old age).[35] Thiering also presented her views at length in an Australian documentary, *The Riddle of the Dead Sea Scrolls* (1990), which was broadcast on an American cable network. Luke Timothy Johnson has aptly described Thiering's book as "poppycock," and she has found precious few defenders. It would be impossible to cite the book as authoritative in any of the scholarly journals devoted to the New Testament, to Jewish Studies, or to the Scrolls. More recently, Thiering ventured further into unexplored territory with her study, *The Book That Jesus Wrote*, claiming that Jesus himself personally directed the writing of the Gospel of John.

Such books have had an impact far beyond their scholarly importance. Eisenman's book is regarded as eccentric by researchers working on either the New Testament or on early Judaism, who would not deem *Deception* or Thiering's work worthy of comment, yet these are the texts likely to be encountered by a consumer seeking information about the latest findings on the Scrolls. When in 1992, *Time* published a detailed special on the Scrolls, Eisenman's work occupied pride of place. The following year, Eisenman's theory received star treatment in a BBC television documentary which was subsequently shown in the United States on PBS's *Nova*. Though Eisenman's critics received fair treatment, the program concluded by a wholesale acceptance of his view of the first Jesus followers not as mystics or protobeatniks, but as lethally armed fanatics assembled in terrorist training camps along the Dead Sea. When examining the implications of his view for mainstream Christianity, the program used recurring visuals of children singing carols around a Christmas tree, symbolizing the naive faith of conventional believers, who were about to receive a rude awakening from incisive scholarship.

Other fringe books received a like degree of respect. When the Canadian magazine *Maclean's* published a typical Christmas special on the theme of "Who Was Jesus?," the two recent scholarly books reviewed for their innovative arguments were *The Dead Sea Scrolls Deception* and Thiering's *Jesus and the Riddle of the Dead Sea Scrolls*.[36] In relation to the scholarly consensus, these ideas are far more outré than the notion of President Truman as transvestite; Truman as UFO pilot would be a better analogy.

The impact of such ideas is magnified through the cumulative effect of related treatments appearing in different types of media. A dramatic theory like Thiering's is proposed in a book, which is then reported in the print media and television news. The reporting might be skeptical, or scornful—*Time* dryly reported that Thiering "tells of a Jesus who was crucified, but secretly revived at the Dead Sea, and who wed a woman bishop at midnight on March 17, A.D. 50."—but this well-known magazine still gave Thiering a prominent role in a story on contemporary Scroll research.[37] The proliferation of accounts gives the impression that this is a powerful and influential theory, which gains the attention of a lay audience that would otherwise pay little attention to academic debate. Thiering's view will be cited as authoritative in discussions in church groups years afterward, as will ideas that the Vatican conspired to conceal the Scrolls. Such canards surface regularly to the puzzlement of academic speakers, who are at a loss to know where lay audiences are picking up such odd ideas. In this field, a chasm separates the assumptions of professionals and lay enthusiasts, even, or especially, if these enthusiasts read widely.

Making News

Why do publishers and media so tend to favor the radical wing of New Testament scholarship, and indeed to be so sympathetic to books from the farthest ends of that spectrum? The dissemination of new theories about the age of Jesus offers a case study of the means by which the media report information about religious scholarship and, to some extent, about the academic world in general. For many reasons, news media and popular culture outlets have a powerful prejudice in favor of scholarly theories that are weird or extreme, and tend to succumb easily to poorly substantiated fads, if their proponents have the skill to present their ideas appropriately.

One obvious factor in explaining media behavior is that religion sells, and can sell very well. The popularity of religious news stories is indicated by the avid attention which newspapers pay to new theories about, for instance, the star of Bethlehem or the location of the Ark of the Covenant.[38] And though media critics unsurprisingly treat the supermarket tabloids as unworthy of serious notice, here, too, a mass readership finds a constant diet of tales about archaeological finds proving the truth of the Bible, new prophecies or miraculous visions, and the recurrent theme of newly discovered documents containing explosive information which could undermine the foundations of contemporary churches. The Dead Sea Scrolls are repeatedly cited as the source of such legends. In 1999, the tabloid *The Sun* headlined, "Forbidden Book of the Bible—*Revealed!* What you were never meant to read!"[39] The main story is a description of the apocryphal Book of Enoch, well known for two centuries, and thus scarcely news. Another issue of the *Sun* reported, "Lost Bible Gospel's End Times Warning," claiming the discovery of a document written by the centurion in charge of the crucifixion: the idea of finding such a text dated back at least to the *Archko Volume* of the 1890s. However ludicrous, these stories demonstrate the continuing existence of a vast potential audience for hidden gospels.

Clearly, the Jesus Quest books are appealing to a totally different level of literacy and critical intelligence, but they are also aiming at a market desperately hungry for new evidence which might shed additional light on matters of religious truth. Harper does not publish works like *The Five Gospels* out of a dedicated urge to subvert the foundations of orthodox Christianity, but rather operates on a shrewd commercial judgment that such books will sell well. *The Five Gospels* itself remained on the religion best-seller list of

Publishers' Weekly for an impressive nine months. Publishers' projections are confirmed by the fact that these books are often reprinted, and this success encourages the firm to support similar ventures by other authors from the same school of thought. If an author who has produced a best-selling title gives a favorable reading to another manuscript by a like-minded colleague or pupil, that review is likely to carry a great deal of weight. Success builds upon success.

For the news media, too, radical views make their impact because they are newsworthy and generate income, and not because journalists and editors are following a preconceived religious agenda. The more radical claims are reported precisely because they are new, and not specifically because they challenge Christianity; indeed, some of the most sensational claims in recent years have had implications that are highly conservative and even fundamentalist, such as Drosnin's *Bible Code* and Thiede's *Eyewitness to Jesus*. The media seek after exciting or innovative stories about Biblical matters, and as these do not tend to be produced from the core of that profession, they will instead emerge from the margins, often from maverick scholars. If even the wild and wonderful books on the Scrolls can be treated seriously, then we should not be surprised at the rapturous receptions granted to the better accredited works of the Jesus Seminar.

Newsworthiness is all. A book by a major religious scholar arguing for an essentially conservative recounting of the Jesus story is usually not newsworthy, however magnificent its argument or documentation. An equally able publication suggesting a thorough revision of Christian origins is far more likely to be taken up, especially if it seems relevant to what are considered hot topics in that period—revolutionary militancy in the 1960s, gender issues in the 1980s, sex any time. In this regard, themes of secrecy, concealment, and conspiracy are almost as attractive as sex, so that while Mark is not newsworthy, Secret Mark certainly is. The four known gospels are old news, but even the most dubious candidate for fifth gospel status is a thrilling proposition. The taste for novelty may help explain why radical scholars are so reluctant to admit just how little we have learned from recent textual finds like Nag Hammadi, and indeed how much we knew about Gnosticism many years before. Their public stance, at least, is that the new materials have "broken the story," unearthed exciting new finds, smashed the orthodox conspiracy of silence.

Once a book has been identified as novel and exciting, the

media tend to treat it uncritically because journalists rarely have any idea of the canons of scholarship in the technical and sophisticated world of Biblical studies. The professional mainstream of Biblical scholarship produces work that does not readily lend itself to exciting news stories; it is rarely the stuff of CNN documentaries and special issues of *Newsweek*. In contemporary North America, there are several thousand professional Bible scholars, individuals who hold academic rank in universities or seminaries, and who are usually affiliated with the Society of Biblical Literature. The vast majority of them are committed to precise textual scholarship, in an academic tradition that frowns on drawing broad conclusions too readily, before an idea has been tested and discussed in conference papers and scholarly articles, which reference the existing literature to a degree that an outsider would consider obsessive. Before an article or book can be published, it must pass a rigorous review process, and the merits of the work are again tested when the published work is reviewed and commented on. To that extent, the profession does work on a basis of consensus. This tradition can lead to a snobbish contempt for effective popularization, but it does have the virtue of being highly resistant toward faddish claims, which surface easily in a field in which people have such passionate personal commitment to particular doctrines and approaches. The tradition is thus conservative in its methods, though not necessarily in ideology; the vast majority of Jesus Seminar Fellows follow these same scholarly approaches to the most exacting degree. What differentiates them from the bulk of the profession is that their group, or its leadership, has made the explicit decision to carry their conclusions to a mass audience, to the delight of the media.

Journalists know little of the means by which academic arguments are advanced, debated, and ultimately established, have no sense of the processes of peer review and publication that are so familiar to specialists. Though many news outlets employ religion correspondents, who might be experienced and intelligent observers, all are chosen for this role because of their interest or expertise in contemporary church politics or religious debates. Few, if any, have any background in textual scholarship. When a book appears from a major trade press making a sensational claim about the Scrolls and Christian origins, the journalist assigned to report on the ensuing controversy will rarely have the scholarly tools to analyze the work in question. Journalists will be heavily influenced by the reputation of the publisher—surely a solid firm would not put out a completely harebrained theory?—and by the academic credentials of the author. Unfortunately, remarkably foolish books can emerge from people with positions at good universities. The books taken up as major news items will thus include some solid scholarship, but also a good deal that is worthless; it is a matter of chance.

Other factors contribute to fringe books being taken far more seriously than they should be, not least because journalistic standards require that balanced coverage be given to both the new theory and its critics. Lacking a way to differentiate between daring thinkers and plain cranks, the media will rarely dismiss a contentious new theory as the product of poor research, tendentious theorizing, or simple silliness, but will instead present the views of the author and a mainstream professional critic, with the implication that both carry equal weight. In practice, this means that a dubious argument will be treated far more seriously than it merits, and the fact of inciting controversy will generate more sales and intensified public attention. With the most outré books, such as Thiering's, very few scholars will consider the views worth review or refutation, so that journalists will find it difficult to find experts who will even go on record condemning the book.

We can reliably predict which books or news stories are likely to generate major news coverage. New and daring ideas always attract much more interest than old or traditional scholarship, provided that these new theories do not include elements that blatantly signal outrageous pseudoscience. A book claiming that "Jesus came in a UFO" would immediately encounter skepticism, while there is nothing inherently impossible about the idea that Jesus survived the crucifixion and married Mary Magdalen, or led a secret cult practicing ritual sex, especially if those claims are ostensibly based on newly discovered hidden gospels. Nor is it impossible that the Dead Sea Scrolls might conceivably offer an intricate portrait of the earliest days of Christianity, despite a large scholarly consensus that they do not. Religion journalists report those theories that present radical ideas in simple and easily comprehended form, rather than more complex or elaborate ones. The basic idea of Thiede's *Eyewitness*—that the gospels reached their final form far earlier than most scholars think—is not only easy to digest, it also has a natural appeal for the reading public, many of whom are delighted to see traditional views affirmed.

Once new ideas generate a controversy, the media find themselves in an enviable position, since public battles of this kind make good copy: a headline like "Storm over Jesus Book" is bound to create and sustain public interest. As Luke Timothy Johnson has noted, much of the coverage of the long-running Jesus Seminar saga consists of defensive quotes from conservative clergy who are portrayed as struggling against potentially devastating revelations about the newly revealed historical Jesus. For the lay reader, the obvious question is, what do they have to fear?[40] News accounts concerning religion are thought lifeless if they lack some element of controversy, and so much of the debate within the world of professional Bible scholars appears nitpicking to the lay audience. The temptation is therefore to seek for the daring, innovative scholar, the heretic or iconoclast, who challenges the weight of academic or ecclesiastical opinion. In the contemporary lexicon, both heretic and iconoclast have come to be synonymous with heroic individualism, just as "orthodoxy" signifies staid conformity.

Long media tradition exalts the idea of exposing the misdeeds of large and oppressive organizations, and this reporting is often accomplished by focusing on some heroic lone individual who bucks the system by standing for principle. Standing alone against the united weight of scholarly opinion can be viewed either negatively, as stubborn wrongheadedness, or quite positively, as bravely challenging a deadening paradigm, and the media generally prefer to accept the latter view. Media attitudes are illustrated by the reaction to Thomas Thompson's recent book on ancient Israel, which argues that virtually everything reported in the Bible prior to the year 400 B.C. is a literary fiction, so that even kings Solomon and David become basically characters in a vast novel. Though this sweeping thesis attracts the scorn of most of the profession, the book was published by the mainstream firm of Basic Books. A laudatory review in the *Los Angeles Times* was entitled, "A Summation of Cutting-Edge Bible Scholarship," and the reviewer remarked on how long it had taken before "the rest of the academic world caught up with [Thompson's] revolutionary ideas."[41]

The media love a good heretic, which is ironic given the very low threshold which corporate news organizations themselves have for insubordinate or deviant attitudes in their own midst. In the academic context, the heretic's enemies are portrayed as an obscurantist, hidebound, and conspiratorial establishment, rigidly resisting fresh ideas. Heterodox writers on the Dead Sea Scrolls make a virtue of their minority status by scornfully describing mainstream interpretations as belonging to the "consensus," the "party line," the implication being that orthodoxy is a slavish group think, or represents obedience to the sinister dictates of ecclesiastical authority. The cover to Eisenman's *James the Brother of Jesus* bears a quotation in which the author is described as "renegade, apostate and heretic," which are clearly to be taken as terms of the highest praise.[42]

Much of the success of the Jesus Seminar reflected the ability of leaders such as Funk and Crossan to cast themselves precisely in this heretic image, as sworn foes of orthodoxy and consensus. Funk seemed to possess an unending stream of neat and controversial phrases that made perfect soundbites: "We should give Jesus a demotion"; the Christian canon should be as open as "the myth of King Arthur and the knights of the round table, or the myth of the American West"; "Biblical scholars went indoors about 1923 and have refused to come out" (1923 seems to be a misdating of the Scopes trial). Crossan summarized Jesus' message as "God says, 'Caesar sucks.'"[43] For Funk, the Seminar sought only "to inquire simply and rigorously after the *voice* of Jesus, after what he really said." What rational person could object to that agenda? Enemies, meanwhile, were caricatured as ignorant reactionaries: his critics "really object to having Jesus say anything about Christianity. They think we should stick to a creed that denies Jesus any voice at all."[44] (On closer examination, the charge is dubious: could one really find any Bible scholar, past or present, who has ever argued against presenting the words of Jesus on particular issues?)

Even more promising for journalists, Funk offers a melodramatic and conspiratorial picture of the difficulties faced by radical scholars in their quest for truth. He suggests that though all competent scholars recognize the truth of radical Jesus scholarship, they have been intimidated into suppressing the truth. By operating the Seminar outside the context of churches, seminaries, and universities, the Fellows were said to be working "at considerable risk to [them]selves": they "took some additional risk in talking to reporters and appearing on talk shows."[45] He even turns to populist advantage the numerous attacks on the Seminar's questionable and much ridiculed procedure of voting to determine the authenticity of words or deeds attributed to Jesus: "Dropping colored beads into a box became the trademark of the Seminar, and the brunt of attack for many elitist academic critics who deplored the public face of the Seminar."[46] Funk's astonishing claims inevitably provoke an angry response, which in turn contributes to the heroic image of the radical dissenter.

A media-savvy scholar can draw on a rich rhetorical arsenal by invoking phrases which carry a potent and even mythological significance, which convey an image of heroic resistance against oppressive institutions. The scholar might be compared to Galileo battling the Inquisition, to John Scopes defending the idea of evolution against a Bible Belt court, even to a victim of McCarthyism. Funk and the editors of *The Five Gospels* ostentatiously dedicated their volume to Galileo, Thomas Jefferson, and David Friedrich Strauss. The book's introduction announced that "the Christ of creed and dogma, who had been firmly in place in the Middle Ages, can no longer command the assent of those who have seen the heavens through Galileo's telescope."[47] A work like *The Five Gospels* can be attacked from many points of view, and certainly not just by fundamentalists, but the authors can immediately respond that such innovative work is bound to attract protests from a threatened establishment: remember Galileo.

Critics can also be stigmatized by various potent labels implying fanaticism. Denouncing a hostile academic mainstream for rigid "fundamentalism" is an excellent means of mobilizing liberal sympathies for one's cause. This is all the more effective when the issue in question can be linked to the politically progressive stances that the media affect on issues such as race, gender, and sexual orientation, as when an iconoclastic scholar is pressing radical views on issues like the role of women in the early church. Embattled scholars can often use the powerful images of Inquisition and witch-hunt, as each in its way conjures images of specifically religious intolerance and fanaticism. And there are newer images: in one recent case, a Methodist minister disciplined for performing a same-sex marriage claimed to be the victim of "denominational cleansing," which recalled the horrors of the ethnic warfare and intolerance then under way in the Balkans.[48] Tags of this sort can usefully be applied when conservatives within a given denomination attack a cleric who has espoused radical teachings or scriptural interpretations.

Though the actual new evidence that can be drawn from the recently found gospel texts is quite limited, this is not something we would learn from the treatments in the mass media. Once a group of scholars decided to make their extravagant claims in the public arena, rather than merely in academe, they found that they possessed every conceivable advantage. Advocates of the hidden gospels were dealing with topics in which the media already had a powerful interest, and they presented their conclusions in terms which could not fail to win the sympathy of both journalists and readers, as they ably mobilized so many contemporary prejudices. Failure was all but impossible: even the most forceful conservative counterattack could be turned to advantage, by suggesting that the very depth of hostility proved the strength and dangerousness of the radical arguments. At every stage, the methods and working assumptions of the media resulted in preferential, uncritical treatment for the heretics, past and present.

9

The Next New Gospel

Neither will the Lord God suffer that the Gentiles shall forever remain in that awful state of blindness, which thou beholdest they are in, because of the plain and most precious parts of the gospel of the Lamb which have been kept back by that abominable church, whose formation thou hast seen.

BOOK OF MORMON, 1 NEPHI 13: 32

AT LEAST SINCE THE ENLIGHTENMENT, religious reformers have tried to uncover the original Jesus buried beneath the super-structures of Christianity, and have sought out the "real Christians" who followed this figure, whether these were identified with Essenes, Gnostics, Ebionites, or Celtic monks. Usually, the best candidates for this role were the ones about whom the least was known, which is why the Essenes remained idealized for so long before the inconvenient outpouring of information in their own words from Qumran. At least the ambitious recent attempts to rehabilitate the Gnostics are based on extensive writings of that sect, but Gnostics too can be fitted into the desired historical role only by ignoring a great deal of contrary evidence about the group's attitudes and world-view. In terms of their potential value for reconstructing earliest Christianity, the ancient heresies are of strictly limited value. The more we know about them, the more we can see that their flaws, limitations, and contradictions were much like those of the orthodox church, only writ large. As with the heresies, so with their new and rediscovered scriptures, which provide each age with a basis on which to recreate Jesus in its own image. Such texts were traditionally drawn from within the New Testament itself, like the purified core of supposedly authen-tic gospel passages and Pauline texts excavated by nineteenth-century German scholars, but in the twentieth century, the authentic Jesus was increasingly located by means of new and extracanonical documents. Each new gospel enjoyed its vogue, but on closer examination, each proved to contain far less than was originally boasted.

A glance at past quests brings out the common flaws of method and assumption which pervade them and, above all, the overwhelming ideological agendas which become apparent in these efforts, the same tendencies to read evidence in light of prevailing assumptions. A common stereotype posits a stark dichotomy between critical academics and traditional or orthodox religious believers, the believers supposedly living in terror of the incisive research of the iconoclastic scholars, and fearing the insights of objective science. The entire rhetoric of the Jesus Seminar group is founded upon such romantic imagery. In examining the successive battles between orthodox and radicals, though, it is far from clear which group really merits the dubious title of "true believers." At least as much as traditional believers, successive seekers have tended to idealize those who uphold a particular religious tradition, to extol them as pristine voices of truth, to believe that certain scriptures represent primitive realities, and to maintain these perceptions in face of massive evidence to the contrary. Though they differ from the orthodox in vaunting the deviant rather than the mainstream, what emerges is advocacy rather than analysis. To a striking extent, the iconoclasts in New Testament study exemplify the worst features of the faithful at their most credulous.

Excessive claims about new gospels now have a track record nearly two centuries long, giving us abundant evidence of how such texts are discovered or reconstructed, used and abused, and the evidence that will likely be drawn from them. This story has its own intrinsic interest, in making us us ask why the pursuit for "real Christianity" and hidden gospels has proved so enduring and, it seems, so permanent an obsession. If nothing else, that phenomenon teaches us a great deal about the Christian assumptions still underlying American society: after so much alleged secularization, the faith that people are struggling to disprove is still Christianity. In practical terms, studying the quest for new gospels is valuable for churches and scholars who have to confront future claims. A historical perspective is critical when facing one of the periodic waves of expectation that some new document is going to rewrite the story of Christianity. Based on past quests, we can identify a series of obvious questions which need to be asked, and issues to be raised, to determine whether contemporary claims are any more plausible than their many predecessors.

Heroes and Villains

One common pattern of the gospel quests is the habit of identifying heroes and villains, to idealize particular individuals and movements fairly uncritically. Because of the deeply held emotions stirred by religious matters, there is a natural tendency to romanticize great figures of the past, to assume, for instance, that the figures of Christian antiquity must have been particularly heroic because they lived so close to the time of Jesus. These ideas are obvious in popular culture depictions, which regularly attempt the all-but-impossible task of using speech and garb to convey sanctity. We are all painfully aware of the undistinguished genre of cinematic Bible epics, in which apostles and martyrs are instantly recognizable from their cotton-wool beards, white robes, and heroic gazes, while persecutors are the familiar villains of melodrama. Often, these productions were so blandly simplistic that the enemies of Christianity could be identified immediately because they quite literally wore black.[1]

While such stereotypical portraits rightly attract mockery, they are uncomfortably reminiscent of modern images of the other side in the great Christian debates, namely, the heretics and Gnostics. Just as orthodox Christians have their idealized martyrs, so do skeptics and radicals, and both sides tend to back-project their own contemporary concerns. During the nineteenth century, liberals and modernists saw Catholic Christianity as the archenemy of scientific progress, and attacked their rivals by means of historical fiction set in the early church. Charles Kingsley's novel *Hypatia* glorified the pagan woman philosopher murdered by a fanatical Christian mob, and in the process made her a far younger and more glamorous figure than she actually was. He also used the incident to attack orthodox fanaticism of the sort he attributed to the Roman Catholics of his own day—the book is significantly subtitled "New Foes with an Old Face." Mediterranean races, who were "effeminate, over-civilized, . . . morbid, self-conscious, physically indolent, incapable then as now of personal or political freedom, . . . afforded material out of which fanatics might easily be made, but not citizens of the kingdom of God." For Kingsley, they were natural Catholics. His book provoked a series of rival novels about Christian martyrs, including Cardinal Newman's *Callista* and Cardinal Wiseman's *Fabiola*. (Hypatia still has a powerful modern reputation as a feminist martyr, and gives her name, for instance, to a current journal of feminist philosophy.)[2]

Much modern writing on the early Church follows faithfully in Kingsley's footsteps, with portrayals of the Gnostics as noble free-thinking individuals, extolled by powerful words from the contemporary lexicon such as "creative" and "intuitive" (not to mention "heretical"). The Gnostics reputedly practiced *spirituality*, while their orthodox opponents succumbed to mere *religion*. In the unlikely event that recent books on the hidden gospels ever were to inspire popular films, then it is surely the Gnostics who would be allocated the white robes and the heavenly gazes, especially the heroic women characters, the "dialectical daughters" who occupy such an honorable position in the current martyrology. They would be depicted with sympathy as they faced the tragedies of persecution, book-burning, and ostracism, and being forced to assume the roles of traditional domesticity. On the other side, the villainous characteristics which older films assigned to Roman emperors and persecuting prefects would in the new productions be given to the orthodox clergy. Judging by recent historical writing, bishops such as Ignatius and Athanasius both cry out for portrayal as villains of the most extreme kind. Constantine would fill the familiar role of the persecuting emperor, though in a future depiction, his darkest deed would be the official establishment of Christian orthodoxy.

If such hypothetical images sound like gross parody, they are not too far removed from the portraits offered in recent television documentaries, or in the scholarly books from which the ideas are derived. Much modern writing on the hidden gospels and their authors is utterly partisan, with well-defined heroes and villains who are represented quite as starkly and stereotypically as the white-robed saints of motion picture notoriety. Though these value judgments so thoroughly inform much recent writing on early Christianity, they need to be treated with skepticism. Though we should not imitate Cardinal Newman's idealized treatment of the Catholic tradition, it is equally misleading to attribute a similar perfection to the heterodox. If the orthodox were not as saintly and impeccable as their admirers have liked to believe, then neither were the heretics.

We often read that the exclusion of heterodox movements was a historical tragedy, which contributed to the bigotry and obscurantism for which the medieval churches became notorious. It is always difficult to imagine alternative historical realities, but based only on what we know about the major heresies, their pass-ing should not perhaps inspire too much grief. Far from con-demning the early Christian leaders who struggled against their doctrinal rivals, a modern audience should find much to sympa-thize with in their positions.

The Gnostics in particular exemplified many of the worst fea-tures for which the later Catholic church would be criticized, and did so to a far higher degree than the orthodox. Fairly or other-wise, modern readers often weary of early and medieval Christian theological debate, from the Trinitarian struggles of antiquity to the worst aspects of logic-chopping in scholasticism, yet on every count, the Catholic Church produced little that could compete with their Gnostic rivals. Already by the second and third cen-turies, the Gnostic scriptures were utterly opaque and prolix. In fact, one of the main scholarly discoveries about Gnosticism over the last century has been the incredulous realization that the early Fathers were not exaggerating when they described the rococo nature of that movement's scriptures, or its imagined cosmic hier-archies. Irenaeus, for example, describes the system proposed by Valentinus, in which "a certain perfect, preexistent Aeon" named Depth sent forth lesser beings, who in turn gave rise to other fig-ures, who together compose the thirty Aeons of the Pleroma, the Fullness. They bear names like Logos (Word), Zoe (Life), Anthro-pos (Man), Ekklesia (Church), Aletheia (Truth), and so on, and references to these terms in the Gospels are always taken to refer symbolically to the heavenly Aeons. The New Testament is also presumed to confirm the details of the heavenly hierarchy, as the Pleroma comprises three hierarchical groups, respectively of eight beings (the Ogdoad), another of ten (the Decad), and another of twelve (the Duodecad):

> They maintain also, that these thirty Aeons are most plainly indicated in the parable of the laborers sent into the vine-yard. For some are sent about the first hour, others about the third hour, others about the sixth hour, others about the ninth hour, and others about the eleventh hour. Now, if we add up the numbers of the hours here mentioned, the sum total will be thirty: for one, three, six, nine, and eleven, when added together, form thirty.[3]

Gnostic texts from Nag Hammadi and elsewhere show that Ire-naeus was accurately portraying both the world-view, and the weird Biblical exegesis on which it was founded. For the Gnostics, the Bible was a dense codebook open only to properly initiated cryptographers.

It is difficult to convey just how arcane the Gnostic scriptures are without quoting documents in full, particularly since they require knowledge of a whole mythological vocabulary, but here is a typical example from one of the Nag Hammadi texts, the *Letter of Peter to Philip*. The dialogue begins when "the apostles answered and said, 'Lord, we would like to know the deficiency of the aeons and their pleroma.'" And: "How are we detained in this dwelling place?" Jesus replies,

> First of all concerning the deficiency of the aeons, this is the deficiency, when the disobedience and the foolishness of the mother appeared without the commandment of the majesty of the Father. She wanted to raise up aeons. And when she spoke, the Arrogant One followed. And when she left behind a part, the Arrogant One laid hold of it, and it became a deficiency. This is the deficiency of the aeons. Now when the Arrogant One had taken a part, he sowed it. And he placed powers over it and authorities. And he enclosed it in the aeons which are dead. And all the powers of the world rejoiced that they had been begotten.[4]

And so on, for many turgid pages. Reading these passages, we might be reminded of the comments of an earlier generation of Western writers on the scriptures of Islam: Carlyle declared the Quran "as toilsome reading as I ever undertook: a wearisome, confused jumble, crude, incondite. Nothing but a sense of duty could carry any European through the Koran." However unfair these remarks are to the Quran, they neatly epitomize the reaction of most readers struggling through the majority of Gnostic texts.[5]

The passage quoted from the *Letter of Peter* gives an accurate impression of the obscurity of the Gnostic works, which are deliberately written for a spiritual and, perforce, an intellectual elite. Fundamental to the whole system was a threefold division between human beings, from the matter-bound *hylikoi* to the somewhat higher *psychikoi*, and the highest spiritual grade, the *pneumatikoi*. The contrast with orthodox ideas is neatly illustrated by comparing the treatment of Jesus' parable about the draught of fishes in Matthew and Thomas. In Matthew, we hear that "the kingdom of heaven is like a net that was thrown into the sea and caught fish of every kind": some were kept, and others rejected, and this symbolizes the division between good and evil mortals which will occur at the final judgment. In *Thomas*, however, the story tells how the fisherman finds "a fine large fish," and easily decides to keep that one, while throwing the rest back.[6] This is exactly in keeping with the elitist Gnostic theme that spiritual treasure was reserved to the very, very few; to big fish like themselves.

It was the orthodox Christian Church that denied this hierarchical view, just as it it insisted on keeping the Christian religion rooted in historical realities rather than the random mythologies reinvented at the whim of each rising Gnostic sage. The church was struggling to retain the idea of Jesus as a historical human being who lived and died in a specific time and place, not in a timeless never-never land. The orthodox were fighting for the whole notion of history as a scene of divine action, recorded in scriptures that for better or worse tried to record actual historical events, rather than purely symbolic conflicts within the Pleroma. Among other things, this effort meant defending the whole Hebrew and Old Testament heritage in Christianity, which was perhaps the most vulnerable aspect of the religion in the second and third centuries. The Old Testament tradition was detested by Gnostics, Marcionites, and others, who affirmed that Jesus had come to destroy the works of the evil creator God worshiped by the Jews. If the Gnostics did not exactly have a devil, then the Yahweh of the Old Testament was a close parallel. They were not necessarily anti-Semitic, which is an anachronistic term presuming an ethnic basis for hatred, but most of the major heresies did have a profoundly anti-Judaic component.

And though women famously play so crucial a role in Gnostic texts, the religious system as a whole had nothing good to say of women, whose reproductive function so obviously served the purposes of the evil beings who kept humanity in thrall. If Paul was reputed to have said that women could be "saved through childbearing," Gnostics felt the exact opposite, that the act of childbirth exemplified woman's role in the conspiracy to keep humanity enslaved: was one view more misogynistic than the other? The Gnostic Jesus had come to provide spiritual liberation, and repeatedly in the texts, we find variants on the theme that the Savior had come "to destroy the works of the female." In *The Dialogue of the Savior*, we read, typically that "Judas said, . . . 'When we pray, how should we pray?' The Lord said, 'Pray in the place where there is no woman.'" The *Book of Thomas the Contender* preaches, "Woe to you who love intimacy with women, and polluted intercourse with it."[7] Though contemporary scholars so often attack early orthodox Fathers such as Augustine for his condemnation of sexuality, we should remember that Augustine was heavily influenced by his early contacts with heresies like Manichaeanism. It is bizarre to denounce Christianity for celibacy and hatred of the body, while ignoring exactly the same flaws in Gnosticism and cognate movements.[8] The fact that Gnosticism placed such heavy emphasis on female divinities and supernatural figures does not necessarily indicate that a Gnostic church would have been any more sympathetic to women's aspirations in the real world. For all its veneration for goddesses and the Divine Mother, Hinduism has often been associated with severe repression of women.

Gnosticism may have contributed to the very features of late Christianity that moderns find so unattractive, especially in its renunciation of the world and the flesh. Continuities are particularly suggestive in Egypt. Even in the time of Jesus, the region around Alexandria was home to the Jewish ascetic movement of the Therapeutae, who renounced their worldly belongings and practiced strict self-denial in pursuit of wisdom. In the second and third centuries, Egypt was a stronghold of a Gnostic tradition which condemned sexuality and preached, in the words of *Thomas*, "Blessed are the elect and the solitary," the word for solitary being *monachos*. In the third and fourth centuries, Egypt produced countless new *monachoi*, celibate monks, who were the vanguard of the revolutionary movement of Christian monasticism, which ultimately spread throughout the Roman world and beyond. Even if there are not direct linkages between the successive movements, it is at least plausible that Gnostics and Christian celibates were drawing on the same underlying cultural themes.[9]

The medieval Christian church has been criticized for many failings, prominent among which would be clerical elitism, anti-Semitism, misogyny, an excessive taste for theological quibbling, and a rejection of the natural world. Since these sins were already so rife, or at least emerging, in Gnostic texts before 250, it is unlikely that a hypothetical Gnostic church would have been any better. It would likely have been far worse. We would have to imagine a Gnostic Christianity that not only practiced these failings, but amply justified them from their scriptures. The movement would also have been utterly submerged in magic and occult speculation. Just what aspect of Gnosticism should we feel sorry to have lost?

The Everlasting Quest

Just as groups such as the Gnostics prove on closer examination to be considerably less attractive than even the worst stereotypes of orthodoxy, so the various candidates for new gospels are uniformly disappointing. Their failings as historical sources include all those of the canonical documents, on which they almost always depend; worse, the alternative gospels add several layers of ideological rewriting and theological interpretation on top of what already exists in the texts we know. Nor is there anything new about this observation. The more people examine the new gospels, the more they tend to detect these flaws. A historical perspective shows that many other sources have in their day attracted the kind of overoptimism we witness today about *Thomas*, and that faddish enthusiasm fades over time. In fifty years, the contemporary fascination with works such as *Thomas* and *Mary* may well seem as quaint as the interest in *Peter* and the *Pistis Sophia* at the start of the last century.

So why do such works continue to attract so much attention, to be touted as the last word on Christian origins? For well over a century, various documents have been put forward more or less seriously as candidates for gospel status, equal to the canonical texts. The steady nature of this process is not difficult to understand. Many people care intensely about Christianity, and at least since the Reformation, millions have believed that absolute truth is to be found in scriptures. As societies change over time, there is bound to be concern about how, or whether, new issues are dealt with in the canonical texts, and when they are not, it is not surprising to observe dissatisfaction, a quest for more. This feeling is strengthened by the obvious successes of scholarship in uncovering ever more dramatic finds about great civilizations of the past: why can we not know a great deal more about Jesus? The hunger for additional knowledge is illustrated by the popular tendency to leap upon any find or fragment which promises, on however slender grounds, to shed new light on Christian origins.

We can also see commonsense reasons why ancient documents should so readily be accepted as authentic records of early Christianity, on grounds that seem highly dubious to scholars. Nonspecialists find it difficult to comprehend that documents from what is loosely called the New Testament period might not feature references to figures and issues referred to in Christian history. If individuals such as Jesus, Peter, and Paul are so important in Christian memory, and indeed in world history, then surely they must have been celebrated at the time, and must somehow be referred to in written sources? On these grounds, it seems incredible that the community which wrote the Dead Sea Scrolls, and which was active in the age of Jesus, should have written nothing at all about him or his movement, although almost all scholars believe that this was the case. Hence the willingness to believe the maverick writers who argue that Christian themes run through the Scrolls. There is something counterintuitive about the statement that we can know nothing about, say, the lives or deaths of most of the apostles, or of the Virgin Mary herself, and that if such records ever existed, they perished irretrievably many centuries ago. It is much more satisfying to believe that enough facts are available to provide the kind of rounded biographies that a modern audience expects, or that these facts might yet be discovered.

Also enhancing the popular credibility of the hidden gospels is the widespread failure to appreciate the length of the historical period that constituted the ancient world. People who know little of ancient history—a group that comprises a very large majority of the population—tend not to appreciate the quite substantial differences which separate, say, the first and the third centuries. To the popular mind, both periods are equally "ancient," and therefore part of a seamless whole. A commonsense logic suggests that a secret hoard of early Christian texts, conveniently labeled "ancient gospels," must contain some authentically valuable material about the time of Jesus, even if, on further examination, they prove to have been written far later than that era. If so many ancient texts and artifacts are available, it seems astonishing that they should not offer crucial clues about the greatest of religious mysteries.

The lay public has a strong natural predisposition to accept that additional information is (or should be) available about Jesus, that the truth is out there, and this gives a definite advantage to those scholars who make claims about supposed new sources, new gospels. Recognizing these public tastes encourages the media to take up and publicize such claims, which remain in public discourse long after the original academic theories have been refuted or withdrawn. In fact, successive claims gain strength by a kind of cumulative process, as each new theory evokes popular expectations based upon memories of earlier discoveries. Assertions about the Nag Hammadi finds met an enthusiastic response from a public well accustomed to remarkable statements about the recent finds from Qumran, and familiar with repeated news stories about the Christian-related materials said to be contained therein.

Next Time Around?

Ideas and fantasies concerning hidden gospels will continue to flourish as long as people are interested in the figure of Jesus, and as long as they wish to root their beliefs in some acceptable scripture. Even when the scholarly world cools toward the *Gospel of Thomas*, the belief in a primitive fifth gospel is now so widely held that the idea has become almost archetypal, and it will surely shape responses to any future claims. We can also predict that other gospels will indeed be discovered in the future, possibly other substantial collections such as those of Nag Hammadi or Qumran, and that these documents, too, will attract excitement like that surrounding *Thomas*. (Judging by the frequency of ancient references, the *Gospel of Matthias* would be a truly dramatic find, and early writers tended to mention the work in the same context as *Thomas*.)[10] Foretelling such discoveries is not a matter of mystical or apocalyptic prophecy, but rather a logical extrapolation from the history of archaeology and New Testament research over the last century or so. Major finds have occurred quite regularly, and there is no reason to believe that the two most famous manuscript hoards were the only ones of their kind. We can be equally sure that the claims made for new texts, the latest codex or scroll, will be just as extravagant as those for *Peter* and *Thomas* in their respective periods of glory. Quite probably, there will at that future date be yet another candidate for a fifth gospel, a document or source which allegedly threatens to overthrow the assumptions of Christianity. If historical trends are anything to go by, the "real Jesus" reconstructed from these documents will be found to speak precisely to the issues and concerns of that particular era, and will thus be a potent rhetorical weapon in the controversies of the day.

But as surely as past experiences allow us to predict this development, they also provide us with means to assess these claims and, ideally, to combat the more outrageous misstatements which will likely emerge. The most important point is to recognize the "hidden gospel" idea for the cultural and religious phenomenon which it is, and to understand the underlying mythological structure which determines how that text is viewed. In this context, exaggerated hopes and expectations are inevitable, and early media reports will almost certainly feature florid claims about the implications of a putative new gospel, ideas which will crumble upon closer examination. Such ideas can have a wide public impact, but to put this in context, it is helpful to recall the fantastic charges made on the basis of other documentary finds in bygone years: remember how the Dead Sea Scrolls had "disproved Christianity"? In reality, they did nothing of the sort, so why should any later finds, the latest hidden gospel *du jour*?

Assertions about both the dating and independent authority of any new hidden gospel need to be scrutinized carefully, since it is essential to the whole narrative that the rediscovered text must be of unparalleled importance and antiquity. Amazing statements about a new gospel need to be looked at all the more closely when the source in question seems just too relevant to the needs of modern-day interest groups, too valuable for contemporary debates. And does the source—*Matthias*, perhaps—really offer evidence that is as entirely novel or epoch-making as it appears? Diligent exploration of the very large literature of New Testament scholarship over the last century or so might suggest that the "new" insight is nothing of the kind, however conveniently the work of past generations will be overlooked. As we have seen, a kind of historical amnesia is a necessary feature of the whole myth of concealment and discovery. It is pleasing to think of scholars of the mid-twenty-first century boasting that their own daring speculations would have been inconceivable to any previous generation of Biblical researchers, naive fundamentalists that they all were. Who knows, perhaps they will also believe themselves to be the first generation since antiquity to have rediscovered Gnosticism.

The more we study the hidden gospel theme, the better able we are to understand the waves of excitement which will be aroused by future finds and, ideally, the better to place them in proper context. Realistically, though, looking at the remarkable subculture generated by *Thomas* and its like in our own era, we should not be too optimistic about any possible efforts we might make. Is it too much to hope that next time—and there assuredly will be a next time—new gospels might be evaluated on their merits, and not solely for their value in cultural battles? Perhaps the question answers itself. In a society in which Christianity plays such a critical role as modern North America, the public is likely to feel that new gospels are simply too important to be left to scholars.

Notes

Note on dating style: Unless otherwise stated, all dates throughout are A.D:, or Common Era.

Abbreviations

ANCF   Alexander Roberts and James Donaldson, eds., *Ante-Nicene Christian Fathers*, 10 Vols. (Edinburgh: T. and T. Clark, and Grand Rapids, Mich.: Eerdmans, 1989–90)

CC   *Christian Century*

CT   *Christianity Today*

LAT   *Los Angeles Times*

SPCK   Society for Promoting Christian Knowledge

Chapter 1. Hiding and Seeking

Epigraph: Origen, quoted in E. Hennecke and W. Schneemelcher, *New Testament Apocrypha* (London: SCM Press, 1973), I: 56.

1. Russell Shorto, *Gospel Truth* (New York: Riverhead Books, 1997), 121, quoting *Gospel of Thomas*, saying 97; Robert W. Funk, Roy W. Hoover, and the Jesus Seminar, *The Five Gospels* (New York: Macmillan, and Sonoma, Calf.: Polebridge Press, 1993), 523–24.

2. This is taken from the first episode of *Christianity: The First Thousand Years*, a television documentary broadcast on A & E, Nov. 29–30, 1998.

3. Elaine H. Pagels, *The Gnostic Gospels* (New York: Random House, 1979); James M. Robinson, *The Nag Hammadi Library in English*, 4th rev. ed. (Leiden: E. J. Brill, 1996). Compare John Dart, *The Laughing Savior* (New York: Harper & Row, 1976); John Dart, *The Jesus of Heresy and History* (San Francisco: Harper & Row, 1988). For other collections of "new gospels," see Ron Cameron, *The Other Gospels* (Philadelphia: Westminster, 1982); Willis Barnstone, ed., *The Other Bible* (San Francisco: Harper San Francisco, 1984); John Dominic Crossan, *Four Other Gospels* (Minneapolis: Winston Press, 1985); Marvin Meyer, *The Secret Teachings of Jesus: Four Gnostic Gospels* (New York: Vintage Books 1986); Ron Cameron, *The Apocryphal Jesus and Christian Origins* (Atlanta, Ga.: Scholars Press, 1990); Ricky A. Mayotte, ed., *The Complete Jesus* (South Royalton, Vt.: Steerforth Press, 1997). Compare Graham N. Stanton, *Gospel Truth?* (Valley Forge, Pa.: Trinity Press International, 1995).

4. For the idea of "the Way," see Mark 1: 1–3; John 14: 6; Acts 9: 2, 22.4.

5. Gregory J. Riley, *One Jesus, Many Christs: How Jesus Inspired Not One True Christianity, but Many* (San Francisco: Harper San Francisco, 1997). Gerd

Lüdemann, *Heretics: The Other Side of Early Christianity* (Louisville, Ky.: Westminster John Knox Press 1996); Keith Hopkins, *A World Full of Gods* (New York: Free Press, 2000).

6. E. Hennecke and W. Schneemelcher, *New Testament Apocrypha*, 2 vols. (London: SCM Press, 1973), I:25; J. K. Elliott, *The Apocryphal New Testament* (Oxford: Clarendon, 1993). The orthodox Fathers mentioned are Irenaeus and Tertullian. The title of James H. Charlesworth's *Authentic Apocrypha* (North Richland Hills, Tex.: BIBAL 1998) plays on the paradox of "apocrypha" being ipso facto unauthentic.

7. Funk et al., *The Five Gospels*, p. 35.

8. Pagels, *Gnostic Gospels*, xxxv.

9. Albert Schweitzer, *The Quest of the Historical Jesus* (Baltimore, Md.: Johns Hopkins Univ. Press, 1998); Gregory W. Dawes, ed., *The Historical Jesus Quest* (Louisville, Ky.: Westminster John Knox Press, 2000). The "third quest" can conveniently be dated to about 1985, with the formation of the Jesus Seminar, and the publication of books such as Marcus J. Borg, *Conflict, Holiness and Politics in the Teachings of Jesus* (New York: Edwin Mellen Press, 1984), and Thomas Sheehan, *The First Coming* (New York: Random House, 1986). For modern-day quests, see Hershel Shanks, ed., *The Search for Jesus* (Washington, D.C.: Biblical Archaeology Society, 1994); Claudia Setzer, "The Quest for The Historical Jesus," *Tikkun*, July 17, 1995, p. 73; Michael R. McAteer and Michael G. Steinhauser, *The Man in the Scarlet Robe* (Etobicoke, Ontario: United Church Pub. House, 1996); Shorto, *Gospel Truth*; Charlotte Allen, *The Human Christ* (New York: Free Press, 1998); Donald Harman Akenson, *Surpassing Wonder* (Montreal: McGill Queens Univ. Press, 1998); Gerd Theissen and Annette Merz, *The Historical Jesus* (Minneapolis: Fortress Press, 1998); Mark Allan Powell, ed., *Jesus as a Figure in History* (Louisville, Ky.: Westminster John Knox Press, 1998); Raymond Martin, *The Elusive Messiah* (Boulder, Colo.: Westview, 1999); Charles W. Hedrick, *When History and Faith Collide* (Peabody, Mass.: Hendrickson, 1999); Stephen J. Patterson, *The God of Jesus* (Harrisburg, Pa.: Trinity Press International, 1999); Bart D. Ehrman, *Jesus: Apocalyptic Prophet of the New Millennium* (New York: Oxford Univ. Press, 1999); W. Barnes Tatum, *In Quest of Jesus* (Nashville, Tenn.: Abingdon Press, 1999); Walter P. Weaver, *The Historical Jesus in the Twentieth Century—1900–1950* (Harrisburg, Pa.: Trinity Press International, 1999); James H. Charlesworth and Walter P. Weaver, *Jesus Two Thousand Years Later* (Harrisburg, Pa.: Trinity Press International, 2000); Robert M. Price, *Deconstructing Jesus* (Amherst, N.Y.: Prometheus Books, 2000). For critiques of the whole idea of a historical quest, see Luke Timothy Johnson, *The Real Jesus* (San Francisco: Harper San Francisco, 1996), and *Living Jesus* (San Francisco: Harper San Francisco, 1999).

10. Stevan L. Davies, *The Gospel of Thomas and Christian Wisdom* (New York: Seabury Press, 1983), 1.

11. Robert W. Funk, *Honest to Jesus* (San Francisco: Harper San Francisco, 1996), 74. For the work of the Jesus Seminar, see Robert W. Funk, Bernard Brandon Scott, and James R. Butts, *The Parables of Jesus*

(Sonoma, Calif.: Polebridge Press, 1988); Robert W. Funk with Mahlon H. Smith, *The Gospel of Mark: Red Letter Edition* (Sonoma, Calif.: Polebridge Press, 1991); Robert W. Funk, ed., *The Acts of Jesus* (Sonoma, Calif.: Polebridge Press and San Francisco: Harper San Francisco, 1998); Robert W. Funk and the Jesus Seminar, *The Gospel of Jesus According to the Jesus Seminar* (Sonoma, Calif.: Polebridge Press, 1999).

12. Funk et al., *The Five Gospels*, xiii.

13. Robert J. Miller, ed., *The Complete Gospels*, rev. and expanded ed. (Sonoma, Calif.: Polebridge Press, 1994), cover.

14. John Dart and Ray Riegert, *Unearthing the Lost Words of Jesus* (Berkeley, Calif.: Seastone, 1998).

15. Ian Bradley, *Celtic Christianity* (Edinburgh: Edinburgh Univ. Press, 1999).

16. For "equal access," see Pagels, *Gnostic Gospels*, 42; for "original creative invention," ibid., 19.

17. *From Jesus to Christ*, broadcast April 6–7, 1998. An important collection of documents relating to this program was presented on the Internet, at http://www.pbs.org/wgbh/pages/frontline/shows/religion/.

18. Johnson, *Real Jesus*, 88–89; John P. Meier, *A Marginal Jew* (New York: Doubleday, 1991); Michael J. Wilkins and James P. Moreland, eds., *Jesus under Fire* (Grand Rapids, Mich.: Zondervan, 1995).

19. G. R. S. Mead, ed., *Pistis Sophia: A Gnostic Miscellany* (1896; London: J. M. Watkins, 1921); Philip Jenkins, *Mystics and Messiahs* (New York: Oxford Univ. Press, 2000); Richard Smoley and Jay Kinney, *Hidden Wisdom* (New York: Penguin USA, 1999).

20. N. T. Wright, "A Return to Christian Origins (Again)," *Bible Review*, December 1999, p. 10.

21. Introduction to Thich Nhat Hanh, *Living Buddha, Living Christ* (New York: Riverhead Books, 1995), xxiii, xxv.

22. Pagels, *Gnostic Gospels*, xx–xxi. For Buddhist parallels to Christianity, see Marcus J. Borg and Ray Riegert, *Jesus and Buddha* (Berkeley, Calif.: Seastone Press, 1999); Thich Nhat Hanh, *Going Home: Jesus and Buddha as Brothers* (New York: Riverhead Books, 1999).

23. Even in a matter as radical and innovative as same-sex marriage, advocates were galvanized by the work of John Boswell, who argued that the Christian Church supposedly had a long practice of blessing such unions. An argument from ancient tradition still appears to carry weight. See John Boswell, *Same-Sex Unions in Premodern Europe* (New York: Villiard Books, 1994).

24. Bruce Bawer, *Stealing Jesus* (New York: Crown, 1997).

25. For the construction of historical memory, see Raphael Samuel, *Theatres of Memory*, vol. 1 (London: Verso, 1994); Edwin M. Yoder, *The Historical Present* (Jackson: Univ. Press of Mississippi, 1997); Pierre Nora, *Realms of Memory: Rethinking the French Past*, 3 vols. (New York: Columbia Univ. Press, 1996–98).

26. Nachman Ben-Yehuda, *The Masada Myth* (Madison: Univ. of Wisconsin Press, 1995).

27. Michael Owen Wise, Martin G. Abegg, and Edward M. Cook, eds., *The Dead Sea Scrolls* (New York: HarperCollins, 1999), 3.

28. Thomas C. Römer, "Transformations in Deuteronomistic and Biblical Historiography," in *Zeitschrift für Alttestamentliche Wissenschaft* 109 (1997): 1–11. I owe this reference to my colleague, Gary Knoppers.

29. 2 Kings chapter 22; 2 Chron. chapter 34.

30. Frances Yates, *The Rosicrucian Enlightenment* (London: Routledge and Kegan Paul, 1972).

31. John L. Brooke, *The Refiner's Fire* (New York: Cambridge Univ. Press, 1994); Richard N. Ostling and Joan K. Ostling, *Mormon America* (San Francisco: Harper San Francisco, 1999).

32. The story of the discovery is conveniently summarized in Dart and Riegert, *Unearthing the Lost Words of Jesus*.

Chapter 2. Fragments of a Faith Forgotten

1. Robert J. Miller, ed., *The Complete Gospels*, rev. and expanded ed. (Sonoma, Calif.: Polebridge Press, 1994), 3.

2. Elaine H. Pagels, *The Gnostic Gospels* (New York: Random House, 1979), xxii, xxxv.

3. Robert W. Funk, *Honest to Jesus* (San Francisco: Harper San Francisco, 1996), 71.

4. Throughout this book, I am using patristic translations from the Ante-Nicene Christian Fathers, as found in *ANCF*. References to Irenaeus are also taken from *ANCF*. See J. T. Nielsen, ed., *Irenaeus of Lyons versus Contemporary Gnosticism* (Leiden: E. J. Brill, 1977); Robert M. Grant, *Irenaeus of Lyons* (London: Routledge, 1997).

5. Gerd Lüdemann and Martina Janssen, *Suppressed Prayers* (Harrisburg, Pa.: Trinity Press International 1998); Alastair H. B. Logan, *Gnostic Truth and Christian Heresy* (Edinburgh: T. and T. Clark, 1996); Gerd Lüdemann, *Heretics: The Other Side of Early Christianity* (Louisville, Ky.: Westminster John Knox Press 1996); Pheme Perkins, *Gnosticism and the New Testament* (Minneapolis: Fortress Press, 1993); Bentley Layton, *The Gnostic Scriptures* (Garden City, N.Y.: Doubleday, 1987).

6. W. H. C. Frend, *The Rise of Christianity* (Philadelphia: Fortress, 1984), 195–215.

7. Layton, *The Gnostic Scriptures*; Edwin Yamauchi, *Pre-Christian Gnosticism* (London: Tyndale, 1973).

8. E. Hennecke and W. Schneemelcher, *New Testament Apocrypha*, 2 vols. (London: SCM Press, 1973), I: 164 (the Tabor reference) and 166–67 (dialogue with Salome).

9. Marvin Meyer, ed., *The Unknown Sayings of Jesus* (San Francisco: Harper San Francisco, 1998); William L. Petersen, Johan S. Vos, and Henk J. de Jonge, eds., *Sayings of Jesus* (Leiden: Brill, 1997); William G. Morrice, *Hidden Sayings of Jesus* (Peabody, Mass.: Hendrickson Publishing, 1997); Hennecke and Schneemelcher, *New Testament Apocrypha*, I: 89; Joachim Jeremias, *Unknown Sayings of Jesus*, 2nd English ed. (London: SPCK, 1964)

10. "Sayings of Jesus Not in the Gospels," *American Monthly Review of Reviews* 9, Feb. 1894, p. 208.

11. Joseph Jacobs, *As Others Saw Him* (Boston and New York: Houghton,

Mifflin, 1895); Charles George Griffinhoofe, *The Unwritten Sayings of Christ* (Cambridge: W. Heffer and Sons, 1903); Bernhard Pick, ed., *The Extra-canonical Life of Christ* (New York: Funk and Wagnalls, 1903); Roderic Dunkerley, *The Unwritten Gospel* (London: Allen and Unwin, 1925).

12. Kurt W. Marek, *Gods, Graves, and Scholars*, 2nd ed. (New York: Knopf, 1967).

13. Carolyn Osiek, *Shepherd of Hermas* (Minneapolis: Fortress Press, 1999); Kurt Niederwimmer, *The Didache* (Minneapolis: Fortress Press, 1998); Kirsopp Lake, *The Apostolic Fathers* (New York: Putnam, 1912–13).

14. Bernard P. Grenfell and Arthur S. Hunt, eds., *New Sayings of Jesus and a Fragment of a Lost Gospel from Oxyrhynchus* (London: H. Frowde, 1904); Walter Lock and William Sanday, *Two Lectures on the "Sayings of Jesus" Recently Discovered at Oxyrhynchus* (Oxford: Clarendon Press, 1897).

15. Hugh G. Evelyn White, *The Sayings of Jesus from Oxyrhynchus* (Cambridge: Cambridge Univ. Press, 1920), xxix-xxx; Kirsopp Lake, "The New Sayings of Jesus and the Synoptic Problem," *Hibbert Journal* 3 (1905): 332–41; R. Ogden, "New Sayings of Jesus," *Nation* 65, August 5, 1897, p. 104.

16. For the "vastly important logia," see B. P. Grenfell, "Discovery of the Oldest Record of Christ," *American Monthly Review of Reviews* 16, October 1897, pp. 455–56.

17. H. I. Bell and T. C. Skeat, *The New Gospel Fragments* (London, 1935); Sir Frederic George Kenyon, *The Chester Beatty Biblical Papyri*, 8 vols. (London: Emery Walker, 1933–41); Graham N. Stanton, *Gospel Truth?* (Valley Forge, Pa.: Trinity Press International, 1995).

18. J. Rendel Harris, "A New Gospel and Some New Apocalypses," *Contemporary Review*, Dec. 1899, pp. 803–18; J. Rendel Harris, *The Newly-Recovered Gospel of St. Peter* (New York: James Pott and Co., 1893); H. B. Swete, ed., *Euaggelion kata Petron: The Akhmim Fragment of the Apocryphal Gospel of St. Peter* (London and New York: Macmillan, 1893). For modern discussions of the significance of *Peter*, see chapter 4.

19. Solomon Schechter, *Documents of Jewish Sectaries*, vol. 1: *Fragments of a Zadokite Work* (Cambridge: Cambridge Univ. Press, 1910); Michael Owen Wise, Martin G. Abegg, and Edward M. Cook, eds., *The Dead Sea Scrolls* (New York: HarperCollins, 1999), 49–74; Charlotte Allen, *The Human Christ* (New York: Free Press, 1998), 314.

20. Edgar J. Goodspeed, *Strange New Gospels* (Chicago: Univ. of Chicago Press, 1931), 1.

21. E. J. Dillon, "The Primitive Gospel," *Contemporary Review*, June 1893, pp. 857–70; J. Rendel Harris, "The New Syriac Gospels," *Contemporary Review* 66, Nov. 1894, pp. 654–73; "Sayings of Jesus Not in the Gospels," *American Monthly Review of Reviews* 9, Feb. 1894, p. 208; Benjamin W. Bacon, "Are the New Sayings of Christ Authentic?," *Outlook*, July 31, 1897, pp. 785–89; R. Ogden, "New Sayings of Jesus," *Nation* 65, Aug. 5, 1897, p. 104; J. Rendel Harris, "A New Gospel and Some New Apocalypses," *Contemporary Review*, Dec. 1899: 802–18; "Alleged New Sayings of Jesus," *Harper's Weekly*, Nov. 28, 1903, p. 1893; "Sayings of Jesus Not in the Bible," *American Monthly Review of Reviews*, Sept. 1904, p. 366; Vernon

Bartlet, "Oxyrhynchus Sayings of Jesus," *Contemporary Review,* Jan. 1905, pp. 116–25; "The New Gospel Fragment," *Independent* 64, Jan. 1908, pp. 107–9; C. O. Morison, "Was Jesus a Peasant?," *Outlook* 89, May 1908, pp. 223–24; E, McClure, "Latest Light from Egypt on the Holy Scriptures," *Nineteenth Century* 70, Dec. 1911, pp. 1135–46.

22. Quoted in Walter W. Wessel, "Voting Out the Fourth Beatitude," *CT,* Dec. 12, 1986, p. 34.

23. Ogden, "New Sayings of Jesus."

24. E. J. Dillon, "The Primitive Gospel," *Contemporary Review,* June 1893, pp. 857–70, at 857; Harris, "A New Gospel and Some New Apocalypses," 803; Layton, *Gnostic Scriptures,* 205.

25. Dillon, "The Primitive Gospel," 857.

26. Harris, "A New Gospel and Some New Apocalypses," 802–3.

27. Francis Legge, ed. and translator, *Philosophumena: or, The Refutation of All Heresies . . . Formerly Attributed to Origen, but Now to Hippolytus, Bishop and Martyr,* 2 vols. (London: SPCK, 1921). For other scholarship on Gnostic writings in this era, see F. Lamplugh, ed., *The Gnosis of the Light: A Translation of the Untitled Apocalypse Contained in the Codex Brucianus* (London: J. M. Watkins, 1918); Charlotte A. Baynes, ed., *A Coptic Gnostic Treatise Contained in the Codex Brucianus* (Cambridge: Cambridge Univ. Press, 1933).

28. Anthony Ashley Bevan, *The Hymn of the Soul Contained in the Syriac Acts of St. Thomas* (Cambridge: Cambridge Univ. Press, 1897); W. Wright, *Apocryphal Acts of the Apostles,* 2 vols. (London: Williams and Norgate, 1871).

29. Carl Schmidt and Viola MacDermot, eds., *Pistis Sophia* (Leiden: Brill, 1978); for the attribution to Valentinus, see Annie Besant, *Esoteric Christianity* (New York: J. Lane, 1902), 96.

30. Allen, *Human Christ,* 235–36. G. R. S. Mead, *Echoes from the Gnosis* (London: Theosophical Pub. Society, 1906–8); Mead, *The Gnostic John the Baptizer* (London: J. M. Watkins, 1924).

31. Francis Legge, *Forerunners and Rivals of Christianity,* 2 vols. (1915; New York: Peter Smith, 1950), ii: 13.

32. Yamauchi, *Pre-Christian Gnosticism.*

33. George Horner, ed., *Pistis Sophia* (London: SPCK/Macmillan, 1924).

34. *ANCF.*

35. Alexander Walker, *Apocryphal Gospels, Acts and Revelations* (Edinburgh: T. and T. Clark, 1873). For some modern studies of the apocryphal acts, see Francois Bovon, Ann Graham Brock, and Christopher R. Matthews, eds., *The Apocryphal Acts of the Apostles* (Cambridge, Mass.: Harvard Univ. Center for the Study of World Religions, 1999); Jan N. Bremmer, *The Apocryphal Acts of Peter* (Leuven: Peeters, 1998); Bremmer, ed., *The Apocryphal Acts of Paul and Thecla* (Kampen: Kok Pharos Pub. House, 1996).

36. M. R. James, *The Apocryphal New Testament* (Oxford: Clarendon Press, 1924). James was using the portions of *Thomas* in the Oxyrhynchus papyri: the verses then available were 1–7, 24, 26–33, 36–39, and 77. Compare White, *The Sayings of Jesus from Oxyrhynchus.* Arthur Stanley, ed., *The Bedside Book* (London: Gollancz, 1940), 801.

37. Charles William King, *The Gnostics and Their Remains* (London: Bell and Dalby, 1864).

38. G. R. S. Mead, *Fragments of a Faith Forgotten* (London: Theosophical Publishing Society, 1900); Legge, *Forerunners and Rivals of Christianity,* I: 196n, II: 134–202.

39. F. C. Burkitt, *Church and Gnosis* (Cambridge: Cambridge Univ. Press, 1932); George A. Gaskell, *Gnostic Scriptures Interpreted* (London: C. W. Daniel Co., 1927); Louis Gordon Rylands, *The Beginnings of Gnostic Christianity* (London: Watts, 1940).

40. James Beaven, *An Account of the Life and Writings of S. Irenaeus, Bishop of Lyons and Martyr* (London: Rivington, 1841); Henry Longueville Mansel, *Gnostic Heresies of the First and Second Centuries* (1875; New York: AMS Press, 1980).

41. J. B. Lightfoot, *Saint Paul's Epistles to the Colossians and to Philemon* (1875; London: Macmillan, 1897), 71–111.

42. Allen, *Human Christ,* 143–64; Stephen Neill and Tom Wright, *The Interpretation of the New Testament, 1861–1986,* 2nd ed. (New York: Oxford Univ. Press, 1988).

43. Washington Gladden *Who Wrote the Bible?* (Boston: Houghton, Mifflin, 1891); Charles Augustus Briggs, *The Authority of Holy Scripture,* 2nd ed. (New York: Scribner, 1891); R. Ogden, "New Sayings of Jesus," *Nation* 65, Aug. 5, 1897, p. 104; *Essays in Modern Theology and Related Subjects, Gathered and Published as a Testimonial to Charles Augustus Briggs . . . by a Few of His Pupils, Colleagues and Friends* (New York: C. Scribner's, 1911); Martin E. Marty, *Modern American Religion I: The Irony of It All* (Chicago: Univ. of Chicago Press, 1986); Mark Stephen Massa, *Charles Augustus Briggs and the Crisis of Historical Criticism* (Minneapolis: Fortress Press, 1990).

44. Walther Bauer, *Orthodoxy and Heresy in Earliest Christianity* (London: SCM Press, 1972), 203–4.

45. Bauer's *Orthodoxy and Heresy* was not translated into English until 1971. For critical analyses based on local case studies, see, for example, Colin H. Roberts, *Manuscript, Society, and Belief in Early Christian Egypt* (New York: Oxford Univ. Press, 1979).

46. Henry Chadwick, ed., *Contra Celsum* (Cambridge: Cambridge Univ. Press, 1953), 345–49. Aleister Crowley, *Magick in Theory and Practice* (New York: Castle Books, n.d., c. 1970), 354, 210; R. Van Den Broek and Wouter J. Hanegraaff, eds., *Gnosis and Hermeticism from Antiquity to Modern Times* (State Univ. of New York Press, 1997); Philip Jenkins, *Mystics and Messiahs* (New York: Oxford Univ. Press, 2000). For neo-Gnostic writings, see R. Swinburne Clymer, *The Divine Mystery . . . According to Pistis Sophia* (Allentown, Pa.: Philosophical Publishing Co., 1910).

47. H. P. Blavatsky, *Isis Unveiled,* 2 vols. (1877; New York: J. W. Bouton, 1886), II: 288–338.

48. Anna B. Kingsford, *The Credo of Christendom* (London: John M. Watkins, 1916), 88.

49. Besant, *Esoteric Christianity;* Alice Bailey, *The Reappearance of the Christ* (New York: Lucis, 1948); Rudolf Steiner, *From Jesus to Christ* (London: Rudolf Steiner Press, 1973); Rudolf Steiner, *Esoteric Christianity and the Mission of Christian Rosenkreutz,* 2nd ed. (London: Steiner, 1984); Robert

S. Ellwood, *The Cross and the Grail* (Wheaton, Ill.: Theosophical Pub. House, 1997).

50. Albert J. Edmunds, *Buddhist and Christian Gospels Now First Compared from the Originals* (Philadelphia, 1902); G. Shann, "Jesus Christ and Buddhism," *Nineteenth Century* 54, July 1903, pp. 120–125; Elmar Gruber and Holger Kersen, *The Original Jesus: The Buddhist Sources of Christianity* (Shaftesbury, Dorset: Element Books Limited, 1995); Marcus J. Borg and Ray Riegert, *Jesus and Buddha* (Berkeley, Calif.: Seastone Press, 1999); Marcus J. Borg and Ray Riegert, "East Meets West," *Bible Review,* Oct. 1999, pp. 18–29; Richard Hughes Seager, *The World's Parliament of Religions* (Bloomington: Indiana Univ. Press, 1994).

51. Arthur Lillie, *Buddhism in Christendom: or, Jesus, the Essene* (London: Kegan Paul, Trench and Co., 1887), 75; Lightfoot, *Saint Paul's Epistles to the Colossians and to Philemon,* 81–96, 114–79.

52. Ernst von Bunsen, *The Angel-Messiah of Buddhists, Essenes, and Christians* (London: Longmans, Green, 1880).

53. Frederick the Great is quoted from Michael Baigent and Richard Leigh, *The Dead Sea Scrolls Deception* (London: Corgi, 1991), 246; Blavatsky's views are from *Isis Unveiled,* I: 26; for other occult interpretations of Jesus based on the Essene connection, see Allen, *Human Christ,* 221–22; Legge, *Forerunners and Rivals,* I: 156.

54. G. K. Chesterton, *The Everlasting Man* (New York: Image Books, 1955), 200.

55. William D. Mahan, *The Archko Volume: or, The Archeological Writings of the Sanhedrin and Talmuds of the Jews . . . Translated . . . from Manuscripts in Constantinople, and the Records of the Senatorial Docket Taken from the Vatican at Rome* (New Canaan, Conn.: Keats Pub., 1975); compare William Hone, *The Lost Books of the Bible* (New York: Alpha House, 1926); Edmond B. Székely and Purcell Weaver, *The Gospel of Peace of Jesus Christ by the Disciple John,* 2nd ed. (Ashingdon, Essex: C. W. Daniel, 1947); Edmond B. Székely and Purcell Weaver, *The Essene Code of Life* (San Diego: Academy Books, 1973); Edmond B. Székely, *The Discovery of the Essene Gospel of Peace* (San Diego: Academy Books, 1975). For the debate over how the Book of Mormon came to be composed, see Richard N. Ostling and Joan K. Ostling, *Mormon America* (San Francisco: Harper San Francisco, 1999), 261–77.

56. Nicholas Notovitch, *The Unknown Life of Jesus Christ, from Buddhistic Records* (New York: G. W. Dillingham, 1894), 155–218; Goodspeed, *Strange New Gospels,* 10; Per Beskow, *Strange Tales about Jesus* (Philadelphia: Fortress Press, 1985).

57. Levi H. Dowling, *The Aquarian Gospel of Jesus the Christ* (Los Angeles: Royal Publishing Co., 1908); Rudolf Steiner, *The Fifth Gospel,* 3rd ed. (London: Rudolf Steiner Press, 1995); Jenkins, *Mystics and Messiahs;* Elizabeth Clare Prophet, *The Lost Years of Jesus* (Malibu, Calif.: Summit Univ. Press, 1984).

58. Goodspeed, *Strange New Gospels;* Beskow, *Strange Tales about Jesus.*

59. Jenkins, *Mystics and Messiahs.*

60. Theodore Ziolkowski, *Fictional Transfigurations of Jesus* (Princeton, N.J.: Princeton Univ. Press, 1972).

61. Albert Schweitzer, *The Quest of the Historical Jesus* (Baltimore, Md.: Johns Hopkins Univ. Press, 1998), 326.

62. *The Crucifixion and the Resurrection of Jesus, by an eyewitness* (Los Angeles, Calif.: Austin Publishing, 1919).

63. Guy Thorne, *When It Was Dark* (New York: G. P. Putnam's, 1905), 112–13.

64. James Hogg Hunter, *The Mystery of Mar Saba* (New York: Evangelical Publishers, 1940).

65. Ben Witherington, *The Paul Quest* (Downers Grove, Ill.: InterVarsity Press, 1998); Richard A. Horsley and Neil Asher Silberman. *The Message and the Kingdom* (New York: Grossett/Putnam, 1997).

66. George Moore, *The Brook Kerith* (New York: Macmillan), 386.

67. Ibid., 318 (on Paul), 357 (term "Christ"), and 367 (mustard).

68. Frank Harris, "The Miracle of the Stigmata," in Charles G. Waugh and Martin H. Greenberg, eds., *Cults!* (New York: Barnes and Noble, 1983), 5–17.

69 D. H. Lawrence, "The Man Who Died."

70. Robert Graves, *King Jesus* (London: Cassell, 1946), 238–39.

Chapter 3. The First Gospels? Q and *Thomas*

1. Marvin Meyer, *The Gospel of Thomas: The Hidden Sayings of Jesus* (San Francisco: Harper San Francisco, 1992); Stephen J. Patterson, *The Gospel of Thomas and Jesus* (Sonoma, Calif.: Polebridge Press, 1993); Richard Valantasis, *The Gospel of Thomas* (New York: Routledge, 1997); Risto Uro, ed., *Thomas at the Crossroads* (Edinburgh: T. and T. Clark, 1998); Bart D. Ehrman, *Jesus: Apocalyptic Prophet of the New Millennium* (New York: Oxford Univ. Press, 1999), 65–83. Herbert C. Merillat, *The Gnostic Apostle Thomas*, on the Internet at http://members.aol.com/didymus5/toc.html. The use of *Thomas* by the Jesus Seminar is discussed in Robert J. Miller, *The Jesus Seminar and Its Critics* (Santa Rosa, Calif.: Polebridge Press, 1999).

2. For the emergence of the Q idea, see Stephen Neill and Tom Wright, *The Interpretation of the New Testament, 1861–1986*, 2nd ed. (New York: Oxford Univ. Press, 1988).

3. Eusebius, *History of the Church*, iii 39.

4. John Dominic Crossan, *The Historical Jesus* (San Francisco: Harper San Francisco, 1991), 429.

5. R. Ogden, "New Sayings of Jesus," *Nation* 65, Aug. 5, 1897, p. 104.

6. Adolf von Harnack, *The Sayings of Jesus* (New York: G. P. Putnam's, 1908). Today, it is common to refer to a Q passage in terms of where it appears in Luke, so that the Lord's Prayer, which appears in Luke's chapter 11, verses 2–4, can be cited as Q, 11: 2–4.

7. Luke Timothy Johnson *The Real Jesus* (San Francisco: Harper San Francisco, 1996).

8. John S. Kloppenborg, *The Formation of Q* (Philadelphia: Fortress Press, 1987); Kloppenborg, *Q Parallels* (Sonoma, Calif.: Polebridge Press, 1988); John S. Kloppenborg, Marvin W. Meyer, Stephen J. Patterson, and Michael G. Steinhauser, *Q–Thomas Reader* (Sonoma, Calif.: Polebridge

Press, 1990); Arland D. Jacobsen, *The First Gospel* (Sonoma, Calif.: Pole-bridge Press, 1991); John S. Kloppenborg and Leif E. Vaage, *Early Christianity, Q and Jesus* (Atlanta: Scholars Press, 1992); John S. Kloppenborg, ed., *The Shape of Q* (Minneapolis: Fortress Press, 1994); John S. Kloppenborg, ed., *Conflict and Invention* (Valley Forge, Pa.: Trinity Press International, 1995); C. M. Tuckett, *Q and the History of Early Christianity* (Edinburgh: T. and T. Clark, 1996); Dale C. Allison, *The Jesus Tradition in Q* (Harrisburg, Pa.: Trinity Press International, 1997); Alan Kirk, *The Composition of the Sayings Source* (Leiden: Brill, 1998); John S. Kloppenborg Verbin, *Excavating Q* (Minneapolis: Fortress, 2000).

9. Q/Luke 11: 2–4; Matthew 6: 9–13. However, the early form of the prayer can also be traced from the version presented in the *Didache*.

10. Q/Luke 11: 29–32.

11. Matthew 12: 40, my emphasis.

12. See, for example, *Thomas*, saying 34.

13. E. Hennecke and W. Schneemelcher, *New Testament Apocrypha*, 2 vols. (London: SCM Press, 1973), I: 303: Quotations from Thomas also appear in many apocryphal works through the centuries: see M. R. James, *The Apocryphal New Testament* (Oxford: Clarendon Press, 1924), 36. For early traditions about the apostle Thomas, see James H. Charlesworth, *The Beloved Disciple* (Valley Forge, Pa.: Trinity Press International, 1995).

14. Q/Luke 17: 24; Matthew 24:40.

15. Q/Luke 17: 21; Q/Luke 11: 9.

16. *Thomas*, saying 113.

17. *Thomas*, sayings 42, 49.

18. *Thomas*, saying 3.

19. Luke 14: 34–35. Kloppenborg, *The Formation of Q*; Kloppenborg, ed., *The Shape of Q*.

20. James M. Robinson, "On Bridging the Gulf from Q to the *Gospel of Thomas*," in Charles W. Hedrick and Robert Hodgson, eds., *Nag Hammadi, Gnosticism and Early Christianity* (Peabody, Mass.: Hendrickson, 1986), 127–76.

21. Stevan L. Davies, *The Gospel of Thomas and Christian Wisdom* (New York: Seabury Press, 1983) 146.

22. Funk et al., *The Five Gospels*, 539.

23. L. Michael White is quoted from the symposium on the *Frontline* series *From Jesus to Christ—The First Christians*; the text is found on the related website at http://www.pbs.org/wgbh/pages/frontline/shows/religion/symposium/; Ben Witherington, *The Jesus Quest* (Downers Grove, Ill.: InterVarsity Press, 1995), 51–52.

24. Funk et al., *The Five Gospels*, 492–93.

25. Q/Luke 22: 30; Matthew 19: 28.

26. Q/Luke 14: 27.

27. Kirsopp Lake, "The New Sayings of Jesus and the Synoptic Problem," *Hibbert Journal* 3 (1905): 339; Gregory J. Riley, *Resurrection Reconsidered: Thomas and John in Controversy* (Minneapolis: Fortress Press, 1994).

28. Burton L. Mack, *The Lost Gospel* (San Francisco: Harper San Francisco, 1993), 4; Burton L. Mack, *Who Wrote the New Testament?* (San Francisco:

Harper San Francisco, 1995); Helmut Koester, *Ancient Christian Gospels* (Philadelphia: Trinity Press International, 1990), 86; John Steinbeck, *The Grapes of Wrath* (1939; New York: Viking ed., 1967), 436.

29. Stevan Davies is quoted from *The Gospel of Thomas and Christian Wisdom*, 81; Jack Miles is quoted from the cover of Mack, *Lost Gospel*; for the "pre-Christian gospel," see Robert J. Miller, ed., *The Complete Gospels*, rev. and expanded ed. (Sonoma, Calif.: Polebridge Press, 1994), 250; Funk's remark about the Christian overlay is from Robert W. Funk, *Honest to Jesus* (San Francisco: Harper San Francisco, 1996), 135.

30. Funk et al., *The Five Gospels*, 128.

31. Crossan, *The Historical Jesus*, 421–22.

32. *Thomas*, sayings 52, 88. For a firm reassertion of Jesus' Jewish identity, see Paula Fredriksen, *Jesus of Nazareth, King of the Jews* (New York: Knopf, 1999). Compare Donald Herman Akenson, *Saint Saul* (New York: Oxford Univ. Press, 2000).

33. Witherington, *Jesus Quest*, 160–96. Witherington, *Jesus the Sage* (Minneapolis: Fortress, 1994).

34. 1 Cor 1: 19; *Thomas*, saying 17, may conceivably be reflected in 1 Cor. 2: 9.

35. Gerd Theissen, *Sociology of Early Palestinian Christianity* (Philadelphia: Fortress Press, 1978); Burton L. Mack, *A Myth of Innocence* (Philadelphia: Fortress Press, 1988); Francis G. Downing, *Cynics and Christian Origins* (Edinburgh: T. and T. Clark, 1992); Leif E. Vaage, *Galilean Upstarts* (Valley Forge, Pa.: Trinity Press International, 1994); Witherington, *Jesus Quest*, 58–92, 138–41; Gregory Boyd, *Cynic, Sage or Son of God?* (Wheaton, Ill.: Victor Books, 1995); Ekkehard W. Stegemann and Wolfgang Stegemann, *The Jesus Movement* (Minneapolis: Fortress Press, 1999). Luke 14: 26; Marianne Sawicki, *Crossing Galilee* (Harrisburg, Pa.: Trinity Press International, 2000).

36. Shorto, *Gospel Truth*, 120.

37. Charlotte Allen, *The Human Christ* (New York: Free Press, 1998), 275; John Dominic Crossan, *Jesus: A Revolutionary Biography* (San Francisco: Harper San Francisco, 1994), 198.

38. Mack, *The Lost Gospel*, 2.

39. Witherington, *Jesus Quest*, 48–57; Bart D. Ehrman, *Jesus: Apocalyptic Prophet of the New Millennium* (New York: Oxford Univ. Press, 1999); Dale C. Allison, *Jesus of Nazareth: Millenarian Prophet* (Minneapolis: Fortress Press, 1999).

40. E. P. Sanders, *Jesus and Judaism* (Philadelphia: Fortress Press, 1985); W. Barnes Tatum, *John the Baptist and Jesus* (Sonoma, Calif.: Polebridge Press, 1994).

41. Witherington, *Jesus Quest*, 48–57; John P. Meier, *A Marginal Jew* (New York: Doubleday, 1991), vol. i, 124–41. Perhaps responding to criticisms concerning the authority of *Thomas*, Robert J. Miller frequently denies or understates the work's importance for the work of the Jesus Seminar, and rightly points out that the group does not accept that many of its sayings are likely to derive from Jesus himself (*The Jesus Seminar and Its Critics* (Santa Rosa, Calif.: Polebridge Press, 1999). However, the exis-

tence of *Thomas* is absolutely pivotal to the Seminar's wider approach to Q and "original Q," and the consequent denial of the "Doomsday Jesus."

42. Martha Lee Turner, *The Gospel According to Philip* (Leiden: E. J. Brill, 1996); Bentley Layton, *The Gnostic Scriptures* (Garden City, N.Y.: Doubleday, 1987), 339.

43. Howard Clark Kee, "A Century of Quests for the Culturally Compatible Jesus," *Theology Today* 52, No. 1 (1995): 17. For the controversy over the Gnostic elements in *Thomas*, see Davies, *The Gospel of Thomas and Christian Wisdom*; April D. De Conick, *Seek to See Him* (Leiden; New York: E. J. Brill, 1996).

44. *Thomas*, sayings 21, 61, 114.

45. Henry Chadwick, ed., *Contra Celsum* (Cambridge: Cambridge Univ. Press, 1953), 345–49n; James M. Robinson, *The Nag Hammadi Library in English* (Leiden: E. J. Brill, 1977), 104; *Thomas*, saying 7, quoted in Stephen J. Patterson and James M. Robinson, *The Fifth Gospel* (Harrisburg, Pa.: Trinity Press International, 1998), 43.

46. Benjamin W. Bacon, "Are the New Sayings of Christ Authentic?," *Outlook*, July 31, 1897, pp. 785–89.

47. De Conick, *Seek to See Him*, 26.

48. Robert M. Grant and David Noel Freedman, *The Secret Sayings of Jesus* (Garden City, N.Y.: Doubleday, 1960), 143.

49. Meier, *Marginal Jew*, 137; Craig Blomberg, "Where Do We Start Studying Jesus?," in Michael J. Wilkins and James P. Moreland, eds., *Jesus under Fire* (Grand Rapids, Mich.: Zondervan, 1995), 18–50.

50. Witherington, *Jesus Quest*, 176, 289 n32.

51. "The Meaning of Jesus," in *Books and Culture*, March-April 1999, p. 43.

52. N. T. Wright, *The New Testament and the People of God* (Minneapolis: Fortress Press, 1996) and Wright, *Jesus and the Victory of God* (Minneapolis: Fortress Press 1997).

53. *Thomas*, saying 12.

54. Gayle White, "Scholar to Speak on 'Secret Words' of Jesus," *Atlanta Journal-Constitution*, March 5, 1998.

55. Clement, *Stromata*, I, xii in *ANCF*.

56. The quote about *mysteria* is from Luke 8: 10/Matthew 13.11; compare Origen, *Contra Celsum*, I, ch. 7.

57. John Stevenson, ed., *A New Eusebius* (London: SPCK, 1977), 143.

58. Paul F. Bradshaw, "The Gospel and the Catechumenate in the Third Century," *Journal of Theological Studies* 50, no. 1 (1999): 143–52.

59. In the early third century, Origen asked, "Who is ignorant of the statement that Jesus was born of a virgin, and that He was crucified, and that His resurrection is an article of faith among many?" Henry Chadwick, ed., *Contra Celsum* (Cambridge: Cambridge Univ. Press, 1953).

60. Luke i, 3–4.

61. Kirsopp Lake, "The New Sayings of Jesus and the Synoptic Problem," *Hibbert Journal* 3 (1905): 338–39; quote from Hugh G. Evelyn White, *The Sayings of Jesus from Oxyrhynchus* (Cambridge: Cambridge Univ. Press, 1920), xxix.

62. 1 Cor. 15: 5–8; Riley, *Resurrection Reconsidered*.

63. Galatians 1.

64. Raymond E. Brown, *The Birth of the Messiah* (New York: Doubleday, 1993), Brown, *The Death of the Messiah* (New York: Doubleday, 1994); Meier, *Marginal Jew*.

65. *From Jesus to Christ* documentary.

66. Thomas Sheehan, *The First Coming* (New York: Random House, 1986).

67. The Scroll texts in question are 1QSa, 1Q28a, 4Q521, in Michael Owen Wise, Martin G. Abegg, and Edward M. Cook, eds., *The Dead Sea Scrolls* (New York: HarperCollins, 1999), 147, 420–22.

68. Philippians 2: 6–11; Colossians 1: 15–17.

Chapter 4. Gospel Truth

1. Helmut Koester, *Ancient Christian Gospels* (Philadelphia: Trinity Press International, 1990), xxx.

2. Bruce C. Metzger, *The Canon of the New Testament* (New York: Oxford Univ. Press), 1987. A large literature discusses the making of the Biblical apocrypha, but chiefly in the context of those books which in some traditions but not others are accepted as part of the Old Testament. These contested works include books such as *Tobit, Judith, the Wisdom of Solomon, Ecclesiasticus,* and the first and second *Books of Maccabees.* As we see below, churches have been far less liberal about accepting works on the fringes of the New Testament.

3. Gustav Niebuhr, "Nonbiblical Texts Gain Credence, Exposure," *Austin American Statesman,* Dec. 27, 1997.

4. James P. Carse, *The Gospel of the Beloved Disciple* (San Francisco: Harper San Francisco, 1997), introduction.

5. William L. Petersen, *Tatian's Diatessaron* (Leiden: E. J. Brill, 1994).

6. John Stevenson, ed., *A New Eusebius* (London: SPCK paperback ed., 1977), 122.

7. Eusebius, *History of the Church,* Book VI: 12; E. Hennecke and W. Schneemelcher, *New Testament Apocrypha* 2 vols. (London: SCM Press, 1973), I: 166–70, 179–87.

8. Eusebius, *History of the Church* VI: 25; Hennecke and Schneemelcher, *New Testament Apocrypha,* I: 52–56.

9. For the suppression of the *Diatessaron,* see John Stevenson, ed., *Creeds, Councils and Controversies* (London: SPCK, 1973), 308. Eusebius, *History of the Church,* Book III: 25; Hennecke and Schneemelcher, *New Testament Apocrypha,* vol I: 56–60, 158–65. Noncanonical gospels might have retained greater status in distant corners of the Christian world such as Ireland, where as late as the tenth century, texts such as the "Gospel of James son of Alphaeus" were used in the liturgy: M. McNamara, *The Apocrypha in the Irish Church* (Dublin: Institute for Advanced Studies, 1975), 51. The Irish also made much use of a "Gospel of the Hebrews," though it is not clear what exactly this work was; it was not the text cited by Eusebius.

10. Hennecke and Schneemelcher, *New Testament Apocrypha,* I: 45, 60.

11. Other volumes produced by the Jesus Seminar offer similar lists of lost gospels, candidates for a new canon. See, for example, Robert W. Funk with Mahlon H. Smith, *The Gospel of Mark: Red Letter Edition* (Sonoma,

Calif.: Polebridge Press, 1991), viii-xi. For a still more recent candidate for a primitive gospel (albeit very fragmentary), see Charles Hedrick and Paul Mirecki, *The Gospel of the Savior* (Santa Rosa, Calif.: Polebridge Press, 1998). Compare Graham N. Stanton, *Gospel Truth?* (Valley Forge, Pa.: Trinity Press International, 1995)

12. Crossan is quoted from the front cover of Robert J. Miller, ed., *The Complete Gospels*, rev. and expanded ed. (Sonoma, Calif.: Polebridge Press, 1994).

13. Miriam T. Winter, *The Gospel According to Mary* (New York: Crossroad, 1993), 24.

14. Elisabeth Schüssler Fiorenza, *But She Said* (Boston: Beacon Press, 1992), 73–76.

15. Reynolds Price, *The Three Gospels* (New York: Scribner, 1996); Price, "Jesus of Nazareth—Then and Now," *Time*, Dec. 6, 1999, pp. 84–94; James P. Carse, *The Gospel of the Beloved Disciple* (San Francisco: Harper San Francisco, 1997); Karen King, "Back to the Future," presentation at conference on "The Once and Future Jesus," held by the Westar Institute, Santa Rosa, Calif., Oct. 22, 1999.

16. Edward Beutner, in Russell Shorto, *Gospel Truth* (New York: Riverhead Books, 1997), 36.

17. Bentley Layton, *The Gnostic Scriptures* (Garden City, N.Y.: Doubleday, 1987), 194–98; Frank Williams, ed. and translator, *The Panarion of Epiphanius of Salamis*, 3 vols. in 2 (Leiden: E. J. Brill, 1987–94).

18. Miller, ed., *The Complete Gospels*, 405.

19. John Dominic Crossan, *The Cross That Spoke* (San Francisco: Harper and Row, 1988); similar observations were made by E. J. Dillon, "The Primitive Gospel," *Contemporary Review*, June 1893, pp. 857–70.

20. Robert W. Funk, ed., *The Acts of Jesus* (Sonoma, Calif.: Polebridge Press, and San Francisco: Harper San Francisco, 1998).

21. Compare John P. Meier, *A Marginal Jew* (New York: Doubleday, 1991), 116–18.

22. Ben Witherington, *The Jesus Quest* (Downers Grove, Ill.: InterVarsity Press, 1995), 267–68.

23. Koester, *Ancient Christian Gospels*, 220.

24. C. M. Tuckett, *Nag Hammadi and the Gospel Tradition* (Edinburgh: T. and T. Clark, 1986).

25. Koester, *Ancient Christian Gospels*; Ron Cameron, *Sayings Traditions in the Apocryphon of James* (Philadelphia: Fortress Press, 1984).

26. John Dominic Crossan, *The Birth of Christianity* (San Francisco: Harper San Francisco, 1998), 32.

27. James M. Robinson, *The Nag Hammadi Library in English* (Leiden: E. J. Brill, 1977), 29–36.

28. Stephen Emmel, Helmut Koester, and Elaine Pagels, eds., *Nag Hammadi Codex III, 5: The Dialogue of the Savior* (Leiden: Brill, 1984).

29. James H. Charlesworth, *Jesus within Judaism* (Garden City, N.Y.: Doubleday, 1988); E. P. Sanders, *Jesus and Judaism* (Philadelphia: Fortress Press, 1985); N. T. Wright, *The New Testament and the People of God* (Minneapolis: Fortress Press, 1996), and Wright, *Jesus and the Victory of God* (Minneapolis: Fortress Press, 1997).

30. Robert W. Funk, Roy W. Hoover, and the Jesus Seminar, *The Five Gospels* (New York: Macmillan 1993), 22; Robert J. Miller, *The Jesus Seminar and Its Critics* (Santa Rosa, Calif.: Polebridge Press, 1999), 50–51.

31. Meier, *Marginal Jew*, 116–23.

32. John Dominic Crossan, *The Historical Jesus* (San Francisco: Harper San Francisco, 1991), 428–29; Miller, ed., *The Complete Gospels*, 427–29; compare Hennecke and Schneemelcher, *New Testament Apocrypha*, I: 163

33. Crossan, *The Historical Jesus*, 422, 428.

34. Crossan, *The Birth of Christianity*, 115.

35. Ibid., 33; Douglas M. Parrott. ed., *Nag Hammadi Codices III,3–4 and V,1 with Papyrus Berolinensis 8502,3 and Oxyrhynchus Papyrus 1081: Eugnostos and the Sophia of Jesus Christ* (Leiden: E. J. Brill, 1991); James M. Robinson, *The Nag Hammadi Library in English* (Leiden: E. J. Brill, 1977), 207; compare Douglas M. Parrott, "Gnostic and Orthodox Disciples in the Second and Third Centuries," in Charles W. Hedrick and Robert Hodgson, eds., *Nag Hammadi, Gnosticism and Early Christianity* (Peabody, Mass.: Hendrickson, 1986); Hennecke and Schneemelcher, *New Testament Apocrypha*, vol. I: 248.

36. Morton Smith, *The Secret Gospel* (London: Gollancz, 1974); "The Secret Gospel," *Time*, Jan. 6, 1961, p. 48.

37. Witherington, *Jesus Quest*, 80–81; Meier, *Marginal Jew*, 120–22; Joseph A. Fitzmyer, "How to Exploit a Secret Gospel," *America*, June 28, 1973, pp. 570–72.

38. John 20: 31.

39. Majella Franzmann, *Jesus in the Nag Hammadi Writings* (Edinburgh: T. and T. Clark, 1996).

40. Elaine H. Pagels, *The Gnostic Gospels* (New York: Random House, 1979), 19, 23.

41. Hennecke and Schneemelcher, *New Testament Apocrypha*, I: 233.

42. Ibid., i, 55, for Origen; ibid., i, 60, for Athanasius.

43. Ronald F. Hock and Ray Riegert, eds., *The Life of Mary and Birth of Jesus* (Berkeley, Calif.: Ulysses Press, 1997); Ronald F. Hock, ed., *The Infancy Gospels of James and Thomas* (Sonoma, Calif.: Polebridge Press, 1996).

44. Miller, ed., *The Complete Gospels*, 370.

45. Robert W. Funk, "The Coming Radical Reformation: Twenty-One Theses," *The Fourth R* 11, no. 4 (July/Aug. 1998).

46. As Reynolds Price remarks of the noncanonical texts, "any dogged attempt to read them is apt to leave the reader with one prime reaction—those second and third century Christian editors who decided on the final contents of the New Testament were above all else, superb literary critics" (Price, "Jesus of Nazareth—Then and Now," 87).

Chapter 5. Hiding Jesus: The Church and the Heretics

1. Ian Bradley, *Celtic Christianity* (Edinburgh: Edinburgh Univ. Press, 1999). For the Protestant commemoration of the Albigensians and similar groups, see, for instance, the *Martyrs' Mirror* beloved of Mennonites and like-minded German sects.

2. Francis Legge, ed. and translator, *Philosophumena: or, The Refutation of All*

Heresies . . . Formerly Attributed to Origen, But Now to Hippolytus, Bishop and Martyr, 2 vols. (London: SPCK, 1921), II: 34; Pagels is quoted from http://www.pbs.org/wgbh/pages/frontline/shows/religion/why/.

3. Karen King, "Back to the Future," presentation at conference on "The Once and Future Jesus" held by the Westar Institute, Santa Rosa, Calif., Oct. 22, 1999; Elaine H. Pagels, *The Gnostic Gospels* (New York: Random House, 1979), xxiii.

4. John Stevenson, ed., *A New Eusebius* (London: SPCK, 1977), 181; Pagels is quoted from http://www.pbs.org/wgbh/pages/frontline/shows/religion/why/.

5. Rosemary Radford Ruether, *Women and Redemption* (Minneapolis: Fortress Press, 1998), 51, 55.

6. Gayle White, "Scholar to Speak on 'Secret Words' of Jesus," *Atlanta Journal-Constitution,* March 5, 1998.

7. Ruether, *Women and Redemption,* 50–51; Robert W. Funk, "The Coming Radical Reformation: Twenty-One Theses," *The Fourth R* 11, no. 4 (July/Aug. 1998).

8. Peter Lampe, *From Paul to Valentinus* (Minneapolis: Fortress Press, 1999); Rodney Stark, *The Rise of Christianity* (San Francisco: Harper San Francisco, 1997); Walter H. Wagner, *After the Apostles: Christianity in the Second Century* (Minneapolis: Fortress Press, 1994); Robert M. Grant, *Jesus after the Gospels* (Louisville, Ky.: Westminster/John Knox Press, 1990).

9. Karen Jo Torjesen, "You Are the Christ," in Marcus J. Borg, ed., *Jesus at 2000* (Boulder, Colo.: Westview, 1998), 85–86; Paula Frederiksen, *From Jesus to Christ,* 2nd ed. (New Haven, Conn.: Yale Univ. Press, 2000).

10. William Dalrymple, *From the Holy Mountain* (New York: Henry Holt, 1997), 68.

11. John Stevenson, ed., *Creeds, Councils and Controversies* (London: SPCK, 1973), 160.

12. James M. Robinson, *The Nag Hammadi Library in English* (Leiden: E. J. Brill, 1977), 50–53; Gerd Lüdemann, "From Faith to Knowledge," presentation at conference on "The Once and Future Jesus" held by the Westar Institute, Santa Rosa, Calif.: Oct. 23, 1999. See 2 Timothy 2: 17–18.

13. Robinson, *The Nag Hammadi Library in English,* 131; Martha Lee Turner, *The Gospel According to Philip* (Leiden: E. J. Brill, 1996).

14. Pagels, *The Gnostic Gospels,* 24.

15. Kurt Niederwimmer, *The Didache* (Minneapolis: Fortress Press, 1998). It would be very useful if we could provide reliable dates for the Pastoral epistles attributed to Paul, since these include important references to episcopacy and church organization, but opinions about dating these texts vary widely. For controversies over the dating of Timothy and the Pastorals, see Luke Timothy Johnson, *The Writings of the New Testament* (Minneapolis: Fortress Press, 1999), 423–52; Ben Witherington, *The Paul Quest* (Downers Grove, Ill.: InterVarsity Press, 1998), 110–14.

16. 1 Clement, 42–44.

17. The quotation about "the mind of Jesus Christ" is from Ignatius' letter to the Ephesians, 3–4; "the medicine of immortality" is from ibid., 20; William R. Schoedel, *Ignatius of Antioch,* ed. Helmut Koester (Philadelphia: Fortress Press, 1985).

18. Ignatius' Letter to the Smyrnaeans, 7–8.
19. Stephen Neill and Tom Wright, *The Interpretation of the New Testament, 1861–1986*, 2nd ed. (New York: Oxford Univ. Press, 1988), 45–58.
20. Legge, ed. and translator, *Philosophumena*, II: 66.
21. Betty Radice, ed., *Letters of the Younger Pliny* (London: Penguin Classics 1969), 294.
22. Clayton N. Jefford, *The Sayings of Jesus in the Teaching of the Twelve Apostles* (Leiden: E. J. Brill, 1989); Clayton N. Jefford, ed., *The Didache in Context* (Leiden: E. J. Brill, 1995); Jonathan A. Draper, ed., *The Didache in Modern Research* (Leiden: E. J. Brill, 1996).
23. *Didache*, 9: 2–4.
24. *Didache*, 11: 1–2.
25. G. K. Chesterton, *The Everlasting Man* (New York: Image Books, 1955), 222.

Chapter 6. Daughters of Sophia

1. Elaine H. Pagels, *The Gnostic Gospels* (New York: Random House, 1979), 69.
2. Biblical passages most frequently condemned as misogynistic include 1 Tim. 2: 9–14. Elizabeth Cady Stanton, *The Woman's Bible* (Boston: Northeastern Univ. Press, 1993). Other Victorian women took more extreme positions than Stanton, feeling that Christianity was too closely related to patriarchy to be worth saving; this was the message of Matilda J. Gage's *Women, Church and State* (1893). See Elisabeth Schüssler Fiorenza, *Sharing Her Word* (Boston: Beacon Press, 1998), 50–74.
3. Francis Legge, ed. and translator, *Philosophumena: or, The Refutation of All Heresies . . . Formerly Attributed to Origen, But Now to Hippolytus, Bishop and Martyr*, 2 vols. (London: SPCK, 1921), I: 121.
4. Henry Chadwick, ed., *Contra Celsum* (Cambridge: Cambridge Univ. Press, 1953), 312.
5. Bentley Layton, *The Gnostic Scriptures* (Garden City, N.Y.: Doubleday, 1987), 213–14.
6. Deirdre Good, "Pistis Sophia," in Elisabeth Schüssler Fiorenza, Ann Brock, and Shelly Matthews, eds., *Searching the Scriptures*, 2 vols. (New York: Crossroad, 1993–94), II: 678–707.
7. G. R. S. Mead, ed., *Pistis Sophia: A Gnostic Miscellany* (1896; London: J. M. Watkins, 1921), 318.
8. J. Rendel Harris, *The Odes and Psalms of Solomon* (Cambridge: Cambridge Univ. Press, 1909); James H. Charlesworth, ed., *The Odes of Solomon* (Oxford: Clarendon Press, 1973); Susan Ashbrook Harvey, "The Odes of Solomon," in Schüssler Fiorenza et al., eds., *Searching the Scriptures*, II: 86–98; Rosemary Radford Ruether, *Womanguides* (Boston: Beacon Press, 1985), 24–25, 29–31.
9. *Acts of Thomas*, ch. 50, in M. R. James, *The Apocryphal New Testament* (Oxford: Clarendon Press, 1924), 388; compare W. Wright, *Apocryphal Acts of the Apostles*, 2 vols. (London: Williams and Norgate, 1871), 189–90, though this latter translation omits the feminine emphasis of the passage.

10. Ibid., II: 116–45; Sheila E. McGinn, "The Acts of Thecla," in Schüssler Fiorenza et al., eds., *Searching the Scriptures*, II: 800–828. For the writing of the Acts of Thecla, see the passage of Tertullian in John Stevenson, ed., *A New Eusebius* (London: SPCK, 1977), 184.

11. Frances Swiney, *The Esoteric Teachings of the Gnostics* (London: Yellon, Williams, 1909); Swiney, *The Cosmic Procession: or, The Feminine Principle in Evolution* (London: E. Bell, 1906); Swiney, *The Awakening of Women, or, Woman's Part in Evolution*, 2nd ed. (London: W. Reeves, 1908).

12. Swiney, *Esoteric Teachings of the Gnostics*, 3–4 (Gnostics as first Christians), 9 (mutilated relics).

13. Ibid., 5 (persecutions), 15 (femininity of the Holy Spirit), 37n ("It is very suggestive of a sinister motive . . .), 40 ("persecution, degradation and maltreatment of womanhood").

14. Mary Daly, *Beyond God the Father* (Boston: Beacon 1973); "Desexing the Bible," *Time*, Nov. 8, 1976, p. 100; Rosemary Radford Ruether, *New Woman, New Earth* (New York: Seabury Press, 1975); Karen Armstrong, *The Gospel According to Woman* (New York: Doubleday Anchor, 1987); Rosemary Radford Ruether, *Gaia and God* (San Francisco: Harper San Francisco, 1992); Ursula King, *Women and Spirituality* (University Park: Pennsylvania State Univ. Press, 1993).

15. Carol P. Christ and Judith Plaskow, *Womanspirit Rising* (San Francisco: Harper San Francisco, 1979). The *Journal of Feminist Studies in Religion* dates from 1985.

16. Luise Schottroff, Silvia Schroer, and Marie-Therese Wacker, *Feminist Interpretation: The Bible in Women's Perspective* (Minneapolis: Fortress Press, 1998); Beverly Mayne Kienzle and Pamela J. Walker, eds., *Women Preachers and Prophets Through Two Millennia of Christianity* (Berkeley: Univ. of California Press, 1998); Karen L. King, ed., *Women and Goddess Traditions* (Minneapolis: Fortress Press, 1997); Luise Schottroff and Wolfgang Stegemann, *Jesus and the Hope of the Poor* (Maryknoll, N.Y.: Orbis Books, 1986); Phyllis Trible, *Texts of Terror* (Philadelphia: Fortress, 1984). For the works of Elisabeth Schüssler Fiorenza, see *In Memory of Her* (New York: Crossroad, 1984); Schüssler Fiorenza, *Bread Not Stone* (Boston: Beacon Press, 1984); Schüssler Fiorenza, *But She Said* (Boston: Beacon Press, 1992); Schüssler Fiorenza, *Discipleship of Equals* (New York: Crossroad, 1993); Schüssler Fiorenza et al., eds., *Searching the Scriptures*.

17. Q/Luke 13: 34–35; Matthew 23: 37–39.

18. Wisdom 7: 25–26, ch. 10; Ben Witherington, *The Jesus Quest* (Downers Grove, Ill.: InterVarsity Press, 1995), 160–96; Patrick J. Hartin, "Yet Wisdom Is Justified by Her Children," in John S. Kloppenborg, ed., *Conflict and Invention* (Valley Forge, Pa.: Trinity Press International, 1995), 151–64; Silvia Schroer, "The Book of Sophia," in Schüssler Fiorenza et al., eds., *Searching the Scriptures*, II: 17–38; Deirdre J. Good, *Reconstructing the Tradition of Sophia in Gnostic Literature* (Atlanta, Ga.: Scholars Press, 1987).

19. Stevan L. Davies, *The Gospel of Thomas and Christian Wisdom* (New York: Seabury Press, 1983), 147.

20. For the texts in Philippians and Colossians, see chapter 3 above

21. Stevenson, ed., *A New Eusebius*, 146. The Book of Wisdom is a deutero-canonical text, which means that it is accepted in Roman Catholic Bibles, but is not included in Jewish texts, nor in the Protestant Bibles which rely on the Jewish tradition.

22. The idea of the "fall into patriarchy" is critiqued in Kathleen L. Corley, "Feminist Myths of Christian Origins," in Elizabeth A. Castelli and Hal Taussig, eds., *Reimagining Christian Origins* (Valley Forge, Pa.: Trinity Press International, 1996), 51–67. One controversial theme in the literature concerns charges of anti-Semitism, as feminist writers extolled the egalitarianism of the Jesus movement, and contrasted it with the supposed repressiveness of Judaism. See Judith Plaskow, "Anti-Judaism in Feminist Christian Interpretation," in Schüssler Fiorenza et al., eds., *Searching the Scriptures*, I: 117–29; Katharina von Kellenbach, *Anti-Judaism in Feminist Writings* (Atlanta: Scholars Press, 1994).

23. Karen Jo Torjesen, *When Women Were Priests* (San Francisco: Harper San Francisco, 1993); Torjesen, "Reconstruction of Women's Early Christian History," in Schüssler Fiorenza et al., eds., *Searching the Scriptures*, I: 290–310; Torjesen, "The Early Christian *Orans*," in Kienzle and Walker, eds., *Women Preachers and Prophets*, 42–56.

24. Romans 16: 7 for Junia, 16: 2 for Phoebe. For Lydia, see Luise Schottroff, *Let the Oppressed Go Free* (Louisville, Ky., Westminster/John Knox Press, 1993), 131–37; Luise Schottroff, *Lydia's Impatient Sisters* (Louisville, Ky., Westminster/John Knox Press, 1995); "Hebrews Written by a Woman," *Outlook* 64, April 1900, pp. 895–96.

25. 1 Tim: 12–15; Susanne Heine, *Women and Early Christianity* (Minneapolis: Augsburg, 1988), 43–44.

26. Irenaeus 1:13 from *ANCF*; Pagels is quoted from http://www.pbs.org/wgbh/pages/frontline/shows/religion/first/roles.html.

27. The "fall into patriarchy" is from Schottroff, *Lydia's Impatient Sisters*, 14. Pagels is quoted from the television program *From Jesus to Christ*.

28. Christine Schenk, "Jesus and Women," in http://www.futurechurch.org/jesuswomen.htm.

29. Miriam T. Winter, *The Gospel According to Mary* (New York: Crossroad, 1993), 27.

30. Torjesen, "Reconstruction of Women's Early Christian History," 291; Luke Timothy Johnson, *The Real Jesus* (San Francisco: Harper San Francisco, 1996), 97–98, for the idea of suppressed voices. Rose Horman Arthur, *The Wisdom Goddess* (Lanham, Md.: Univ. Press of America, 1984); Karen L. King, ed., *Images of the Feminine in Gnosticism* (Philadelphia: Fortress Press, 1988).

31. Annti Marjanen, *The Woman Jesus Loved* (New York: E. J. Brill, 1996); Susan Haskins, *Mary Magdalen, Myth and Metaphor* (New York: Harcourt, Brace and Co., 1993), 30–54.

32. Jane Schaberg, "The Case of Mary Magdalen," in Hershel Shanks, ed., *Feminist Approaches to the Bible* (Washington, D.C.: Biblical Archaeology Society, 1995), 85. Schaberg herself wrote *The Illegitimacy of Jesus* (San Francisco: Harper & Row, 1987), which argues that Jesus' mother became pregnant by rape. Mary Rose D'Angelo, "Reconstructing Real

Woman in Gospel Literature," Ross Shepard Kraemer and Mary Rose D'Angelo, eds., *Woman and Christian Origins* (New York: Oxford Univ. Press, 1999), 105–28.

33. Mark 16: 9; Henry Chadwick, ed., *Contra Celsum* (Cambridge: Cambridge Univ. Press, 1953), 109

34. Luke 7: 36–50, John 8: 1–11. Pagels is quoted from http://www.pbs.org/wgbh/pages/frontline/shows/religion/first/roles.html.

35. James M. Robinson, *The Nag Hammadi Library in English* (Leiden: E. J. Brill, 1977), 471–74; Karen L. King, "The Gospel of Mary Magdalen," in Schüssler Fiorenza et al., eds., *Searching the Scriptures*, II: 601–634; King, "Prophetic Power and Women's Authority," in Kienzle and Walker, eds., *Women Preachers and Prophets Through Two Millennia of Christianity*, 42–56.

36. Robert J. Miller, ed., *The Complete Gospels*, rev. and expanded ed. (Sonoma, Calif.: Polebridge Press, 1994), 357; Cullen Murphy, *The Word According to Eve* (Boston: Houghton Mifflin, 1998), 202–14.

37. Karen L. King, "Women in Ancient Christianity," at http://www.pbs.org/wgbh/pages/frontline/shows/religion/first/women.html

38. Ruether, *Womanguides*, 161, 169–72.

39. *Thomas*, saying 114.

40. Robinson, *Nag Hammadi Library in English*, 138; Haskins, *Mary Magdalen*, 38.

41. King, "Women in Ancient Christianity."

42. Miller, ed., *The Complete Gospels*, cover.

43. Ibid. King, "The Gospel of Mary Magdalen," 609. King now places *Mary* in the early second century: Karen King, "Back to the Future," presentation at conference on "The Once and Future Jesus" held by the Westar Institute, Santa Rosa, Calif., Oct. 22, 1999. For the tradition of Christian prophecy, see Antoinette C. Wire, *The Corinthian Women Prophets* (Minneapolis: Fortress Press, 1995); Cecil M. Robeck, *Prophecy in Carthage* (Cleveland, Ohio: Pilgrim Press, 1992); Ronald E. Heine, ed., *The Montanist Oracles and Testimonia* (Macon, Ga.: Mercer Univ. Press, 1989); Edward Carus Selwyn, *The Christian Prophets and the Prophetic Apocalypse* (London: Macmillan, 1900).

44. Rosemary Radford Ruether, *Women and Redemption* (Minneapolis: Fortress Press, 1998), 57. Robert W. Funk and the Jesus Seminar, *The Gospel of Jesus According to the Jesus Seminar* (Sonoma, Calif.: Polebridge Press, 1999), 114.

45. King, "The Gospel of Mary Magdalen," 629 n10.

46. Torjesen, "Reconstruction of Women's Early Christian History," i, 291.

47. Luke 24: 11; Stanton, *Woman's Bible*, 143.

48. Epiphanius, quoted in Bentley Layton, *The Gnostic Scriptures* (Garden City, N.Y.: Doubleday, 1987), 202–9.

49. Pagels, *The Gnostic Gospels*, 60–61.

50. Anne McGuire, "Thunder, Perfect Mind," in Schüssler Fiorenza et al., eds., *Searching the Scriptures*, II: 39–54; Layton, *The Gnostic Scriptures*, 78, 205. For the woman prophet, see King, "Women in Ancient Christianity."

51. M. Waldstein and F. Wisse, ed., *The Apocryphon of John* (Leiden: E. J. Brill, 1995).

52. Karen L. King, "The Book of Norea, Daughter of Eve," in Schüssler Fiorenza et al., eds., *Searching the Scriptures*, II: 66–85.

53. Ruether, *Womanguides*, 122–23. Compare *Thomas*, saying 22; Ruether, *Women and Redemption*.

54. King, "Women in Ancient Christianity."

55. Robinson, *The Nag Hammadi Library in English*, 308.

56. Birger A. Pearson, "The Problem of Jewish Gnostic Literature," in Charles W. Hedrick and Robert Hodgson, eds., *Nag Hammadi, Gnosticism and Early Christianity* (Peabody, Mass.: Hendrickson, 1986); Francis T. Fallon, *The Enthronement of Sabaoth* (Leiden: E. J. Brill, 1978).

57. For the extensive intermingling of Christian and pagan elements in Egypt, see Marvin W. Meyer and Richard Smith, eds., *Ancient Christian Magic* (Princeton, N.J.: Princeton Univ. Press, 1994); C. Wilfred Griggs, *Early Egyptian Christianity* (Leiden: E. J. Brill, 1990).

58. Bentley Layton has argued that *Thunder* should in fact be seen as a riddle, the solution to which is "Eve," but this is open to debate: Layton, "The Riddle of the Thunder," in Hedrick and Hodgson, eds., *Nag Hammadi, Gnosticism and Early Christianity*.

59. See the criticism of Pagels in Heine, *Women and Early Christianity*, 108–17.

60. King, "Women in Ancient Christianity"; Jan N. Bremmer, ed., *The Apocryphal Acts of Paul and Thecla* (Kampen: Kok Pharos Pub. House, 1996). For Thecla as a historical character, see W. M. Ramsay, *The Church in the Roman Empire before A.D. 170* (New York: G. P. Putnam's Sons, 1893).

61. Ruether, *Women and Redemption*, 41–42; Stevan L. Davies, *The Revolt of the Widows* (Carbondale: Southern Illinois Univ. Press, 1980); Virginia Burrus, *Chastity as Autonomy* (Lewiston, N.Y.: E. Mellen Press, 1987).

Chapter 7. Into the Mainstream

Epigraph: Jorge Luis Borges, "From an Apocryphal Gospel," in David Curzon, ed., *The Gospels in Our Image* (New York: Harcourt Brace, 1995), 76.

1. For changes in contemporary American religion, see, for example, Roger Finke and Rodney Stark, *The Churching of America 1776–1990* (New Brunswick, N.J.: Rutgers Univ. Press 1992); Barry A. Kosmin and Seymour P. Lachman, *One Nation under God* (New York: Harmony Books, 1993). For social movement theory, see Marco Giugni, Doug McAdam, and Charles Tilly, eds., *How Social Movements Matter* (Univ. of Minnesota Press, 1999); Enrique Larana, Hank Johnston, and Joseph R. Gusfield, eds., *New Social Movements: From Ideology to Identity* (Philadelphia: Temple Univ. Press, 1994); Anthony Oberschall, *Social Movements: Ideologies, Interests, and Identities* (New Brunswick, N.J.: Transaction, 1993).

2. Lundy is quoted from Parker T. Williamson, "Sophia Upstages Jesus at ReImagining Revival," *Presbyterian Layman*, May-June 1998.

3. Luke Timothy Johnson, *The Real Jesus* (San Francisco: Harper San Francisco, 1996), 72–73.

4. These figures are compiled from reports and statistics presented in *Religious Studies News* during 1995, based on a survey by the Auburn Center for the Study of Theological Education, and the American Academy of Religion.

5. For "the fundamentalist mentality," see Robert W. Funk, Roy W. Hoover, and the Jesus Seminar, *The Five Gospels* (New York: Macmillan 1993), 1. For the actual scale of purges and disciplinary proceedings within the churches, see Martin E. Marty, *Modern American Religion*, vol. I: *The Irony of It All* (Univ. of Chicago Press, 1986) and vol II: *The Noise of Conflict* (Chicago: Univ. of Chicago Press, 1986 and 1991). The remark about "exiting ecclesiastical precincts" is from Robert W. Funk, *Honest to Jesus* (San Francisco: Harper San Francisco, 1996), 67.

6. Stephen Neill and Tom Wright, *The Interpretation of the New Testament, 1861–1986*, 2nd ed. (New York: Oxford Univ. Press, 1988).

7. John Dominic Crossan, *The Historical Jesus* (San Francisco: Harper San Francisco, 1991).

8. Carola Barth's dissertation was published as *Die Interpretation des Neuen Testaments in der Valentinianischen Gnosis* (Leipzig: A. Pries, 1908).

9. http://www.episdivschool.org/. Jackson W. Carroll, Barbara G. Wheeler, and Daniel O. Aleshire, eds., *Being There: Culture and Formation in Two Theological Schools* (New York: Oxford Univ. Press, 1997).

10. The trend is illustrated by the success of Christ and Plaskow's *Womanspirit Rising*, and many subsequent works; Teresa Watanabe, "A Feminist Focus," *LAT*, Jan. 29, 2000.

11. See, for example, the highly specific technical essays in a scholarly collection such as John D. Turner and Anne McGuire, eds., *The Nag Hammadi Library after Fifty Years* (Leiden: E. J. Brill, 1997).

12. Ben Witherington, *The Jesus Quest* (Downers Grove, Ill.: InterVarsity Press, 1995), 42–57; Johnson, *The Real Jesus*, 3.

13. Funk, Hoover, and the Jesus Seminar, *The Five Gospels*.

14. Charlotte Allen, *The Human Christ* (New York: Free Press, 1998), 261. For Claremont, see Watanabe, "A Feminist Focus," Watanabe, "Wealth of Diversity in Faith," *LAT* May 20, 2000.

15. James M. Robinson and Helmut Koester, *Trajectories Through Early Christianity* (Philadelphia: Fortress Press, 1971); Allen, *The Human Christ*, 262.

16. Marty, *Modern American Religion*, vols. I and II.

17. John Shelby Spong, *Rescuing the Bible from Fundamentalism* (San Francisco: Harper San Francisco, 1991); Spong, *Born of a Woman* (San Francisco: Harper San Francisco, 1992); Spong, *This Hebrew Lord* (San Francisco: Harper San Francisco, 1993); Spong, *Resurrection: Myth or Reality?* (San Francisco: Harper San Francisco, 1995); Spong, *Liberating the Gospels* (San Francisco: Harper San Francisco, 1997); Spong, *Why Christianity Must Change or Die* (San Francisco: Harper San Francisco, 1998); Spong, "Christ and the Body of Christ," presentation at conference on "The Once and Future Jesus" held at Santa Rosa, Calif., Oct. 21 1999.

18. Robert Wuthnow, *Sharing the Journey* (New York: Free Press, 1994). My comments about the audience for Jesus Seminar presentations are based on the Westar Institute's conference on "The Once and Future Jesus" in October 1999. Particularly instructive was an informal poll of church affiliations which Marcus Borg carried out at this event.

19. Marcus J. Borg, ed., *Jesus at 2000* (Boulder, Colo.: Westview, 1998).

20. James Ferry, *In the Courts of the Lord* (New York: Crossroad, 1994), introduction by Bishop Spong.

21. George Gallup and D. Michael Lindsay, *Surveying the Religious Landscape* (Harrisburg, Pa.: Morehouse, 2000); David Lyon, *Jesus in Disneyland* (Malden, Mass.: Blackwell, 2000): Kimon H. Sargeant, *Seeker Churches* (New Brunswick, N.J.: Rutgers University Press, 2000); Wade Clark Roof, *Spiritual Marketplace* (Princeton, N.J.: Princeton Univ. Press, 1999); Richard Cimino and Don Lattin, *Shopping for Faith* (San Francisco: Jossey-Bass, 1999); Elizabeth Lesser, *The New American Spirituality: A Seeker's Guide* (New York: Random House, 1999); Tom Beaudoin, *Virtual Faith* (San Francisco: Jossey-Bass, 1998); Robert Wuthnow, *After Heaven* (Berkeley: Univ. of California Press, 1998); Wuthnow, *Sharing the Journey*; Wuthnow, *Christianity in the Twenty-First Century* (New York: Oxford Univ. Press, 1993); Wade Clark Roof, *A Generation of Seekers* (San Francisco: Harper San Francisco, 1993).

22. The focus group survey is reported in Heidi Schlumpf, "Religion vs. Spirituality," in *Publishers Weekly*, Aug. 30, 1999, p. 54. John Dominic Crossan, "Almost the Whole Truth," *The Fourth R* (Sept./Oct. 1993). Hanna Rosin, "Beyond 2000: A Self-Made Deity," *Washington Post*, Jan. 18, 2000.

23. Winifred Gallagher, *Working on God* (New York: Random House, 1999); Nora Gallagher, *Things Seen and Unseen* (New York: Knopf, 1998); Kathleen Norris, *Amazing Grace* (New York: Riverhead, 1998); Frederica Mathewes-Green, *Facing East* (San Francisco: Harper San Francisco, 1997); Bill Moyers, *Genesis* (New York: Doubleday, 1996); Gary Dorsey, *Congregation* (New York: Viking,1995); Matthew Fox, *Illuminations of Hildegard of Bingen* (Santa Fe, N.M., Bear and Co., 1985).

24. Neil Douglas-Klotz, *The Hidden Gospel* (Wheaton, Ill.: Quest Books/Theosophical Pub. House, 1999); Nevill Drury, *Exploring the Labyrinth: Making Sense of the New Spirituality* (New York: Continuum, 1999); Christian D. Amundsen, *Insights from the Secret Teachings of Jesus: The Gospel of Thomas* (Fairfield, Ia.: Sunstar Publishing, 1999); Richard Smoley and Jay Kinney, *Hidden Wisdom* (New York: Penguin USA, 1999); John Baldock, *The Alternative Gospel* (Shaftesbury: Element, 1997); Helen Schucman, *A Course in Miracles*, 2nd ed. (New York: Viking, 1996); James Redfield, *The Celestine Prophecy* (New York: Warner Books, 1994); Jacob Needleman, *Lost Christianity* (Shaftesbury: Element Books 1990); Don Lattin, "Rediscovery of Gnostic Christianity," *San Francisco Chronicle*, April 1, 1989; Robert Winterhalter, *The Fifth Gospel: A Verse-by-Verse New Age Commentary on the Gospel of Thomas* (San Francisco: Harper and Row, 1988). Parallel to the rediscovery of a Gnostic Jesus is the popularization of Qabalistic thought among Jews, although this particular kind of Qabalism appears in a very New Age guise: David Van Biema, "Pop Goes the Kabbalah," *Time*, Nov. 24, 1997, pp. 92–94.

25. Gayle White, "Celtic Spirituality: Nature Oriented Pagans in Ireland of Patrick's Day Accepted and Influenced Christianity," *Atlanta Journal-Constitution*, March 14, 1998. For a critical account of the Celtic spirituality fad, see Ian Bradley, *Celtic Christianity* (Edinburgh: Edinburgh Univ. Press,

1999); Marion Bowman, "Reinventing the Celts," *Religion* 23, no. 2 (1993): 147–56. For the Irish use of noncanonical texts, see M. McNamara, *The Apocrypha in the Irish Church* (Dublin: Institute for Advanced Studies, 1975).

26. From a very large recent literature on Celtic spirituality, see Shirley Toulson, *The Celtic Alternative: The Christianity We Lost* (London: Rider, 1987); Shirley Toulson, *The Celtic Year* (Rockport, Mass.: Element, 1996); Michael Poynder, *The Lost Magic of Christianity: Celtic Essene Connections* (Cork, Ireland: Collins Press, 1997); J. Philip Newell, *Listening for the Heartbeat of God* (New York: Paulist Press, 1997); Nigel Pennick, *The Celtic Cross* (London: Blandford, 1997); John O'Donohue, *Anam Cara* (New York: HarperCollins, 1997); Esther De Waal, *The Celtic Way of Prayer* (New York: Doubleday, 1997); Esther De Waal, *Celtic Light* (London: Fount, 1997); John Matthews, *Drinking from the Sacred Well* (San Francisco: Harper San Francisco, 1998); Edain McCoy, *Celtic Women's Spirituality* (St. Paul, Minn.: Llewellyn Publications, 1998); Timothy J. Joyce, *Celtic Christianity* (Maryknoll, N.Y.: Orbis Books, 1998); J. Philip Newell, *The Book of Creation: An Introduction to Celtic Spirituality* (New York: Paulist Press, 1999); Bruce Reed Pullen, *Discovering Celtic Christianity* (Mystic, Conn.: Twenty-third Publications, 1999); Deborah K. Cronin, *Holy Ground: Celtic Christian Spirituality* (Nashville, Tenn.: Upper Room Books, 1999).

27. The respective websites are "Gospel of Thomas Homepage," http://home.epix.net/~miser17/Thomas.html; "Nazarene Nirvana," http://www.geocities.com/Athens/Styx/8676/files/page1.html; "Gnostic Society Library," http://www.gnosis.org/naghamm/nhl.html); the Celtic sanctuary http://www.anamchara.com/. For a Celtic church, see http://www.coastnet.com/~stdavid/; for "Celtic Orthodox Christian Resources," see http://www.geocities.com/Athens/3374/celtdocs.html.

28. Matthew Fox, *The Coming of the Cosmic Christ* (San Francisco: Harper & Row, 1988); Fox, *Creation Spirituality* (San Francisco: Harper San Francisco, 1991); Fox, *Original Blessing* (Santa Fe, N.M.: Bear and Co. 1996); Fox, *Confessions: The Making of a Post-Denominational Priest* (San Francisco: Harper San Francisco, 1997). Wendy Kaminer, *Sleeping with Extra-Terrestrials* (New York: Pantheon, 2000). For the popularity of New Age beliefs, see Gallup and Lindsay, *Surveying the Religious Landscape*. The variety of contemporary Christian liberalism is suggested by Deborah Brown, ed., *Christianity in the Twenty-first Century* (New York: Crossroad Publishing, 2000), with its essays by Fox, Robert Funk, Karen Armstrong, and others.

29. The remarks about Grace cathedral are taken from the standard visitor's leaflet. Melissa Gayle West, *Exploring the Labyrinth: A Guide for Healing and Spiritual Growth* (New York: Broadway Books, 2000); Jill Kimberly Hartwell Geoffrion and Lauren Artress, *Praying the Labyrinth* (Cleveland, Ohio: Pilgrim Press, 1999); Lauren Artress, *Walking a Sacred Path* (New York: Riverhead Books, 1996); Matthew Fox, *Illuminations of Hildegard of Bingen*, (Santa Fe: Bear and Co. 1985).

30. Charlotte Allen, "The Search for a No-Frills Jesus," *Atlantic Monthly*, Dec. 1996, pp. 51–68.

31. Stephan A. Hoeller and June Singer, *Jung and the Lost Gospels* (Quest Books, 1989); Pagels, *Gnostic Gospels*, 129; Rosemary Radford Ruether, *Womanguides: Readings Toward a Feminist Theology* (Boston: Beacon Press, 1985), 22–23. June Singer, *Knowledge of the Heart: Gnostic Secrets of Inner Wisdom* (Rockport, Mass.: Element Books, 1999).

32. Funk, "Honest to Jesus," cover; "The Meaning of Jesus," in *Books and Culture*, March-April 1999, p. 39; "beyond dogmatic religion" is from the subtitle of Marcus J. Borg, *The God We Never Knew* (San Francisco: Harper San Francisco, 1997).

33. Mack is quoted from Allen, "The Search for a No-Frills Jesus." Robert W. Funk, "The Coming Radical Reformation: Twenty-one Theses," *The Fourth R* 11, no. 4 (July/Aug. 1998); Jeffrey L. Sheler, "Bob Funk's Radical Reformation Roadshow," *U.S. News and World Report*, August 4, 1997, pp. 55–56.

34. Robert W. Funk, Roy W. Hoover, and the Jesus Seminar, *The Five Gospels* (New York: Macmillan 1993), 5.

35. Funk, "The Coming Radical Reformation"; Allen, *Human Christ*, 271.

36. Barbara Brown Zikmund, Adair T. Lummis, and Patricia M. Y. Chang. *Clergy Women* (Louisville, Ky.: Westminster John Knox Press, 1998); Mark Chaves, *Ordaining Women* (Cambridge, Mass.: Harvard Univ. Press, 1997); Paula D. Nesbitt, *Feminization of the Clergy in America* (New York: Oxford Univ. Press, 1997); Catherine M. Prelinger, ed., *Episcopal Women* (New York: Oxford Univ. Press, 1992); Mary Sudman Donovan, *Women Priests in the Episcopal Church* (Cincinnati: Forward Movement, 1988).

37. Lavinia Byrne, *Woman at the Altar* (New York: Continuum, 1999); Denise Lardner Carmody, *The Double Cross* (New York: Crossroad, 1986); Mary Jo Weaver, *New Catholic Women* (San Francisco: Harper San Francisco, 1985).

38. Thomas Reeves, *The Empty Church* (New York: Free Press, 1996).

39. Gustav Niebuhr, "Following Mothers, Women Heed Call to Nation's Pulpits," *New York Times*, April 25, 1999; Larry B. Stammer, "Women Celebrate a Christian Heroine," *LAT*, July 24, 1999; Cullen Murphy, *The Word According to Eve* (Boston: Houghton Mifflin, 1998); Pamela Susan Nadell, *Women Who Would Be Rabbis* (Boston: Beacon Press, 1998).

40. Deirdre Good, "Pistis Sophia," in Elisabeth Schüssler Fiorenza, Ann Brock, and Shelly Matthews, eds., *Searching the Scriptures*, 2 vols. (New York: Crossroad, 1993–1994), II: 704; Haskins is quoted in Josh Simon, "Who Was Jesus?" *Life*, Dec. 1994; Karen Jo Torjesen, *When Women Were Priests* (San Francisco: Harper San Francisco, 1993), 10, 35–36; Karen L. King, "Women in Ancient Christianity," at http://www.pbs.org/wgbh/pages/frontline/shows/religion/first/women.html. Compare Katherine Ludwig Jansen, "Maria Magdalena: Apostolorum Apostola," in Beverly Mayne Kienzle and Pamela J. Walker, eds., *Women Preachers and Prophets through Two Millennia of Christianity* (Berkeley: Univ. of California Press, 1998), 57–98; Esther De Boer, *Mary Magdalene: Beyond the Myth* (Trinity Press International, 1997). There is now a whole alternative genre of "Magdalene Gospels": see Marianne Fredriksson, *According to Mary Magdalene* (Charlottesville, Va.: Hampton Roads Publishing, 1999); Mary

Ellen Ashcroft, *The Magdalene Gospel* (New York: Doubleday 1995); Mary R. Thompson, *Mary of Magdala: Apostle and Leader* (New York: Paulist Press, 1995). For Mary Magdalen as a New Age heroine, see Clysta Kinstler, *The Moon under Her Feet* (San Francisco: Harper San Francisco, 1991); Margaret Starbird, *The Woman with the Alabaster Jar* (Santa Fe, N.M.: Bear and Co., 1993); Starbird, *The Goddess in the Gospels* (Santa Fe, N.M.: Bear and Co., 1998).

41. Stammer, "Women Celebrate a Christian Heroine"; for Future Church, see http://www.futurechurch.org/primer.htm. Pamela Schaeffer, "Groups Promote Mary of Magdala, Women's Roles," *National Catholic Reporter*, April 7, 2000.

42. Reeves, *Empty Church*, 148 for the Christa statue; Teresa Malcolm, "Jesus 2000 Images Stir Reflections in Retreats, Parishes, Colleges," *National Catholic Reporter*, March 3, 2000. For the women's spirituality movement, see Wendy Griffin, ed., *Daughters of the Goddess* (Walnut Creek, Calif.: Altamira Press, 1999); Laurel C. Schneider, *Re-imagining the divine* (Cleveland, Ohio: Pilgrim Press, 1998); Wendy Hunter Roberts, *Celebrating Her: Feminist Ritualizing Comes of Age* (Cleveland, Ohio: Pilgrim Press, 1998); Bill Broadway, "Having Their Say in Growing Spirituality Movement, Women Aim to Assert Their Voice on Religion," *Washington Post*, July 4, 1998; Teresa Watanabe, "Seeking the Feminine Face of God," *LAT*, Oct. 15, 1998; Sue Monk Kidd, *The Dance of the Dissident Daughter* (San Francisco: Harper San Francisco, 1996); Jann Aldredge-Clanton, *In Search of the Christ-Sophia* (Mystic, Conn.: Twenty-Third Publications, 1995); Ursula King, *Women and Spirituality* (Univ. Park, Pa.: Pennsylvania State University Press, 1993); Gustav Niebuhr, "Image of God as 'He' Loses Its Sovereignty in America's Churches," *Wall Street Journal*, April 27, 1992.

43. Uta Ranke-Heinemann, *Eunuchs for the Kingdom of God* (New York: Doubleday, 1991).

44. See, for example, Ivone Gebara, *Longing for Running Water* (Minneapolis: Fortress Press, 1999).

45. *Episcopal Life*, April 1999.

46. "Spirit Quest" was advertised in *Episcopal Life* in Nov. 1997. "The Women Around Jesus," ibid., March 1999; "Maiden, Mother, Crone," ibid., July-Aug. 1998.

47. The New England Women Ministers Association meeting was advertised in *Episcopal Life*, April 1999; The Center for Progressive Christianity event in ibid. May 1998. John L. Allen, "Bishop Shuts Down Women's Series," *National Catholic Reporter*, March 17, 2000.

48. Philip G. Davis, *Goddess Unmasked* (Dallas, Tex.: Spence Publishing, 1998); Cynthia Eller, *Living in the Lap of the Goddess* (New York: Crossroad, 1994); Caitlin Matthews, *Sophia; Goddess of Wisdom* (San Francisco: Harper San Francisco, 1993); Rosemary Radford Ruether, *Women-Church* (San Francisco: Harper, 1985)

49. Lynn Schofield Clark and Stewart M. Hoover, "Controversy and Cultural Symbolism," *Critical Studies in Mass Communication* 14 (1997): 310–31; "Fallout Escalates over Goddess Sophia Worship" *CT*, April 4, 1994, 72.

50. Diane L. Knippers, "Sophia's Children," *Wall Street Journal*, May 8, 1998; Elaine H. Pagels, *Adam, Eve, and the Serpent* (New York: Random House, 1988). The movement which developed from the Re-Imaginings event has a public face in the "Voices of Sophia," which can be found on the Internet at http://www.execware.com/vos/.

51. Carter Heyward, *Saving Jesus from Those Who Are Right* (Minneapolis: Fortress Press, 1999); Heyward, *When Boundaries Betray Us* (San Francisco: Harper San Francisco, 1993); Heyward, *A Priest Forever* (New York: Harper and Row, 1976).

52. "The Re-Imagining Revival" at http://www.banneroftruth.co.uk/News/reimagining_revival.htm.

Chapter 8. The Gospels in the Media

1. For coverage of religious news in the media, see Benjamin J. Hubbard, ed., *Reporting Religion: Facts and Faith* (Sonoma, Calif.: Polebridge Press, 1990), particularly the essay by Kenneth A. Briggs, "Why Editors Miss Important Religion Stories," 47–58; Judith M. Buddenbaum, *Reporting News about Religion* (Ames: Iowa State Univ. Press, 1998); S. Robert Lichter, Linda S. Lichter, and Daniel R. Amundson, *Media Coverage of Religion in America 1969–1998* (Washington, D.C.: Center for Media and Public Affairs, 2000): online at http://www.cmpa.com/archive/Relig2000.htm.

2. Good recent surveys of Scroll scholarship are found in Michael Owen Wise, Martin G. Abegg, and Edward M. Cook, eds., *The Dead Sea Scrolls* (New York: HarperCollins 1999), and Geza Vermes, *The Complete Dead Sea Scrolls in English* (New York: Allen Lane/Penguin Press, 1997). For early reactions, see Edmund Wilson, *The Scrolls from the Dead Sea* (New York: Oxford Univ. Press, 1955); compare Andre Dupont-Sommer, *The Dead Sea Scrolls* (New York: Macmillan, 1952). For media coverage, see "Out of the Desert," *Time*, April 15, 1957, pp. 60–62; "Oldest Decalogue," *Time*, Sept. 29, 1958, p. 47; A. D. Tushingham, "Men Who Hid the Dead Sea Scrolls," *National Geographic*, Dec. 1958, pp. 784–808; "Another Psalm," *Time*, March 16, 1962, p. 73; "Essenes or Zealots?," *Newsweek*, Feb. 10, 1964, p. 72; "Explaining the Scrolls," *Newsweek*, June 15, 1964, p. 67.

3. Stephen Neill and Tom Wright, *The Interpretation of the New Testament, 1861–1986*, 2nd ed. (New York: Oxford Univ. Press, 1988), 323; Joseph A. Fitzmyer, "The Dead Sea Scrolls: The Latest Form of Catholic-Bashing," *America*, Feb. 15, 1992, p. 119; Joseph A. Fitzmyer, *The Dead Sea Scrolls and Christian Origins* (Grand Rapids, Mich.: William B. Eerdmans, 2000). For the work of John M. Allegro, see his *The Dead Sea Scrolls* (London: Penguin Books, 1956); Allegro, *The Dead Sea Scrolls and the Origins of Christianity* (New York: Criterion Books, 1957); Allegro, *The Sacred Mushroom and the Cross* (Garden City, N.Y.: Doubleday, 1970); Allegro, *The Dead Sea Scrolls and the Christian Myth* (Buffalo, N.Y.: Prometheus Books, 1984).

4. Stephen J. Patterson and James M. Robinson, *The Fifth Gospel* (Harrisburg, Pa.: Trinity Press International, 1998), 2; A. Guillaumont, H.-C. Puech, G. Quispel, W. Till, and Y. Abd-al Masih, *The Gospel According to Thomas* (New York: Harper & Row, 1959); R. McL. Wilson, *Studies in the*

Gospel of Thomas (London: A. R. Mowbray, 1960); Robert M. Grant and David Noel Freedman, *The Secret Sayings of Jesus* (Garden City, N.Y.: Doubleday, 1960); Jean Doresse, *The Secret Books of the Egyptian Gnostics* (New York: Viking Press, 1960); Bertil Gärtner, *The Theology of the Gospel of Thomas* (London: Collins, 1961); Henry E. W. Turner and Hugh Montefiore, *Thomas and the Evangelists* (Naperville, Ill.: A. R. Allenson, 1962). For press reaction, see "New Sayings of Jesus," *Time*, March 30, 1959, p. 38; "New Words of Jesus Found in Egypt," *CC*, April 1, 1959, pp. 381–82; J. J. Collins, "Fifth Gospel?," *America*, May 23, 1959, pp. 365–67; "St. Thomas' Gospel," *Time*, Nov. 9, 1959, p. 46; Otto A. Piper, "A New Gospel?," *CC*, Jan. 27, 1960, pp. 96–99

5. "The Secret Gospel," *Time*, Jan. 6, 1961, p. 48; compare the later "Jesus as Magician," *Newsweek*, June 4, 1973, p. 73; see above, chapter 4, for the controversy over Morton Smith's work.

6. "New Words of Jesus?," *Time*, Jan. 7, 1966, p. 70; "Temple Scroll," *Time*, Nov. 3, 1967, p. 83; "Eyewitness Mark?," *Time*, May 1, 1972, p. 54; Susan C. Cowley and Scott Sullivan, "Fifth Gospel?," *Newsweek*, March 3, 1975; "Newest of the Dead Sea Scrolls," *Time*, Jan. 24, 1977, pp. 57–58; Kenneth L. Woodward and Joseph B. Cumming, "Books the Bible Left Out," *Newsweek*, Nov. 28, 1977.

7. "The Gospels Revised," *Newsweek*, Feb. 4, 1963, p. 46; "The New Search for the Historical Jesus," *Time*, June 21, 1963, pp. 68–69; "Christ's Sexuality," *Time*, April 9, 1965, p. 59; "Heretic or Prophet?," *Time*, Nov. 11, 1966, pp. 56–58; "A Political Patriotic Jesus," *Time*, Jan. 3, 1969, pp. 54–55; "A Married Christ?," *Newsweek*, March 24, 1969, p. 90; John G. Gibbs, "Possibly," *CC*, March 3, 1971, p. 299; William E. Phipps, *Was Jesus Married?* (New York: Harper & Row, 1971).

8. A. Ripp, "Jesus Kissed Mary Magdalen on the Mouth," *People*, Nov. 12, 1979, pp. 141ff.

9. James Hall Roberts, *The Q Document* (London: J. Cape, 1965); Irving Wallace, *The Word* (New York: Simon and Schuster, 1972); J. G. Sandom, *Gospel Truths* (New York: Perfect Crime, 1992); Wilton Barnhardt, *Gospel* (New York: St. Martin's Press, 1993); Larry Witham, *The Negev Project* (College Park, Md.: Meridian Books, 1994); Paul L. Maier, *A Skeleton in God's Closet* (Nashville: T. Nelson Publishers, 1994); Alan Gold, *The Lost Testament* (New York: Harper Paperbacks, 1996). See Thomas G. Walsh, "Imagining the Lost Gospels," *Houston Chronicle*, Jan 7, 1995. Fictionalized accounts of rediscovered "Jesus scrolls" continue to appear; see now David Howard, *The Last Gospel* (Sarasota, Fla.: Disc-us Books, 2000).

10. Jeffery L. Sheler, *Is the Bible True?* (San Francisco: Harper San Francisco, 2000); Kenneth L. Woodward, "2000 Years of Jesus," *Newsweek*, March 29, 1999, pp. 52–65; Charlotte Allen, "The Search for a No-Frills Jesus," *Atlantic Monthly*, Dec. 1996, pp. 51–68; Russell Shorto, "Cross Fire," *GQ*, June 1994, pp. 116–23; Cullen Murphy, "Women and the Bible," *Atlantic Monthly*, Aug. 1993, pp. 39–64; Jeffery L. Sheler, "Cutting Loose the Holy Canon," *U.S. News and World Report*, Nov. 8, 1993, pp. 75; R. N. Ostling, "Who Was Jesus?," *Time*, Aug. 15, 1988, pp. 37–42.

11. For criticisms of the Jesus Seminar, see James R. Edwards, "Who Do

Scholars Say That I Am?," *CT*, March 4, 1996; Robert J. Hutchinson, "The Jesus Seminar Unmasked," *CT*, April 29, 1996; Birger Pearson, "The Gospel According to the Jesus Seminar," 1996: http://id-www.ucsb.edu/fscf/library/pearson/seminar/home.html; Robert L. Thomas, "Did the Jesus Seminar Draw from Faulty Assumptions?," *LAT*, April 13, 1991. For defenses by Seminar members, see Robert J. Miller, *The Jesus Seminar and Its Critics* (Santa Rosa, Calif.: Polebridge Press, 1999). For debates between advocates and critics of the group, see, for example, Marcus J. Borg and N. T. Wright, *The Meaning of Jesus* (San Francisco: Harper San Francisco, 1998); Paul Copan, ed., *Will the Real Jesus Please Stand Up?* (Grand Rapids, Mich.: Baker Book House, 1998); John Dominic Crossan, Luke Timothy Johnson, and Werner H. Keller, *The Jesus Controversy* (Harrisburg, Pa.: Trinity Press, 1999).

12. For the origins of the Jesus Seminar, see Marcus J. Borg, *Jesus in Contemporary Scholarship* (Valley Forge, Pa.: Trinity Press International, 1994); Gustav Niebuhr, "Iconoclastic Scholars of Jesus to Consider Doctrinal Revision," *New York Times*, Nov. 25, 1996; Niebuhr, "The Jesus Seminar Courts Notoriety," *CC*, Nov. 23, 1988, p. 1060.

13. Luke Timothy Johnson, *The Real Jesus* (San Francisco: Harper San Francisco, 1996); Robert W. Funk, Bernard Brandon Scott, and James R. Butts, *The Parables of Jesus* (Sonoma, Calif.: Polebridge Press, 1988); Robert W. Funk with Mahlon H. Smith, *The Gospel of Mark: Red Letter Edition* (Sonoma, Calif.: Polebridge Press, 1991); Robert W. Funk, ed., *The Acts of Jesus* (San Francisco: Harper San Francisco, 1998); Robert W. Funk and the Jesus Seminar, *The Gospel of Jesus According to the Jesus Seminar* (Sonoma, Calif.: Polebridge Press, 1999).

14. See, for example, Larry B. Stammer, " Do You See What I See?," *LAT*, Dec. 19, 1998; Jeffrey L. Sheler, "In Search of Jesus," *U.S. News and World Report*, April 8, 1996.

15. David Van Biema, "The Gospel Truth?," *Time*, April 8, 1996, pp. 52–59.

16. L. Michael White is quoted from the symposium on the *Frontline* series *From Jesus to Christ—The First Christians*: the text is found at http://www.pbs.org/wgbh/pages/frontline/shows/religion/symposium/.

17. Judith Plaskow, *Standing Again at Sinai* (San Francisco: Harper San Francisco, 1991); Lynn Gottlieb, *She Who Dwells Within* (San Francisco: Harper San Francisco, 1995); Ellen Frankel, *Five Books of Miriam* (San Francisco: Harper San Francisco, 1998); Michael O. Wise, *The First Messiah* (San Francisco: Harper San Francisco, 1999).

18. Carol P. Christ and Judith Plaskow, *Womanspirit Rising* (San Francisco: Harper San Francisco, 1992); Caitlin Matthews, *Sophia: Goddess of Wisdom* (San Francisco: Harper San Francisco, 1993).

19. John Dart and Ray Riegert, *Unearthing the Lost Words of Jesus* (Berkeley, Calif.: Seastone, 1998); Marcus J. Borg et al., eds., *The Lost Gospel Q* (Berkeley, Calif.: Ulysses Press, 1996).

20. Michael Drosnin, *The Bible Code* (New York: Simon and Schuster, 1997); "Bible Code Debunked by Scholars," *New York Times*, Sept. 10, 1999; Jeffery L. Sheler, *Is the Bible True?* (San Francisco: Harper San Francisco, 2000).

21. Carsten Peter Thiede and Matthew D'Ancona, *Eyewitness to Jesus* (New York: Doubleday, 1996); Gary Burge, "Indiana Jones and the Gospel Parchments," *CT*, Oct. 28, 1996; Geza Vermes, "Books: The Gospel Truth?," *The Guardian*, May 24, 1996; Graham N. Stanton, *Gospel Truth?* (Valley Forge, Pa.: Trinity Press International, 1995).

22. Bruce Nolan, "Scholar Argues Age of Gospel—Could Have Been Work of Witness," *New Orleans Times–Picayune*, April 7, 1996; "Matthew Put Much Closer to Jesus' Time," *Dallas Morning News*, Oct. 12, 1996; John Elson, "Eyewitnesses to Jesus?," *Time*, April 8, 1996.

23. R. N. Ostling, "Secrets of the Dead Sea Scrolls," *Time*, Aug. 14, 1989, pp. 71–72; James H. Charlesworth, "Sense or Sensationalism? The Dead Sea Scrolls Controversy," *CC*, Jan. 29, 1992, p. 92; Randall Price, *Secrets of the Dead Sea Scrolls* (Eugene, Ore.: Harvest House Publishers, 1996); Gayle White, "Dead Sea Scrolls: Sensationalism or Serious Insight?" *Atlanta Journal-Constitution*, Marsh 23, 1997; Sheler, *Is the Bible True?* For earlier conspiracy theories, see, for instance, Donovan Joyce, *The Jesus Scroll* (New York: New American Library, 1974).

24. Charlesworth, "Sense or Sensationalism?" For the outpouring of books following the "release" of the Scrolls, see Fitzmyer, *The Dead Sea Scrolls and Christian Origins*; Martin G. Abegg, Peter W. Flint and Eugene Charles Ulrich, eds., *The Dead Sea Scrolls Bible* (New York: HarperCollins, 1999); Wise et al., eds., *The Dead Sea Scrolls*; Wise, *The First Messiah*; Neil Asher Silberman, *The Hidden Scrolls* (New York: Riverhead Books, 1996); Robert H. Eisenman, *The Dead Sea Scrolls and the First Christians* (Rockport, Mass.: Element 1996); John Joseph Collins, *The Scepter and the Star* (New York: Anchor, 1995); Lawrence H. Schiffman, *Reclaiming the Dead Sea Scrolls* (New York: Doubleday Anchor, 1995); Robert H. Eisenman and Michael Wise, *The Dead Sea Scrolls Uncovered* (New York: Penguin, 1993);

25. 1QSa, 1Q28a, in Wise et al., eds., *The Dead Sea Scrolls*, 144–47.

26. Wise et al., eds., *The Dead Sea Scrolls*, 34.

27. 4Q521, in ibid., 420–22; Vermes, *The Complete Dead Sea Scrolls in English*, 391–92.

28. Kevin D. Miller, "The War of the Scrolls" *CT*, Oct. 6, 1997; James H. Charlesworth, ed., *Jesus and the Dead Sea Scrolls* (New York: Doubleday, 1995).

29. Edwin Yamauchi, in Michael J. Wilkins and James P. Moreland, eds., *Jesus under Fire* (Grand Rapids, Mich.: Zondervan, 1995), 208–11.

30. 4Q285, 11Q14, in Wise et al., eds., *The Dead Sea Scrolls*, 291–93; Charlesworth, "Sense or Sensationalism?"

31. 4Q246, in Wise et al., eds., *The Dead Sea Scrolls*, 268–70; Vermes, *The Complete Dead Sea Scrolls in English*, 576–77.

32. The quote is from a publisher's flier for Robert H. Eisenman, *James the Brother of Jesus* (New York: Penguin, 1998).

33. Michael Baigent and Richard Leigh, *Holy Blood, Holy Grail* (New York: Dell, 1983); Michael Baigent and Richard Leigh, *The Messianic Legacy* (New York: Dell 1989); Michael Baigent and Richard Leigh, *The Dead Sea Scrolls Deception* (London: Corgi, 1991). For a spate of books on related and equally improbable themes, see Richard Andrews and Paul Schel-

lenberger, *The Tomb of God* (Boston: Little, Brown, 1996); Christopher Knight and Robert Lomas, *The Hiram Key* (Shaftesbury: Dorset, Element, 1998); Lynn Picknett and Clive Prince, *The Templar Revelation* (New York: Touchstone Books, 1998). The idea of Jesus' surviving the crucifixion, and living to participate in the Jewish War, was also presented in Joyce, *Jesus Scroll.*

34. Baigent and Leigh, *Dead Sea Scrolls Deception*, 130.
35. Barbara Thiering, *Jesus and the Riddle of the Dead Sea Scrolls* (San Francisco: Harper San Francisco, 1992); Thiering, *Jesus the Man* (New York: Doubleday, 1993); Thiering, *Jesus of the Apocalypse* (New York: Doubleday, 1995); Thiering, *The Book That Jesus Wrote* (London: Corgi, 1998).
36. Nora Underwood, "Who Was Jesus?," *Maclean's*, Dec. 21, 1992.
37. "Is Jesus in the Dead Sea Scrolls?," *Time*, Sept. 21, 1992, p. 56; Charlesworth, *Jesus and the Dead Sea Scrolls.*
38. Graham Hancock *The Sign and the Seal* (New York: Touchstone Books 1993).
39. *The Sun*, Aug. 10, 1999.
40. Johnson, *Real Jesus*, 9–11.
41. Thomas L. Thompson, *The Mythic Past* (New York: Basic Books 1999); Jonathan Kirsch, review of *The Mythic Past*, in *LAT*, June 12, 1999.
42. The quote is taken from Baigent and Leigh, *Dead Sea Scrolls Deception.*
43. Robert W. Funk, *Honest to Jesus* (San Francisco: Harper San Francisco, 1996), 54; David Van Biema, "The Gospel Truth?" *Time*, April 8, 1996, pp. 52–59; John Dominic Crossan, *A Long Way from Tipperary* (San Francisco: Harper San Francisco, 2000).
44. Walter W. Wessel, "Voting Out the Fourth Beatitude," *CT*, Dec. 12, 1986, pp. 34–35.
45. Robert W. Funk, "The Once and Future Jesus," presentation at conference on "The Once and Future Jesus" held by the Westar Institute, Santa Rosa, Calif., Oct. 20, 1999.
46. http://westarinstitute.org/Jesus_Seminar/jesus_seminar.html
47. Funk et al., *The Five Gospels*, 2.
48. "Church Discipline on Trial," *CT*, May 24, 1999, pp. 38–39.

Chapter 9. The Next New Gospel

1. W. Barnes Tatum, *Jesus at the Movies* (Sonoma, Calif.: Polebridge Press; 1998).
2. Charles Kingsley, *Hypatia; or, New Foes with an Old Face*, 13th ed. (New York: Macmillan and Co., 1880), xvi. For the continuing myth and memory of Hypatia, see Margaret Alic, *Hypatia's Heritage* (London: Women's Press, 1986); Maria Dzielska, *Hypatia of Alexandria* (Cambridge: Harvard Univ. Press, 1995); Linda Lopez McAlister, ed., *Hypatia's Daughters* (Bloomington: Indiana Univ. Press, 1996).
3. Irenaeus, i, *ANCF.*
4. James M. Robinson, *The Nag Hammadi Library in English* (Leiden: E. J. Brill, 1977), 394–98.
5. Quoted in Huston Smith, *The World's Religions*, rev. ed. (New York: HarperCollins, 1991), 233.

6. Matt 13: 47; *Thomas*, saying 8.

7. E. Hennecke and W. Schneemelcher, *New Testament Apocrypha*, 2 vols. (London: SCM Press, 1973), I: 166–67; Robinson, *The Nag Hammadi Library in English*, 237, 193.

8. Peter Brown, *The Body and Society* (New York: Columbia Univ. Press, 1988).

9. James E. Goehring, *Ascetics, Society, and the Desert* (Harrisburg, Pa.: Trinity Press International, 1999); Leif E. Vaage and Vincent L. Wimbush, eds., *Asceticism and the New Testament* (Routledge, 1999); C. Wilfred Griggs, *Early Egyptian Christianity* (Leiden: E. J. Brill, 1990); Birger A. Pearson, *Gnosticism, Judaism and Egyptian Christianity* (Harrisburg, Pa.: Trinity Press International, 1990).

10. For the comments of Origen and Eusebius on the *Gospel of Matthias*, see Hennecke and Schneemelcher, *New Testament Apocrypha*, I: 56–57.

Index

Abortion controversy, 19

Academic profession. *See* American Academy of Religion (AAR); Seminaries; Society for New Testament Studies; Society of Biblical Literature (SBL); Universities

Acts of the Apostles, 74

Acts of Jesus, 96. *See also* Jesus Seminar

Adam, Apocalypse of, 145

Africa, 132

Alawites, 30

Alexandria, 49, 52, 145. *See also* Clement of Alexandria; Egypt; Origen

Allegro, John M., 180, 189, 191

Allen, Charlotte, 66–67, 168

American Academy of Religion (AAR), 152, 154, 187

Andrew, Apostle, 136

Ante-Nicene Christian Library, 38

Anti-Catholicism, 18–19, 41, 46–47, 107–8, 163, 182–83, 195, 207

Antichrist, 50, 123

Anticlericalism, 18. *See also* Anti-Catholicism

Antioch. *See* Ignatius

Anti-Semitism and anti-Judaism, 22, 30, 50, 166, 169, 211, 235n22. *See also* Gnosticism; Marcion

Apocalyptic ideas, 24, 38, 60–61, 65, 69, 168, 186. *See also* Q (gospel source); John, Revelation of; Peter, Revelation of

Apocrypha, concept of, 7, 229n2. *See also* Canon, New Testament; Gospel, concept of

Apocryphon of James. *See James, Apocryphon of*

Apocryphon of John. *See John, Apocryphon of*

Apostolic Constitutions, 76

Apostolic Fathers. *See Barnabas, Epistle of; Clement of Rome, Epistles of; Didache* ("Teaching of the Twelve Apostles"); Ignatius; Polycarp

Apostolic Succession, 119–21

Aquarian Gospel of Jesus the Christ, 27, 47–48, 89–90

Archaeology, 32, 35

Archko Volume, 46, 48, 197

Aristides, Apology of, 34

Asia Minor, 42, 67, 128, 133. *See also* Bithynia; Ephesus; Phrygia; Smyrna

Asian religions. *See* Buddhism; Hinduism; Taoism; Tibet; Zen Buddhism

Athanasius, 84–85, 87, 114–15, 208

Atonement, doctrine of, 63, 167

Augustine, 212

Avircius Marcellus, 75

Bahrdt, Karl Friedrich, 49

Baigent, Michael, 194–96

Bardesan and Bardesanites, 42–43

Barnabas, Epistle of, 32, 86

Barnhardt ,Wilton, 182

Barth, Carola, 154

Basilides, 29, 40, 43, 104, 121

Bauer, Walter, 42–43, 158

Benares, 27